The Fraser

Bruce Hutchison

Introduction by Vaughn Palmer

OXFORD
UNIVERSITY PRESS

OXFORD
UNIVERSITY PRESS

8 Sampson Mews, Suite 204, Don Mills, Ontario M3C 0H5
www.oupcanada.com

Oxford University Press is a department of the University of Oxford.
It furthers the University's objective of excellence in research, scholarship,
and education by publishing worldwide in

Oxford New York

Auckland Cape Town Dar es Salaam Hong Kong Karachi
Kuala Lumpur Madrid Melbourne Mexico City Nairobi
New Delhi Shanghai Taipei Toronto

With offices in

Argentina Austria Brazil Chile Czech Republic France Greece
Guatemala Hungary Italy Japan Poland Portugal Singapore
South Korea Switzerland Thailand Turkey Ukraine Vietnam

Oxford is a trade mark of Oxford University Press
in the UK and in certain other countries

Published in Canada by Oxford University Press

Library and Archives Canada Cataloguing in Publication
Hutchison, Bruce, 1901-1992

The Fraser / Bruce Hutchison ; introduction by Vaughn Palmer.

(The Wynford Project)

Includes bibliographical references.

ISBN 978-0-19-543892-5

1. Fraser River (B.C.). I. Title. II. Series: Wynford Project

FC3845.F73H88 2009   971.1'3   C2009-905930-4

Illustrated by Richard Bennett

Oxford University Press is committed to our environment. This book is printed on Forest
Stewardship Council certified paper, harvested from a responsibly managed forest.

www.oupcanada.com

1 2 3 4 – 13 12 11 10

The Fraser

To *Dorothy, Joan* and *Robert*
Companions of the Long River

PUBLISHER'S NOTE

The Fraser was first published in 1950. This facsimile edition faithfully reproduces the original text of the book. In the six decades since, society's attitudes toward Canada's First Nations peoples and indeed the very terms used to denote those societies have changed greatly. So have historical views of first contact between Europeans and the First Nations, as well as social attitudes toward gender and ethnicity. Mr. Hutchison was remarkably modern in his views but *The Fraser* is, like any creative work, an artifact of its time, and the twenty-first century reader may stumble across the occasional expression no longer in common use.

AUTHOR'S NOTE

Most of the work of research for this book was done over a period of three years by Christine Fox, of the Provincial Library at Victoria. Without her diligence as a librarian and her knowledge of the history of her native province the book would not have been written. I am indebted also to many able officials of the British Columbia government, who provided information in their special fields, particularly Major R.C. Farrow, comptroller of water rights, Dr. John Walker, deputy minister of mines, and George Alexander, deputy commissioner of fisheries; to Ernest and Halcyon Carson, who first took me to the Fraser; and to countless unknown men and women who inhabit the banks of the river and know its lore.

INTRODUCTION TO THE WYNFORD EDITION

There was a time when few Canadian readers would have needed an introduction to the works of Bruce Hutchison.

He was one of our most honoured writers. Three Governor-General's awards for non-fiction. Three National Newspaper Awards for editorial writing. The Bowater Prize. The Royal Society of the Arts medal. Four honourary degrees. One of the first officers of the Order of Canada. Named, not long before his death in 1992, to the Privy Council.

He was also one of our most successful writers, with books that were best-sellers before we had best-seller lists, that defined the country before there were entire sections of Canadiana in our bookstores.

"I owe him a great debt," said Pierre Berton (whose own books topped the best-seller lists from the '60s till the start of the twenty-first century), "for it was he who first taught me that the Canadian past could be interesting. His books of popular history have been my single most important influence."

Exhibit A: the popular history you are holding. *The Fraser*, first published in 1950: Hutchison's third book, and one of his most enduring.

For a sense of what Berton was talking about, turn to chapter seven, a vivid retelling of the saga of the Overlanders, "the maddest chapter in the Fraser's history and the most pitiful."

Hutchison's account is gripping as well as instructive. After reading it, you'll understand why no wagon trains—and few overland travelers of any kind—were involved in the early settling of British Columbia.

Though *The Fraser* delivers an instructive slice of British Columbiana for those who wish to know the province and its history better, the book began as a commission from an American publisher, part of the long-running "Rivers of America" series. (W.H. Clarke, who in those days ran the Canadian branch of Oxford University Press as, in effect, an affiliate of his own publishing house, Clarke, Irwin, secured the Canadian rights.)

The founding editor, Constance Lindsay Skinner, envisaged "a literary, not a historical series." In selecting Hutchison to write the 42nd of what eventually became 65 books published between 1937 and 1974, the publisher chose someone whose first two books, *The Unknown Country* (1942), a work of non-fiction about Canada, and *The Hollow Men* (1944), a novel set in the vicinity of the Fraser, were both reviewed favourably south of the border.

INTRODUCTION

Hutchison knew British Columbia as well as anyone. His mother gave birth to him at her family home in Prescott, Ontario (June 5, 1901), but he was borne back to B.C. when just a few weeks old and lived there all of his long life.

He employed a researcher for the historical chapters of *The Fraser*. It was written in his "spare time," while he was editing one newspaper, writing for a second, and contributing regular articles to *Maclean's* and other publications. Still, readers will find ample evidence in these pages of Hutchison's first-hand knowledge of his beloved province.

Turn to chapter 12, "The Old Trail," which opens with his recollection of a trip on horseback—"I learned to ride a horse before I attended school regularly"—to visit Barkerville, terminus of the Cariboo gold rush. The author was just 20 at the time he made the ride. The last miner still working the last diggings could remember the glory days of the 1860s because he'd joined the great rush himself.

As well as the history, the descriptive passages of the book illustrate Hutchison's love of the natural world, that of an author who made the journey from old-fashioned conservationist to fully alert environmentalist through his long life.

"The history of Canada," wrote Hutchison, not long after *The Fraser* was published, "for about 300 years was a struggle to escape from the wilderness, and for the last half century has been a desperate attempt to escape into it."

When *National Geographic* published a look at the Fraser in the mid-1980s, Hutchison was one of the first people interviewed by writer David Boyer for an article that was, in part, an update of his view of the river.

The Fraser is, of course, history. Since Hutchison wrote the book, much has changed. But, remarkably, not always for the worst.

Readers will note that in the final chapter ("The Future of the River") the author suggests the inevitability of huge hydroelectric dams on the Fraser. The Columbia, its neighbor, to the south and east, was already so constricted, with more dams on the way. The Peace, to the north and east, would be hobbled soon enough.

Although spoiled in some ways, changed irrevocably in others, the Fraser still runs free. And in that respect, the great river is still as "virginal" as when Hutchison sent his manuscript to the publishers 60 years ago.

Vaughn Palmer
September 2009

CONTENTS

PRINCE RUPERT

↤ TO PRINCE RUPERT

The
FRASER
River

BRITISH

TATLA
LAKE

CHILCOTIN

Pacific Ocean

VANCOUVER I.

HARRISON TRAIL ●●●●●●●●●●●●●●●●●
ORIGINAL CARIBOO ROAD ▬▬▬▬▬▬

0   50   100   150

Scale of Miles

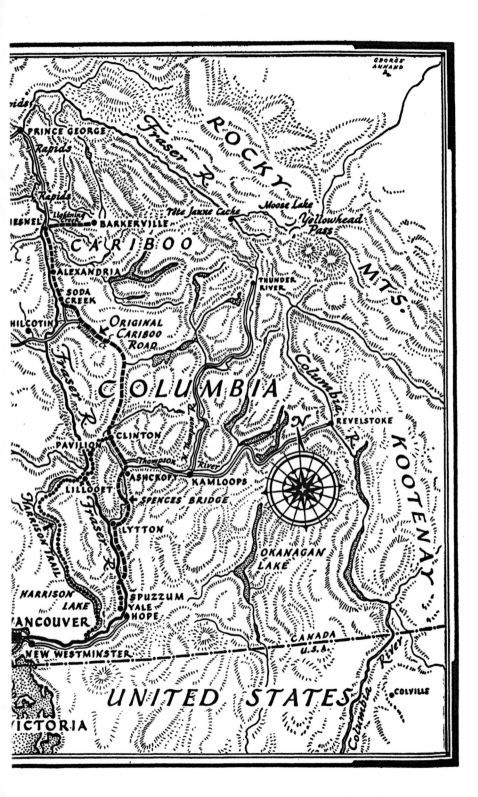

1   The River

No MAN STANDS BESIDE THE FRASER RIVER WITHOUT SENSING THE precarious hold of his species upon the earth. This fact is disclosed, perhaps, by all of nature's larger spectacles, but here it is thrust upon you with a special clarity. In this grisly trench, bored out of solid rock through unimaginable time by the scour of brown water, the long history of lifeless matter, the pitifully brief record of life, the mere moment of man's existence, are suddenly legible. And here, in this prodigal waste of energy, nature's war on all living creatures is naked, brutal and ceaseless.

Of all America's great rivers the Fraser is probably the most unfriendly to mammalian life. The fish it tolerates and breeds in countless swarm. The vegetable growth it burrows out and sweeps away wherever its tides can reach. The animal touches these waters at its peril. Among the animals, the river has seen man for a fragment of time hardly worth recording in the ages of its experience and it holds him in contempt. It crushes his vessels. It tugs and chews forever at his bridges. It heaves its avalanches against his fragile railways. It gnaws his little plots of habitable land, overwhelms his dikes, silts up his harbors, and awaits the day of his going.

In this lash and spill of water, in the slow grinding of rock and cliff, in the perpetual slide of mountain and forest, in the erosion of mountain and gumbo rangeland, in the impact of whirlpool and winter ice, the river is forever mad, ravenous and lonely.

Like many other species which have lived beside it and disappeared, man, though he may build a few dams and tunnels, is a helpless spectator of this process. He cannot look upon it without knowing that he, too, will disappear in due time, he and all his kind, leaving only a few scratches on the shore. These the river will erase at leisure.

The Fraser's experience with man, while short, is filled with adventure, toil, treasure and war. Yet, unlike other great rivers, it has produced no songs, no myths, not even a special type of riverman.

The Fraser has carved through its gorges the shape of the Canadian and American nations. Yet it is unknown, except as a ragged line on the map, to most of the inhabitants of both countries.

The Fraser has seen captains and kings, millionaires and stagecoach robbers, empire builders, soldiers, dance hall girls, and an uncounted company of gold miners who left their bones along its banks for a thousand miles. Yet nearly all of them are forgotten as if the river could not tolerate their fame.

The Fraser is one of the basic political and economic facts of America. Yet its place in the scheme and civilization of the continent is little understood by governments and seldom mentioned in history books.

For song and story, for the record of men's labor, wealth and defeat, for any intimate association with his business, the Fraser is too violent, hurried and solitary. But man in America can never escape the Fraser.

The life of Canada from the beginning has flowed mainly down two channels, the St. Lawrence in the east and the Fraser in the west. Alike in their political and economic effects, the rivers differ in everything else. The calm and hospitable eastern stream, broken by one great falls and easily navigable by canals, floats out from the hinterland the goods of men's labor and takes his ships into the center of the continent. The Fraser hurls itself from the high mountains to the sea and carries nothing but its water, its freight of dissolving earth, and the eroded dust of rock and gold. Yet each has borne its equal cargo of events.

Canada began as a cluster of settlements on the St. Lawrence, a part of the Atlantic community. Canada burst into the Pacific basin through the Fraser's canyon and this narrow passage still carries the lifestuff of the nation. The St. Lawrence was the natural line between Canada and the United States in early times and it divides North America permanently into two great states. Though the boundary falls a little to the southward, on an imaginary line of latitude, the Fraser, though few realized it at the time, became the determining factor in the western division of the continent. The political and economic pattern of the New World is bisected by these two rivers.

The Fraser is a Canadian river. All its waters move through Canadian territory. But in the story of Americans who have struggled against it, and in its effects on their nation, the Fraser is almost an American river. In any case, nothing which has created and now maintains the state of Canada, the United States' closest neighbor and most essential ally, can be unimportant to Americans, and few things have contributed more to the structure and health of Canada than the Fraser. Measured by size, by economic consequence, by political influence, the Fraser is a continental force.

In shape it is an elongated letter S; in length 850 miles without its vast mesh of tributaries; in aspect ugly and sublime; in character violent and treacherous; in potential usefulness the largest source of electrical power left in North America.

Its first waters drip from the melting snows of the Rockies' central range, some 300 miles north of the American border, latitude 52° 45′, and hard by the upper reaches of the Columbia, which almost duplicates the Fraser's seaward journey farther to the south. The milky sweat of glaciers, the oozings of the mountain mosses, the clean upland puddles, and the tiny cataracts among the rock slides form the first creeks which, joining in a

narrow lake, begin a leisurely and deceptive passage northwestward through British Columbia. Fresh from the snow and well-
washed mountainsides, the little river is green and cleanly.

At the top of its northern arc the Fraser almost slips over
the northern watershed of the continent. A few miles away, the
first small members of the great Mackenzie family are beginning
their long voyage to the arctic. A minute tilt of land would join
the Fraser to this northern flow, but the little elevation along
the arc turns it southward. Thus barely escaping the pull of the
arctic drainage basin, the Fraser, now a mighty river and growing
with every mile, searches for a passage to the Pacific.

Between it and the ocean lie the several ranges of the Coast
mountains, some of them higher than the Canadian Rockies. For
more than four hundred miles there is no direct opening through
this barrier. The Fraser is forced to move southward across the
broad inland plateau, where it easily digs for itself a yawning
ditch through the yielding gumbo.

In the early stages its journey is monotonous. It moves
among somber hills, dark with forests of spruce and jack pine,
and every mile is the same. By now it is gathering volume and
speed. Its load of sediment has turned its water to the color of
pale treacle.

At its southward turn it absorbs its first great tributary,
the Nechako, from the lake country to the west. Now its canyon is deepening and widening but at one famous danger point
its current is suddenly compressed in a narrow gate of rock to
spill over a few miles of rapids, where the skeletons of ancient
ships and barges still lie across the sand bars. Having passed this
first obstruction, the river is soon running free again.

Now it is swollen by the Quesnel, which it sucks in from the
eastward. From the west it swallows the Chilcotin out of the
coastal snow. It has left the timbered country and is cutting
through an open rangeland of bunch grass and sagebrush.

It is still growing. Some hundred miles to the south it meets
its only serious rival, the Thompson, whose northern branch has

risen not far from the Fraser's own source in the Rockies but has moved down an eastern trench and then swung west through the Dry Belt.

At their junction the Thompson looks almost as large and tumultuous as the Fraser but is instantly engulfed in the main

current with a gaudy blend of color. Its leagues of clay have turned the Fraser to a deep and oily brown. The Thompson, cleansed by its filtering lakes to the eastward, is a hard blue-green. As it surges into the Fraser at Lytton the Thompson cuts a sharp line across the muddy substance of its parent, like a vein of precious metal on a bed of dull ore. The margin of this clean water is so fixed and solid that you can almost believe that the two rivers are made of different elements. But at the edge of this bubbling mixture the Thompson suddenly disappears.

The character of the Fraser has changed. Its direction is still south but it has collided for the first time with the Coast Range, which runs from the southeast to the northwest sideways along the edge of the continent. Seeking a pass to the sea, the current moves in a quickened pace but yet parallel to the coast. It is now squeezed tight within the mountains and turns furious at its imprisonment. Its channel here is cut out of the living rock, its trench dug ever deeper to accommodate its distended body, its water convulsed in whirlpool, back eddy and hidden cavern.

This is the black canyon of the Fraser, where even the salmon is often hurled bodily from the current, where the first explorers crawled on hands and knees along the edges of the precipice, where the Indians traveled on dangling ladders, where the gold rush hauled its freight by a road built on stilts, where the engineers blasted their railway grades out of the naked cliffs.

The canyon has been called beautiful. If this be beauty, it is the beauty of nightmare. It has been called magnificent, but this is the magnificence of destruction. It has been called sublime, and so it is, with the sublimity of blind and senseless force.

From the road, high up the mountains, the river appears as a twisted line of brown, solid and motionless, no wider than a clothesline. The Coast Range around it, unlike the more orderly defiles of the Rockies, sprawls in chaos as if its builders had mislaid their plans—a jumble of ragged peaks, dim gorges, smears of green forest, shadows miles wide in ceaseless shift of pattern.

Hour by hour this jumble of rock, earth, timber and water changes its aspect and almost seems to change its substance in men's sight. At dawn the surface of the mountains thrusts itself out, acquires body and shape and seems to lurch toward the river. At noon, as the shadows move down them, the slopes retreat, fading into dull grays and greens. In the twilight the canyon is hung with ragged curtains of blue and purple, haze streams out of every crevice and the mountains stand solid against the stars, almost within touch of your hand. Always, in daylight or dark, the canyon is clamorous with the voice of its passenger.

In such a closed and wrinkled pocket man and his works are lost. The two railways and the single road have left only a nick on the cliffs, a few feet of level space across the slides. A freight train a mile long is a toiling worm, at night a glow worm, whose spark flickers for a moment and is snuffed out. Only a wink of light from some railway town on the canyon's lip proclaims the presence of any life but the river's.

To observe the dimensions and power of this larger life you must crawl down the rock slides to the riverbank. There the smooth line of water as seen from the mountains turns into a paroxysm of dirty foam, rising and falling in steady pulse. The perpetual mist has coated the canyon walls with slime and the water has worn them smooth, squared them off like old masonry so that in places they might have been built by human hands. A few islands still stand in the channel, whittled down to narrow splinters and already doomed. The final product of this erosion, the white sand pulverized out of the mountainsides, is laid in glistening bars by every back eddy. The dust of gold lies in these bars from the undiscovered mother lode.

All other sounds, the human voice, the whistle of the loco- motive a few yards off, are obliterated by the din of this caldron. The motion of the river seems to set the entire canyon in mo- tion. Before the spectacle of flux, the beholder turns dizzy and, looking up, finds the cliffs closing over his head.

The river is larger than it appears. At the gut of Hell's Gate, where it finally breaches the central spine of the moun- tains, it is only 120 feet wide, but its constricted body has bored a channel for itself 85 feet deep at low water and as deep as 175 feet in summer freshet. It moves here sometimes at the rate of 20 feet a second, too fast even for the passage of salmon.

At last the river has found its outlet to the sea. At Hope it bursts out of the canyon, turns straight west, and pours down the coastal shelf.

Now the character of the river country changes again. Moving in from the Pacific, the clouds have collided with the mountains and dumped their rain on the western slope to nourish the Pacific jungle. The sparse, red-barked pine, the jack pine, the flat juniper and shivering poplar, which have followed the river through the Dry Belt, give way to close-packed fir, hemlock, balsam, maple and alder. After the bare clay of sagebrush and tumbleweed, the ground is rank with fern, salal and devil's club. All at once, in hardly more than a mile, the river emerges from the mountains and the jungle to find itself ample elbowroom in a lush and open valley.

On the silt dumped by the current before he appeared man now grows his crops and feeds his dairy herds. Still the river is not to be trusted. It continually threatens and often overflows the dikes he has built against it. But after the madness of its youth it spends its last years in relative peace. Toward its mouth it tolerates the ships of remote oceans, the tugs and log booms of commerce, and the white flocks of sea gulls feeding on its refuse. Thus past the busy port of New Westminster, across the delta of its own making, by three separate channels heavy with its silt, this weariest river moves somehow safe to sea.

The journey has been long and laborious. The Fraser has traveled nearly a thousand miles. It has drained two mountain ranges and 91,000 square miles of land, more than the area of many great nations, nearly twice the entire space of New York State, nearly one and a half times the size of Washington. It has laid the alluvial site and by its commerce has built the world port of Vancouver. Its power has lighted this city and propelled most of Canada's industry west of the Rockies. Its waters have irrigated a hundred thousand acres. Its silt has provided some of the most fertile farm land in the world. It has altered, as we shall see, the course of man's life in America. Even on the sea it has left its indelible mark, a gout of brown smeared for miles across the green salt waters, as if the Fraser were loath to die.

2 Discovery

IT TOOK THE WHITE MAN A LONG TIME TO FIND THE FRASER—
some two centuries from the beginning of his search.

In December, 1577, Sir Francis Drake sailed from Plymouth
with five ships, built at his own cost from the pillage of the
Spanish Main, with violin and harp players to beguile him at his
meals, with golden plate for his food, the rarest vintage wines of
Europe, and a corps of young noblemen to wait on him. Raiding
and looting his way around the Horn and up the coast of America, he weighted the *Golden Hind* so deep with Spanish treasure
that he was compelled to abandon this congenial piracy and head
reluctantly for home.

As an afterthought he decided to seek out the Strait of
Anian, the Northeast Passage which, as all navigators believed, cut
through the new continent from the Pacific to the Atlantic.
How far north he sailed the *Golden Hind* we do not know, but
by midsummer, 1579, he had satisfied himself that the continental passage was a myth. He turned west, rounded the Cape of
Good Hope and reached Plymouth a year later.

To England he was a hero, to the geographers a failure—he
had missed the great passage. In his own words:

> The Asian and American continents, if they be not
> fully joined, yet seem they to come very neere, from whose
> high and snow-covered mountains the north and north-west
> winds send abroad their frozen nimphes to the infecting of

13

the whole air—hence comes it that in the middest of their summer, the snow hardly departeth from these hills at all; hence come those thicke mists and most stinking fogges— for these reasons we coniecture that either there is no passage at all through these Northerne coasts, which is most likely, or if there be, that is unnavigable.

This the geographers, seated comfortably at home beside their imaginary maps, stoutly denied. The passage, they said, was there and could be found. If they had believed Drake, much money and uncounted lives would have been saved in the next two hundred years.

Drake had not looked for a river but his voyage opened the clash of European imperialisms that finally discovered the Fraser. In the first quarter of the eighteenth century the race between Spain, Britain and Russia, joined later by the newborn United States, for control of the Pacific got seriously under way. It would ferret out all the secrets of the American coast, the Fraser among them.

Peter the Great was the first of the empire builders to grasp the importance of the northern Pacific. Learning the practical side of kingship as a carpenter in the dockyards of the East India Company in England, this earlier Stalin had seen the inpouring treasure of the New World and the power to be bought with it. He wanted his share. Unfortunately, in the struggle to divide the booty, the older empires had got in on the ground floor and occupied most of it. Since he was sealed up in the Baltic, Peter turned eastward across the plains of Siberia and northward to the arctic. He had nowhere else to go.

Here, for the first time, arises the faint rumor of the Fraser and a name which is still attached to it. Shortly after Drake left the stinking fogges of the Pacific for the friendly mists of London, a Greek navigator, Juan de Fuca, sailed a Spanish ship north from the Spanish settlements of California. He came home to tell of a passage inland across what is now British Columbia. Perhaps he lied. Perhaps he had found that great strait which bears his name today and into which the Fraser pours its muddy water—a potential passage through America certainly, but useless until the day of roads and railways. At any rate, Peter had heard of de Fuca and saw a chance to penetrate America and seize an empire.

Peter was sick by now and within five weeks would die, crazy with remorse, haunted by the ghosts of his victims, shrieking for mercy in the corridors of his palace; but he still had time to organize an expedition to America. For this prodigy of labor he chose the Dane, Vitus Bering, who, with a great caravan of sleds, boats, horses, dogs and Cossacks, toiled six thousand miles across Siberia to the sea.

On Kamchatka Bering built his ships and sailed eastward on July 9, 1728, to explore the continent of Gamaland, which was supposed to lie between Asia and America. He went far enough to convince himself that no such continent existed, but the geographers of St. Petersburg, like those of London, still clung to their myths. Bering was ordered to try again.

With an incredible collection of botanists, monks, artists, doctors, soldiers and assorted lunatics this doomed man led his second expedition across Europe and Asia—six hundred men in all, with four thousand pack horses. Three years later the survivors reached the Pacific, built two ships at Petropavlovsk and started out to find Fuca's Strait.

Bering had lost all belief in it, but the lunatics urged him on until, reaching the coast of Alaska, he ran out of provisions. By now he was half mad from the quarrels of his followers and sick in his bed of scurvy. He did not stay to explore the new land. Knowing that the chance of safe return was small, he turned back toward Russia, was wrecked on the Aleutians and died in a pit, wrapped in the furs of wild animals.

Those furs would change the history of the human race from that day forward, through two hundred years of exploration, war and plunder, through revolution in St. Petersburg, communism in China, the Yalta conference, the atomic explosion of Hiroshima, the clash of two worlds in the United Nations, the current struggle for domination of the Pacific, and all the other ironies of the great victory of 1945. But Bering, in his charnel pit, could hardly guess what he had started.

The twoscore survivors of that winter in the Aleutians sailed back to Siberia on a raft, naked but for the skins of animals about their loins and shoulders. They knew not what they wore. But the wise old Chinese merchants from Manchuria, who beheld these men and fingered their furs, looked at one another with a wild surmise—these were the skins of the sea otter, priced beyond pearls. Bering had failed to find the gold and gems of Gamaland as Peter had hoped. He had found something better. Or worse.

Now Fuca's Strait was forgotten as the Russians swarmed over the Aleutians, butchered the fur animals and the human inhabitants impartially and, while butchered themselves in return, as they deserved, yet managed to smear across the North Pacific a spectacle of mass murder on which only modern and civilized man could improve. This story is pallid beside the larger carnage of our enlightened times and does not concern us here, but it began that collision of nations on the Pacific which is still in today's headlines. And it directed men unknowingly toward the Fraser.

During the year of Bering's first voyage James Cook was born in a Yorkshire village, the son of a farm laborer. He went to sea as a boy, sailed in the Baltic, and from the Russians learned of their countrymen's adventures among the fur islands east of Siberia. He also heard of that will-o'-the-wisp called Fuca's Strait.

Cook was not to see these fabled seas for some time. He had yet to navigate Wolfe's ships up the St. Lawrence to capture Quebec and half a continent with one stroke. When the British pushed westward across Canada, when their explorers were dying in the ice and tundra to find the Northwest Passage, when their

Parliament was offering £20,000 to the man who found it, Cook started for the Pacific. The year was 1776, when other strange things were happening among transplanted Britons in the colonies of New England and when, in these same colonies, a baby was being born whose name would someday mark the great western river.

In 1778 Cook passed Fuca's Strait. Like Drake before him, he missed it in the stinking fogges. Fuca's legend seemed such an obvious siren's call to deluded navigators that Cook named the sharp point of land that marked the strait's entrance Cape Flattery. Beyond it lay the river, its golden gravel, its veins of minerals, its timber, farm lands and fish. Cook passed them by, recording in his log that no passage could exist here.

After landing at Nootka, on Vancouver Island, and voyaging northward, but finding no passage there, Cook sailed back to the Sandwich Islands, died with a knife in his back, and was hacked to pieces by the natives. And still the Fraser, which was to become a passage for men's travel across the continent, rolled brown, angry and unsuspected to the sea.

The log of Cook's voyage, despite the great blank in it, set his countrymen afire. England held Canada, it claimed the whole Pacific shore of America as New Albion on the strength of Drake's piracy, and it laughed at Spain's edict which called the Pacific a "closed sea."

The Spaniards, indeed, were becoming troublesome again as they had been in the days of the Armada. They were creeping up the American coast. One of their navigators, Bruno Heceta, had begun to suspect the truth at last—there was no open passage through the continent but a "great river" flowed across it to the western ocean. This was, in fact, only half the truth. There were two great rivers. Anyway, Heceta's theory set the ponderous machinery of British imperialism in faster motion.

The great river, said the British, must be the long-sought link between the Atlantic and the Pacific, the easy route from Hudson Bay to the islands of the sea otter and the seal. For their fur the misguided Chinese would pay absurdly high in tea, which could be swilled in London, thirty cups a day by Dr. Johnson and the other temperance drinkers of the club. Britain must find the Great River to reach the furs and the tea.

British explorers established themselves at Nootka, where Cook had landed. Captain Barkley looked into the Strait of Juan de Fuca and noted it on his maps. Captain Meares pressed some way up this channel but decided that the Great River did not flow into it.

Meanwhile the new American nation was showing an annoying interest in these regions. Captain John Kendrick in the *Columbia* and Captain Robert Gray in the *Lady Washington* sailed out of Boston on October 1, 1787, and next August Gray observed the Olympic Mountains, which flank the sea entrance to the Fraser on the south. He wrote in his log: "I am of opinion that the Straits of Juan de Fuca do exist; for the coast takes a great bend here."

At Nootka the British assured the Americans that the strait led nowhere and that there were no furs to be found thereabouts. It was the usual fur trader's story and the shrewd Yankees were not deceived. They bought furs from the Indians and they nosed up the strait. They did not find its secret.

By now Britain and Spain were both claiming Vancouver Island and the entire coast, but the story of their quarrel, the comic-opera negotiations and drinking parties of their representatives at Nootka, the treachery of the Indians, the coming and going of great ships and bejeweled commanders need not be told here. While these affairs went forward, wiser men were looking for the river.

Having temporarily pushed the British out of Nootka, the Spaniards scoured the coast anew. In the spring of 1792 their most daring pilot, a man named Narvaez, was given a leaky schooner, a crew of thirty wretched Mexican peons and scant supplies. He was told to follow Fuca's Strait to its end, wherever that might be.

Narvaez passed the entrance of Puget Sound, threaded the archipelago to the north of it, and worked his way slowly northward until his eyes rested on a curious sight—a vast brown stain lying, oily and still, upon the sea. A river, obviously, and a large one. He called it Boca de Florida Blanca. The Great River at last? No, it could not be the Great River of Bruno Heceta. It was too far north and too far from the open sea. Another Great River then? Perhaps the true passage!

Narvaez, that forgotten man who actually found the Fraser, was too sick to care about it and his crew was starving. They brought their news and their questions back to Nootka and for their trouble they received neither pay nor fame. Spain knew the importance of the discovery, a possible channel inland, but Spain, having proclaimed the Pacific a "closed sea," did not reveal the secret to its rivals.

Before Spain could exploit Narvaez's news England had returned to the race for control of the Pacific. The Spaniards must be booted out of Nootka first and then a systematic exploration of the coast would be conducted in British style, where the blundering Spaniards had failed. Spain yielded to the mistress of the seas. Nootka (but not the secret of the river) was handed over to Britain. Captain George Vancouver, who had been a midshipman under Cook, was sent out with two ships, the *Discovery* and the *Chatham*, to accept the Spanish surrender.

An unfortunate man, Vancouver. He almost discovered the Columbia on the way north and certainly would have observed it if he had not been blown offshore. Then, later on, England could have claimed Oregon Territory, perhaps with an unanswerable case. Two weeks after Vancouver had passed this way the dauntless Yankee, Gray, recognized Heceta's Great River at last, crossed the Columbia's bar and established his country's rights over one of the richest regions in the world. No one but a few obscure Spaniards, now driven out of the Pacific, suspected that there was still another Great River to be explored.

Vancouver sailed north, entered the Strait of Juan de Fuca and mapped Puget Sound. Still he found no river. When he passed the Fraser's entrance the fog hid it, a stinking fogge indeed. He pushed on and was the first man to circumnavigate the island to which his own name was given, but he never suspected the existence of the Fraser. He went south again, explored the Columbia's mouth, claimed it for England, and declared that "it does not appear that Mr. Gray either saw or was ever within five leagues of the entrance." A greatly mistaken man, Vancouver, but he is remembered by the name of a living Canadian city and an island paradise, while only history books remember Gray.

With Vancouver's voyage the north Pacific coast was safely under British rule, the lines of the future struggle for power in this ocean had narrowed to England, Russia and the United States. And at Fort Chipewyan, on the other side of the Rockies, just beyond the first frail trickle of the Fraser, a young Scot was lying awake in his winter cabin, brooding on a desperate exploit.

3   To the Pacific by Canoe

A LEXANDER MACKENZIE, THE FIRST WHITE MAN TO CROSS THE
land mass of North America and voyage upon the Fraser,
was born in 1764 at Stornoway, on the island of Lewis. He came
from a region celebrated by an early Canadian poet in a rhyme
which yet stirs our Scottish blood:

> From the lone shieling of the misty island
> Mountains divide us, and the waste of seas;
> But still the blood is strong, the heart is Highland,
> And we in dreams behold the Hebrides.

Mackenzie was to dream such dreams in many a curious bed
on the other side of the world. But, by all accounts, from Bos-
well's onward, the Hebrides are a hard sort of country. Perhaps
they helped to prepare Mackenzie for the still harder country
of Canada. He emigrated at sixteen and went to work for the
North West Company, of Montreal. At twenty-two he was a
partner and found himself caught up, while hardly yet of age,
in the bloody fur wars of America.

His first major expedition was northward, and if he had gone
no farther his name would have remained large and indelible on
the map of the continent. In 1789, now twenty-five years old,
he descended the largest northern river to the Arctic Sea. That
river, where he almost perished in the ice, where he saw the midnight sun and the endless leagues of tundra, is the Mackenzie.
The boisterous partners of the North West Company were not

much interested in exploration unless it brought in fur, especially the fur of the Pacific seal and sea otter. Now locked in a life-and-death struggle with the Hudson's Bay Company—a private shooting war which produced arson, massacre and bankruptcy before the Nor' Westers capitulated—Mackenzie's bosses in Montreal almost broke his heart by ignoring his arctic voyage.

When he reached Chipewyan again he began to consider a larger and more desperate plan. The Russians, the Spaniards, the Americans and the British were harvesting the fur of the western ocean. Between his fort and the coast lay a region no man knew how large or how rich. But assuredly it must contain fur and beyond it swam the seal and the otter. The maps showed Mackenzie little more than the rumor of a great river which, if he could find it, would carry him down to the sea. Cooped up in his cabin, almost forgotten by his company, he resolved to take the risk.

To be the first man across the continent, to sail the fabled river of the west—this, more than the prospect of fur, became such an obsession with the young Scotsman that he packed up his gear, paddled down to Montreal, sailed for England, and spent a winter studying astronomy and surveying in London. A Scot from the northern isles, he believed in preparation.

London was too busy just then to take much notice of the man who had explored the Mackenzie and reached the arctic ice floes, but it was interested in western fur. England seemed to be talking of nothing else. The plans for new Pacific voyages, the story of Cook's murder, of another expedition by Vancouver, sent Mackenzie hurrying to Canada, lest someone cross the continent ahead of him.

By the spring of 1792 he was back at Fort Chipewyan outfitting for his expedition. In October he paddled out of Lake Athabaska and up the Peace River to a point near its junction with the Smoky. Here he built a fort and wintered.

In early May, judging the river fit for travel, he prepared to embark. Mackenzie was now a man just short of thirty, of smooth, handsome face, thin nose, cleft chin, curly hair and heavy side whiskers. He had the far-ranging, restless eye of a poet, but he was still a Scot and left nothing to chance. Thus in his diary:

> Having ascertained, by various observations, the latitude of this place to be 56.9 north and longitude 117.35 west, on the 8th day of May, I found that my acrometer was one hour and forty-six minutes slow to apparent time; the mean going of it I had found to be twenty-two seconds slow in twenty-four hours. Having settled this point, the canoe was put in the water . . .

It was seven o'clock on the evening of Thursday, May 9, 1793. A single birchbark canoe, ten men and a dog aboard, a tiny speck on the darkening river—could such a craft hope to climb over the Rockies and slide down to the western sea? Most of Mackenzie's company doubted it.

"My winter interpreter," says the diary, "with another person whom I left here to take care of the fort and supply the natives with ammunition during the summer, shed tears on the reflection of those dangers which we might encounter in our expedition, while our own people offered up their prayers that we might return in safety from it."

At least the canoe was a stout one, specially designed for its work. Since it must carry him where no white man had been before, Mackenzie notes its virtues with satisfaction:

> Her dimensions were twenty-five feet long within; exclusive of the curves of stem and stern; twenty-six inches hold and four feet nine inches beam. At the same time she was so light that two men could carry her on a good road three or four miles without resting. In this slender vessel we shipped provisions, goods for presents, arms, ammunition and baggage to the weight of three thousand pounds, and an

equipage of ten people, viz. Alexander Mackay, Joseph Landry, Charles Ducette, François Beaulieu, Baptiste Bisson, François Courtois and Jacques Beauchamp, with two Indians as hunters and interpreters.

Two fur traders, a half dozen tough French-Canadian voyageurs and a pair of Indian guides, one of the most notable companies in the story of man's roving about the earth, paddled out into the river that night, watched the fort fade into the twilight, and heard the last salute of its guns. Mackenzie waved his hat and turned westward. He would not look back until he had found the ocean.

In the spring freshet the Peace River belies its name. By May 16 the ten men in the big canoe found themselves struggling upward against the power concentrated within the core of the Rockies. They had reached the Rocky Mountain Portage—perpendicular walls, impassable rapids, and a current where no craft could live.

Mackenzie leaped ashore with a towrope tied to his shoulders and slithered up the slippery banks while his companions waited on a rock below. He had made a few yards of progess when the rope broke and the canoe was swept down the rapids. At this instant of disaster, when the whole expedition seemed lost, a wave hurled the canoe onto the bank, where the men were able to pull it up on the narrow rocks.

Now Mackenzie began to hear the first murmurs of mutiny. His paddlers said they would go no farther. He left them to think it over with a "regale" of rum and, clambering up the canyon walls, sought a portage above. He found that the rapids were nine miles long.

The company was feeling better by this time and agreed to try the portage. Carrying the canoe and the supplies in the customary ninety-pound packs, it made exactly one mile the first day and three miles on the second. The men were exhausted and chilled, even in this spring weather, but they found calm water again and paddled on. On the last day of May they reached the junction of two rivers, now called the Finlay and the Parsnip, which together form the Peace.

Here, from a band of Indians, Mackenzie got his first news of the great western river. These natives had heard from others, farther west, of a stream which flowed toward the noonday sun and finally to the "stinking waters." They had heard, too, of white men who sailed on the sea in "huge canoes with sails like clouds" and wore "armour from head to heel." This was hopeful, but which way lay the great river? Should the expedition ascend the Finlay, northwestward, or the Parsnip, southward? Mackenzie talked it over with his guides and determined to go south. That was a lucky choice. If he had followed the Finlay he would have ended hopelessly blockaded in the unbroken coastal range.

The Parsnip, like its parent Peace, was in flood. Again the paddlers, worn out by days of poling and towing, began to complain, but just as they seemed likely to turn back they met another band of Indians who told them of a portage leading to the great river. On June 12 Mackenzie and his company portaged 817 paces over a ridge and found a mountain lake, whose waters drained westward. At last they were in the Pacific drainage basin. By following these waters they must reach the ocean.

Yet where was the great river? Mackenzie could not know it then but he had stumbled into one of the tributaries of the Fraser's north fork. Fraser himself, covering the same route in the next century, christened this stream the Bad River. It deserved that name.

As Mackenzie's canoe sped down the current, the voyageurs singing with delight because the weeks of uphill paddling were over, the river suddenly narrowed into fierce rapids. Before he could land, Mackenzie found himself caught in an eddy which swamped the canoe. He and his companions clung to it and would have drowned that first day on the Pacific waters if the eddy had not carelessly cast them upon a sand bar. The stern of the canoe was stove in, all the supplies soaked and half the ammunition lost.

This, said the paddlers, was the end. They would go back. Mackenzie ignored them and set quietly to work repairing the canoe with resin and oilcloth. Dried out at last, the crew agreed to advance but they had to carry their goods by land while the four best paddlers took the empty canoe downstream. On June 17 they reached the confluence of a larger current. This, Mackenzie guessed, was the great river of the west.

Again the canoe was loaded—heavy now from repeated patching. The going was comfortable enough but, to Mackenzie's alarm, the river was not flowing west. Soon he found himself moving straight south and getting no nearer to the ocean. He was, in fact, sliding down the western arc of the Fraser's great bend. He seems to have missed the Nechako, which flows into the Fraser from the westward just below the top of the bend. The Nechako would have led him westward through the lake country to the headwaters of the Bulkley and the Skeena and down to the sea, but he lost that chance.

Soon he found himself in a deep clay trench, swept southward at high speed and unable to see where he was going. Once again the broken canoe was hurled into some of the worst waters of the north, the three-forked Fort George canyon.

Anyone like the writer of this book who has drifted in a small boat between these foaming gates of rock will realize what kind of man Mackenzie was from his own record, a masterpiece of understatement and Scottish phlegm:

> From the extremity of this point to the rocky and almost perpindicular bank that rose on the opposite shore is not more than forty or fifty yards. The great body of water, at the same time tumbling in successive cascades along the first carrying-place, rolls through this narrow passage in a very turbid current and full of whirlpools.

That is all. The next sentence is comic in its homeliness:

26

On the banks of the river there was plenty of wild onions, which, when mixed up with our pemmican, was a great improvement on it, though they produced a physical effect in our appetites which was rather inconvenient to the state of our provisions.

Wild onions and pemmican beside the vortex of the Fort George canyon! We shall return to these waters later on, in the days when little gas boats crawled through them by the skin of their teeth. For the moment it is sufficient to note that they did not excite Mackenzie. He was thinking of his provisions, now melting away because they were too appetizing with their new onion flavor.

Once past the triple-pronged passage, he drifted down to the Quesnel, which enters the Fraser from the east. Travel was easy but Mackenzie was becoming worried. The great river, if this indeed was it, showed no sign of turning toward the sea. When he saw a tribe of Indians on the bank he resolved to question them.

These were of the Takulli nation, the famous Carriers, so called because the widows of warriors carried their husbands' cremated ashes about with them for three years. The Carriers lived midway between the coastal and mountain peoples and acted as middlemen in trade. They did not welcome the white men. Arrows were shot at the canoe and rocks were rolled down upon it from the canyon walls. Fortunately the Indians' aim was poor.

Mackenzie landed on the shore opposite the Indians, threw his pistols to the ground, together with some glittering trinkets, and made signs of friendship. Never taking unnecessary chances, he sent one of his men across the river secretly to watch the Indians from the rear and shoot them if they seemed dangerous. The Carriers timidly crossed to Mackenzie in an unfamiliar craft, one of the great dugouts of the upper Fraser, made from the easily carved cottonwood tree. They eyed the trinkets eagerly and accepted them with delight.

Having drawn a rough map on the river sand, Mackenzie explained his purpose in sign language—he was seeking the stinking waters of the west. The Carriers understood and drew on the sand the course of the western trail. The trail, as they drew it, branched off from the Fraser along a tributary, some distance north of this point. It was useless, the natives said, to go farther south, for the river plunged into impassable rapids, the noise of which they imitated, alarmingly, in their throats.

Here was a crisis. Should Mackenzie follow the great river on which all his hopes had been set or abandon it and strike westward overland, with no assurance but the word of a few savages who might well be scheming to destroy him?

"The more I heard of the river," says Mackenzie's diary, "the more I was convinced that it would not empty itself into the ocean to the north of what is called the river of the west, so that with its windings, the distance must be very great."

He therefore called his people together and:

. . . after passing a warm eulogium on their fortitude, patience and perseverance, I stated the difficulties that threatened our continuing to navigate the river, the length of time it would require and the scanty provisions we had for such a voyage: I then proceeded for the foregoing reasons to propose a shorter route, by trying the overland road to the sea. . . . I declared my resolution not to attempt it unless they would engage, if we could not after all proceed over land, to return with me, and continue our voyage to the discharge of the waters, whatever the distance might be. At all events, I declared in the most solemn manner that I would not abandon my design of reaching the sea, if I made the attempt alone, and that I did not despair of returning in safety to my friends.

This speech around the campfire to nine ragged and exhausted men was the measure of the young Scot—he would reach the sea if he reached it alone and never returned. He had forgotten the Hebrides. All his dreams were of the Pacific.

The men decided to follow him. Now they had no river to guide them, no assurance of a pass through the mountains that loomed raggedly to the westward, nothing but the word of the Indians. And it was already midsummer. Two months had passed since they paddled out of their winter fort. Would there be time to reach the fort again on the other side of the Rockies before freeze-up?

Not an hour was to be wasted. From the point on the Fraser now called Alexandria, Mackenzie turned northward, giving up one of his greatest hopes, the exploration of the great river. A Carrier went with him and guided the canoe to the Blackwater, which enters from the westward, just north of the Quesnel. On July 4 the canoe could go no farther up this side stream. The last great portage began.

From here on the paddlers had to travel day after day on foot, the earth being for them an unnatural and hostile element. Soon they experienced the Pacific jungle which, sodden by the incoming ocean rains, sprawls dankly along the sea and oozes into the defiles of the coastal range. The Indian trail was poorly marked, the rank underbrush soaked the travelers, mist hung in every valley, and the Carrier guide tried to desert. Mackenzie slept beside him at night—a filthy fellow, covered with vermin and stinking of fish oil—to prevent his escape. The brave company of May was reduced by this time to a band of half-naked, barefooted skeletons, almost too weak to walk.

For two weeks they staggered on until the gigantic size of the forest and the totem poles in the Indian villages along the trail told them they were nearing the sea. When they encountered the Dean River they managed to ford it and soon found themselves on the bank of the Bella Coola.

This stream Mackenzie selected as the route of his final dash to the coast. From an Indian tribe he secured dugout canoes, the universal craft of the coastal people—heavy, finely carved craft, hollowed out of cedar trees, and seaworthy enough to live in almost any storm. In these the expedition paddled down the Bella Coola.

Mackenzie soon noted sure signs that his destination was close. The Indians living along the banks possessed white men's goods and trinkets, obviously secured from the navigators of the Pacific. A lance in the hands of one warrior Mackenzie took to be Spanish or Russian. The assault on the continent from east and west was about to be joined.

On July 20 the canoes turned the last corner of the river. Mackenzie looked out on a blue and shining water and sniffed the flavor of salt. But he was still some distance from the open sea. Next day he descended North Bentinck Arm, passed the south arm, and moved down Burke Channel. Now, beholding the archipelago that hugs the western shore, he decided that he could go no farther without a ship. His work was done.

On a great rock fronting the sea he daubed his final message in red ocher and bear's grease:

"Alexander Mackenzie, from Canada, by land, the twenty-second of July, one thousand seven hundred and ninety-three. Lat. 52° 20′ 48″ N."

There were no heroics in Mackenzie or in his brief monument. The commonplace words on the sea rocks were soon washed off by wind and rain. His trail and camping places disappeared in the long silence that followed him. But he had lived a story that would not be forgotten while the records of North American men survived. He had walked and paddled from ocean to ocean, measured the widest sweep of the continent, reached the Pacific twelve years before the Americans, Lewis and Clark, and claimed the west for the British Empire. That, for a practical Scot, was enough. Mackenzie resolved to go home to the lone shieling of his misty island.

The return was not much easier than the advance. The coastal Indians were hostile. One of them claimed compensation because white sailors (presumably Vancouver's crew, which had explored these waters two months before) had fired on him. With only twenty pounds of pemmican on hand, fifteen pounds of rice and six pounds of moldy flour, Mackenzie had no gifts to spare. The Indians began to hurl spears and for a moment the whole expedition faced massacre, just after reaching its goal. Mackenzie and his men stood firm, the Indians retreated, and the long paddle upstream began. Toward the end of August the company was back at the fort on the Peace River. Soon Mackenzie started eastward, bound for Scotland.

He was tired of the wilderness. Settling down as a Scottish gentleman, he wrote his *Voyages on the River St. Lawrence and through the Continent of North America to the Frozen and Pacific Oceans*, which appeared in 1801, to inform the British people of their unknown western domain. A king who was busy with Napoleon found time to knight the greatest explorer of his time and Mackenzie seems to have lived comfortably enough until 1820. He died at Mulinearn, near Pitlochry, aged fifty-six. The long trails and heavy portages had taken their toll. But he had done precisely what he had set out to do, no more, no less. He had reached the western sea. He had seen the Great River.

4 Simon Fraser

M ACKENZIE WAS SATISFIED, BUT THE FUR TRADERS AND THE British government, after a brief day of jubilation, were not. Though Mackenzie had crossed the continent, he had failed to descend the Great River. He had not traveled far enough south to mark out the bulk of the west for Britain.

This, to an empire struggling with the irrepressible young Americans in the division of America, was becoming a serious business. Where lay the boundary between the new Republic and the British America that had survived the Revolution? No one knew under the vague terms of peace, but assuredly the Columbia, the Great River that Mackenzie apparently had traveled, would largely fix the ultimate line. For Britain it was a tragic error that Mackenzie had not reached the river's mouth and anchored the line before the Americans could dispute it.

The Americans were pressing hard. Jefferson had bought Louisiana from Napoleon for $15,000,000 and Jefferson seemed to think his purchase included everything between the original colonies and the Pacific. To nail down his claim he sent Lewis and Clark overland to the Columbia, which Gray had discovered. The American expedition reached the Pacific in November, 1805.

Thus two thin corridors of exploration and rival ambition stretched clear across the continent—Mackenzie's line far to the north, the line of Lewis and Clark to the Columbia. Between them lay who knew what fur, minerals, timber, farm lands in a space now containing the western border states and half the western provinces of Canada?

Having lost the richest half of America by its own folly, Britain decided to hang on to anything left out of King George's debacle. The first move, obviously, was to fix the Columbia line. Mackenzie, it seemed, had explored the upper river. Now someone must follow it to the sea and make sure that every acre down to the mouth was saved from the Yankees.

For this work another man of Mackenzie's breed was chosen. Simon Fraser, by his portrait in the Parliament Buildings at Victoria, was a dour and homely person of bullet head, sloping brow, tangled hair, heavy eyebrows and massive chin—a solid sort of man with infinite patience and courage but no poetry, and looking in profile rather like the coastal Indians who nearly murdered him. He was of pure Scottish descent, with all the adaptability and stubborn purpose that went with his blood throughout the wilderness of America.

Ironically enough, this man, who was to establish Britain's possessions in the west, came out of the United States. His grandparents, sound stock from Culbochie, had settled at Bennington, Vermont. Here, by a further irony, Simon was born in 1776 just when Jefferson, a kind of invisible opponent throughout his life, was writing the great Declaration.

From the beginning of the trouble in the States the Frasers were on the losing side. Simon's father was a captain in Burgoyne's army, was captured by the revolutionists, apparently at Saratoga, and, though the records are vague, seems to have died in Albany, a prisoner of the Continental Congress. His celebrated son, however, believed that he died on a vessel which carried away the surrendered British army.

At all events, the elder Fraser left a widow, four sons and five daughters. This destitute family, obscure particles in the migration of the United Empire Loyalists, somehow moved north into Canada and settled at St. Andrews, near the Ottawa River.

33

For Simon the widow Fraser evidently had brave hopes. She managed to send him to Montreal for a brief period of schooling and in 1792, aged sixteen, he was articled as a clerk in the North West Company, one of whose junior partners was at that moment getting ready to descend the river that would later bear Simon's name.

The young Fraser moved up fast. By 1802 he was a "bourgeois" or full partner in the company and its managers had picked him as Mackenzie's successor. In 1805, as the race with the Americans quickened, Fraser traveled westward by slow stages. There seemed to be no urgent rush yet, for the British had not heard that Lewis and Clark were on the march. Throughout the race, indeed, neither contestant ever knew the position of the other.

Fraser's route lay along the familiar fur trail from Fort William across the prairies and thence up the Peace in Mackenzie's footsteps. At the awful nine-mile carrying place Fraser built a post which he called Rocky Mountain Portage. In the late autumn he pushed up the Peace and Parsnip to a lake which he called McLeod after his friend, Archibald Norman McLeod. There he built the first post west of the Rockies.

While Fraser went back to his base on the Peace for supplies, he left James McDougall at McLeod. This daring lieutenant, not content to spend the winter under cover, followed Mackenzie's trail to the Bad River, reached the Fraser (or upper Columbia, as he imagined), paddled down the big bend and discovered the Nechako, which Mackenzie had missed. Pressing up the Nechako, McDougall reached the western lake region and may have touched both Fraser and Stuart Lakes, of which no white man had yet heard. Thus when Fraser appeared at Fort McLeod in the spring of 1806 McDougall had a remarkable tale to tell him. Fraser resolved to follow up McDougall's explorations without delay.

Up to now Fraser's journals had often been fragmentary and abounded in long gaps, but now that he was following Mackenzie along the Great River he decided to keep a close check on his predecessor's record. The Fraser diary seems to reveal a touch of jealousy. Thus:

> Trout Lake is a considerable large and navigable river in all seasons. It does not appear to have been noticed by Sir A.M.K. [Mackenzie] as he used to indulge himself in a little sleep. Likely he did not see it and I can account for many other omissions in no other manner than his being asleep at the time he pretends to have been very exact; but was I qualified to make observations and inclined to find fault with him, I could prove he seldom or ever paid the attention he pretends to have done, and that many of his remarks were not made by himself but communicated by his men.

The diary makes light of channels and portages which Mackenzie found almost impassable, and when Fraser reached the mouth of the Nechako, on McDougall's trail, he attacked Mackenzie outright for missing the great tributary:

"Sir A.M.K. appears to have been very inaccurate in the courses or there must have been a vast difference in the compass he made use of and the one we had which is perhaps not very good."

Having put Mackenzie in his place, Fraser abruptly abandoned his diary on July 18, 1806. What Mackenzie, now living a life of ease in Scotland, thought of these comments from a rival it would be interesting to know. Anyway, the first overlander's reputation survived these few tiny blemishes.

By the end of July Fraser and his party had reached Stuart Lake in two huge birchbark canoes. The Carriers, amazed by their first sight of white men, gathered on the lake shore as Fraser and his aide, John Stuart, stepped aground and discharged a volley from their guns to proclaim this superb area of lake and river the property of the British crown. To the Indian braves Fraser gave tobacco but they were puzzled by it and supposed that the smoke emerging from the white men's throats contained the spirits of their dead ancestors. The squaws ate Fraser's soap and frothed at the mouth in an alarming fashion.

This, thought Fraser as he looked across the blue waters of the lake with the snowy mountains behind it, was an ideal site for trade, a natural channel of navigation, the drainage basin of a rich fur land, some of the most pleasant country in America. He christened the lake Stuart after his friend and built a palisaded post which he called Fort St. James. And so entranced were these Scotsmen with the scenery that they gave the name New Caledonia to the whole region.

Stuart had discovered another lake to the south and named it in honor of his chief. Fraser visited it and established his third post there—three posts, be it noted, before any permanent British settlement had appeared on the coast. The Nor' Westers were now open for business on a line running from Montreal almost to the Pacific—but too far north to fit the imperial needs of Britain.

Until now, in the territory left them by the American Revolution, the British had been operating with customary unconcern, only half sure that Canada was an asset and not a liability when they needed all their energies to deal with Napoleon. Since nothing had been heard of Lewis and Clark, no real sense of urgency had developed. It was Fraser who finally had to ask permission to get on with his exploration.

After his successful venture into the lake country he returned to his Peace River base. In January, 1807, he wrote to McDougall at Fort McLeod: "I have another plan in view, that is if it could be done with ease, to get all the goods that will be required for going down the Columbia in the spring." Meanwhile he had written to the company at Montreal and asked for these supplies and permission to follow Mackenzie's river, without further delay, to the sea. The company hesitated no longer, for it had just learned that Lewis and Clark were at the Pacific, with Jefferson claiming everything in sight.

Supplies were shipped to Fraser from Montreal under Jules

Quesnel, but he did not arrive at Fort St. James, on Stuart Lake, until the autumn of 1807. It was too late to face the Great River that year. But the company, after all this delay, wrote Fraser that he must get to the sea as soon as he could. The British lion was awake at last.

Fraser had waited impatiently for this chance. He moved back from the lake country to the Great River, and there, at the mouth of the Nechako, he built a new base, calling it Fort George. Alone among all his posts this was destined, a century later, to become an important town, a roistering railway construction center, and finally an airbase on the flying route to Alaska.

From Fort George, on Saturday, May 22, 1808, Fraser set out on what was to prove perhaps the most desperate expedition in the history of western exploration.

At five in the morning four canoes headed out into the river. They carried Fraser, Stuart, Quesnel, nineteen paddlers and two Indians, twenty-four in all. No company of two dozen men had ever known less where they were going. Fraser still thought they were on the Columbia but he had no idea of its lower course or what lay between him and salt water. If he had known he would not have started out so blithely. Probably he would not have started at all, for no crew would have followed him.

The going was easy at first, as Mackenzie had found, but in the narrow swirl of Fort George canyon the canoes became almost unmanageable. Fraser makes light of it in his diary and repeats Mackenzie's amusing record: "Gathered wild onions for sauce." Onions apparently spiced many a voyageur's adventure in the three-forked sluice.

The first large river on the left Fraser named Quesnel after his second lieutenant, little suspecting how famous that name would become in half a century. All this country, later to be known as the gold field of Cariboo, the voyageurs found to be of "very fine aspect, consisting of extensive plains and behind these hills rising over hills." Many Indians seemed to live along the river, for the canoes constantly passed their villages. The sight of the white men caused wild excitement among the natives, whose grapevine system of communication soon spread the news.

At some point below Mackenzie's most southern penetration the Indians had gathered in such numbers that Fraser paused to parley with them. He set down the incident in his diary:

A woman of the Atnah nation came running towards us, speaking as loud as possible, but our interpreter could not understand her; she nevertheless continued speaking and endeavoured to supply the deficiency in language by signs. She so continued, at times addressing the people on the other side [of the river] then speaking to us.

It turned out that the Indians were not hostile but, having sent out mounted messengers to all the neighboring tribes, wanted Fraser to address a mass meeting and explain his intentions before going downstream. Fraser agreed to pause and presently the Indians were arriving from all directions on horseback. Their news was not good:

According to the accounts we received here, the river below is but a succession of falls and cascades which we would find impossible to pass, not only on account of the difficulties of the channel but from the extreme ruggedness and the mountainous character of the surrounding country. Their opinion, therefore, was that we should discontinue our journey and remain with them. I remarked that our determination of going was fixed; they then informed us that at the next camp the Great Chief of the Atnaugh nation had a slave who had been to the sea and which he might probably give us as a guide.

Fraser began to suspect the good will of the natives and took steps to impress them with his strength:

These Indians had heard of fire arms but had never seen any, and they evinced a great desire of seeing ours and obtaining explanations as to their use. In compliance, we fired several shots whose reports astonished them so as to make them drop off their legs. Upon recovering from their surprise, we made them examine the effect. They appeared quite uneasy on seeing the marks on the trees and observed that the Indians in that quarter were good and peaceable, and would never make use of their arms to annoy white people; yet they remarked that we ought to be on our guard and proceed with great care when approaching villages for, should we surprise the natives, they might take us for enemies and through fear, attack us with their arrows . . . The men of this tribe are of diminutive, active appearance; they dress in skins, prepared in the hair; their weapons are bows and arrows, neatly finished.

The slave recommended by the Indians as a guide was produced the following day, along with gifts of dried salmon and evil-tasting roots. Distrusting the guide's knowledge of the lower river, Fraser spread out an oilcloth and asked him to draw a map on it:

> This he readily undertook, but his endeavours soon convinced me that his stock of knowledge was very slender indeed, for his lines were entirely directed by an elderly man, a relation of the chief, who stood by him. We could, however, plainly see in his sketch a confirmation of what had been told us of the difficulties of the navigation and thereby the necessity of leaving our canoes with as much of our baggage as we could spare in order to continue our journey by land.

But navigation was possible for some distance yet. Fraser was now south of the present village of Soda Creek, the southernmost point that white men regarded as navigable for sternwheelers later on. The river's rage was just beginning. Every rapid and eddy that Mackenzie had seen above was child's play compared with the lower waters. Nevertheless, Fraser resolved to run the river rather than portage it—a foolish and almost fatal decision as it turned out. From the diary of June 1:

> This morning at an early hour all hands were ready and the natives began to appear from every quarter in great numbers. Mr. Stuart, six men and myself went again to visit the rapids; we found it about two miles long with high and steep banks which contracted the channel in many places to forty or fifty yards. This immense body of water, passing through this narrow space in a turbulent manner, forming numerous gulfs and cascades and making a tremendous noise, and an awful forbidding appearance. Nevertheless, since it was considered next to impossible to carry the canoes across the land on account of the height and steepness of the hills, it was resolved to venture them down this dangerous pass.
>
> Leaving Mr. Stuart and two men at the lower end of the rapid in order to watch the motions of the natives, I returned with the other four men to the camp. Immediately on my arrival I ordered the five best men out of the crews into a canoe lightly loaded, and the canoe was in a moment under way. After passing the first cascade, she lost her course and was drawn into the eddy where she was whirled about for a considerable time, seemingly in suspense whether to sink or swim, the men having no power over her. However, she took a favorable turn and by degrees was led from this dangerous vortex again into the stream. In this manner she continued, flying from one danger to another, until the last cascade but one where, in spite of every effort, the whirlpools forced her against a low projecting rock. Upon this the men debarked, saved their own lives and contrived to save the property, but the greatest difficulty was still ahead and to continue by water would be the way to certain destruction.

From the shore Fraser watched the shipwreck in midstream, powerless to prevent it, but he was not the man to desert his crew. Risking his own life at every step, he slid down the bank toward the water's edge. His account of this exploit, as usual, is repressed and dull:

> During this distressing scene we were on shore looking on and anxiously concerned; seeing our poor fellows once more safe afforded us as much satisfaction as to themselves and we hastened to their assistance, but their situation rendered our approach perilous and difficult. The bank was extremely high and steep and we had to plunge our daggers at intervals into the ground to check our speed, as otherwise we were exposed to slide into the river. We cut steps in the declivity, fastened a line to the front of the canoe, with which some of the men ascended in order to haul it up, while others supported it upon their arms. In this manner our situation was most precarious; our lives hung, as it were, upon a thread, as the failure of the line or a false step by one of the men might have hurled the whole of us into Eternity. However, we fortunately cleared the bank before dark.

This was Fraser's first real glimpse of the river's power as it gathered speed for its final journey to the coast. It sobered but did not daunt him. He consulted the Indians again. They urged him to leave the river and travel south by horse until he reached calmer waters near a great eastern tributary (the Thompson). From there on, they said, navigation was easy. As a matter of fact, the worst hazards only began at this point.

Fraser had been instructed to descend the river. Literal and unimaginative, he intended to carry out those instructions:

"Going to the sea by an indirect way was not the object of this undertaking; I therefore would not deviate and continued our route according to our original intention."

The canoes and baggage were lugged along the riverbank by hand, the Indians having promised and failed to produce horses. Three days were spent in this portage; and no sooner had the canoes been launched again than the waters ahead closed in as before. But the voyageurs, tired of packing, shot the new rapids. They were almost swamped and landed their canoes half full of water.

Again Fraser reconnoitered the current ahead:

> On visiting the lower part of it and having found it very strong and full of tremendous whirlpools, we were greatly at a loss how to act. The nature of our situation, however, left us no choice, we were under the necessity either of running down the canoes or of abandoning them. We therefore unloaded and provided each of them with five men.

These indifferent words from a Scotsman's diary cannot quite hide the nature of this crisis. He was now halfway down to the sea and thought himself still nearer to it. To turn back now would be to lose the whole gamble, to fail his instructions, to abandon the great prize when it was almost in sight. To advance farther was to risk his own life and the lives of all his friends in water where no craft seemed likely to survive. Looking at this maelstrom, Fraser must have wondered whether, at the far end of it, anyone would remain alive even to carry his diary home, whether the expedition would not disappear completely in the next half hour and leave all its work to be done from the beginning by someone else. There could be no retreat. Fraser watched the first canoe head into the rapids:

> The canoe which went first having succeeded, the other two immediately followed. The struggles which the men on this trial experienced between the whirlpools and the rocks almost exhausted their strength, the canoes having been in continual danger of sinking or of being broken to pieces; it was a desperate undertaking!

For the first time Fraser permits himself the use of an exclamation mark. "A desperate undertaking!" The words help us to imagine what happened in the canyon that day.

Somewhere between the present towns of Lillooet and Lytton—in a canyon so narrow that the modern road is carved out of solid rock walls, gravel banks, and vast slides of broken stone—the canoes had to be abandoned. Fraser stored them, with some of his provisions, under a pile of brush against thieves. The expedition advanced on foot but still followed the river. The walking was harder, if anything, than the paddling, for the canyon afforded no foothold, its sharp rocks tore the men's boots, and the river lay straight below, ready to receive anyone who stumbled.

One of the men got wedged so tightly between the rocks that he could not move or unload his pack. "Seeing this poor fellow in such an awkward and dangerous predicament," says Fraser, "I crawled, not without great risk, to his assistance and saved his life by causing his load to drop from his back over the precipice into the river. This carrying place, two miles long, so shattered our shoes that our feet became quite sore and full of blisters."

On June 19 they reached the nexus of the river system, where the clear Thompson flows in from the east to join its muddy parent. Here, at a natural center of travel, they found the capital of the Thompson Indians, whom Fraser calls the Hacamaugh. It stood on the high shelf now occupied by the little railway town of Lytton and it seems to have been the hub of a tenuous economic system stretching from the coast to the interior.

Seeing the Indians in possession of white traders' goods, Fraser realized that he had encountered the ancient line of communication that, for centuries, had followed the river from the sea.

The Indians had always carried their own goods from tribe to tribe along this route which, with its salmon hordes, supplied most of their food. Since the white traders had reached the Pacific a few years before, European goods had moved up from the coast in the same fashion. Similar channels of commerce followed the Nass, the Skeena and the Bella Coola but of all these trade and cultural movements that of the Fraser was by far the most important north of the Columbia as it was to be, later on, in the white man's civilization.

The Thompson Indians called their village Camchin, the largest center of habitation in the interior. Fraser regarded its people as more enlightened than any he had met farther north and he consulted them at length about the route ahead. As usual, he was told that it was impassable by water and this time, though he did not believe it, the Indians spoke the truth.

The expedition was now entering the dark and tortuous gulch that the river, swinging west at last, had driven through the coast mountains. No craft could live here. Even for a traveler as experienced as Fraser the next stage of the journey was unimaginable.

Meanwhile he paused at Camchin and committed an interesting historical error in christening the river that swept in here from the east. He named it the Thompson in honor of David Thompson, a partner of the North West Company who, he supposed, was then exploring the headwaters of this same river, eastward among the Rockies. Actually Thompson was on the headwaters of the Columbia, working his way down to the sea—a second and parallel attempt by Britain to anchor the Columbia line. Thompson never saw the river that is now the chief memorial to his fame, nor is it likely he ever knew of the honor conferred on him by Fraser, who, for his part, thought he was following the Columbia.

On June 20, with two new canoes obtained from the Indians, Fraser began the final descent. As you look down from the present highway upon the brown line of the river, boiling up here and there in its caldrons of white foam, you find it hard to believe that any men in their senses would attempt to run these waters. The Indians regarded it as madness but one of them, the Great Chief, or "Little Fellow," finally agreed to go along as guide.

For a few miles the canoes would slide down a navigable current. Then, just in time, they would be pushed ashore before they could be sucked into a whirlpool. Now canoes and baggage would be dragged up sheer cliffs and along the sides of the hills, sometimes far above the river. At this labor the men began to grumble. The Indians who lived on salmon in this region turned hostile and frequently hurled stones down upon the travelers. Having come so far, Fraser refused to pause.

The canyon still narrowed. The river, compressed by its walls of rock, churned deeper with a force which often hurled the salmon clear of the water and flattened them, dead, against the bank. The travelers turned giddy at this spectacle, an unbelievable movement of water. Fortunately, after centuries of experience, the Indians had learned a way around it.

Their trail utilized every flat ledge and when the ledge ended they built a ladder of tree trunks and withes to the ledge above. Up and down from ledge to ledge, all naked, wet and slippery, this crazy series of Jacob's ladders hung from rocks and stumps like some monstrous vine growth. Fraser had seen nothing like this before but, abandoning the canoes, he led his men up the ladders, ninety pounds on his back, the mountains straight above, the clamor of the river below. At last the diary caught the feeling of the Black Canyon:

> Here we were obliged to carry among loose stones in the face of a steep hill between two precipices. Near the top, where the ascent was perfectly perpindicular, one of the Indians climbed to the summit and by means of a long rope drew us up one after another. This work took three hours, and then we continued our course up and down the hills and along the steep declivities of mountains where hanging rocks and projecting cliffs, at the edge of the bank of the river, made the passage so small as to render it, at times, difficult even for one person sideways. Many of the natives from the last camp who accompanied us were of the greatest use on this intricate occasion. They went on boldly with heavy loads in places where we were obliged to hand our guns from one to another, and where the greatest pre-

caution was required in order to pass even singly and free from encumbrance.

It was a trail fit only for natives who had been born beside it, who had spent their lives crawling like spiders on this queer web. The diary again:

I have been for a long period in the Rocky Mountains, but have never seen anything like this country. It is so wild that I cannot find words to describe our situation at times. We had to pass where no human beings should venture; yet in those places there is a regular footpath impressed, or rather indented upon the very rocks by frequent travelling. Besides this, steps which are formed like a ladder or the shrouds of a ship, by poles hanging to one another and crossed at certain distances with twigs, the whole suspended from the top to the foot of the deep precipices and fastened at both extremities to stones and trees, furnish a safe and convenient passage to the natives; but we, who had not had the advantage of their education and experience, were often in imminent danger when obliged to follow their example.

Thus they crawled on the Indian web through the deepest gorges of the Fraser. Gazing upward, they could see a country disordered as by a sudden convulsion. Compared with this welter of mountains, these twisted caverns and senseless heaps of stone, the Rockies were disciplined and regular. Nightmare country, black with shifting shadow, hung with mist, and thunderous with the steady beat of water.

What new horror lay ahead? That Fraser could never guess from hour to hour. The river still narrowed, deepened and grew in fury, for it was now fighting its way through the central substance of the coast mountains. Then, in a final spasm, it broke through the contracted gut of Hell's Gate and cleared the last barrier to the sea.

The worst was over. A little farther down Fraser was able

to use Indian dugouts again. He paused at Spuzzum, which was later to be the main crossing point on the gold-rush road, to examine the Indian burial ground. Here, in one of the few quiet spots along the river, the natives were gathered for burial after their spider life on the canyon walls.

These tombs [Fraser writes] are superior to anything of the kind I saw among savages; they are about fifteen feet long and of the form of a chest of drawers. Upon the boards and posts are beasts and birds carved in a curious but rude manner, pretty well proportioned. These monuments must have cost the workmen much time and labor, as they must have been destitute of proper tools for their execution; round the tombs was desposited all the property of the deceased.

The canyon was beginning to widen out toward the broad coastal delta. If travel was relatively comfortable, the river's course now planted an alarming suspicion in Fraser's mind. At Hope the current had turned sharply west and it did not seem to be turning south again. Yet Fraser knew that the Columbia lay far south of this latitude. For the first time he guessed the truth—this was another river. And if it turned out so, the real purpose of the expedition would be defeated after all these weeks of misery. The line of exploration that was to contain the Americans would be drawn too far north.

The mountain waters calmed down, almost in a single mile, broadened and oozed gently west through a thick forest of cedar, fir and hemlock. Then Fraser noticed that the river was rising and falling in regular tides. He was near the sea but far from the Columbia. When the river forked into a maze of channels between islands of silt there could be no more doubt about it—this was a river which no white man had traveled before.

That Fraser actually reached the river's mouth and saw the Gulf of Georgia and the sharp line between the brown fresh water and the green salt, there can be no doubt, though some early historians disputed it. Fraser distinctly describes the Indian village of Musquiam, which stood at the mouth of the river's north arm, where the southern flank of Vancouver now sprawls. Moreover, David Thompson's famous map of Northwestern America carries this legend opposite the words "Musquiame Village":

"Mr. Simon Fraser and party returned from the sortie of the river."

The sea had been reached, the map of the continent had been revised, a second Great River had been discovered, but Fraser could not pause to weigh his triumph against his disappointment. The coastal Indians were much more dangerous than their distant relatives of the interior. They massed in their village, beat drums and chanted war songs, "howling like wolves and brandishing war clubs." Besides, supplies were running out and there was no chance to purchase more.

Fraser hurriedly confirmed his location as 49° "very nearly," as compared with the Columbia's latitude of 46° 20' and noted: "This river is, therefore, not the Columbia. If I had been convinced of this when I left my canoes I would certainly have returned." For such a man the failure to find the Columbia seems to have outweighed the discovery of an unsuspected river, the forgotten, legendary river of Juan de Fuca.

There was another disappointment—Fraser was unable to see the main body of the Pacific, for the islands of the gulf and the lowering mass of Vancouver Island hid it completely from the mainland. "I must again acknowledge," he writes, "my great disappointment in not seeing the main Ocean, having gone so near as to be almost within view." Mackenzie had not seen the main ocean either. He and Fraser were to have no second chance.

Reluctantly Fraser turned up the river again. His troubles were not over yet. The Indians, who had expected the white men to perish on their downward journey, were now determined to prevent their return. More recklessly than ever the braves harassed the expedition day and night, using arrows in the lower reaches of the river, boulders in the canyon. The details of these attacks we do not know, probably because Fraser was too busy to maintain his diary. They must have been serious since they almost broke the nerve of voyageurs who, by this time, were hardened to peril. On July 6 the entire company threatened to desert. Maddened by the Indians' attacks, the men proposed to abandon the river channel altogether, head eastward overland and hope to escape somehow through the mountains. This was madness indeed. No trail eastward was known, no map covered the wilderness between here and the prairies. By winter everyone would be swallowed up in the unexplored recesses of the Rockies and the results of the expedition would be lost. Fraser met the crisis:

> Considering this scheme as a desperate undertaking, I debarked and endeavoured to persuade the delinquents of their infatuation; but two of them declared in their own names and in the names of the others that their plan was fixed and that they saw no other way by which they could save themselves from immediate destruction than by flying out of the way of danger; for said they, continuing by water, surrounded by hostile nations, who watched every opportunity to attack and torment them, created in their mind a state of suspicion worse than death. I remonstrated and threatened by turns, the other gentlemen joined me in my endeavours to expose the folly of their undertaking and the advantages that would accrue to us all by remaining as we had hitherto done in perfect union for our common safety. After much debate on both sides, they yielded and we all shook hands, resolved not to separate during the voyage.

There they were, two dozen ragged, hungry men, lost in the canyon of an unknown river, thousands of miles from any settlement, surrounded by savages, half mad with fear. Two dozen men who had altered the geography of a continent, laid down the boundary lines of two great nations, and fixed the shape of British America. Two dozen men who, standing on a rock beside the river foam, raised up their hands and shouted their binding oath above the roar of water: "I solemnly swear before Almighty God that I shall sooner perish than forsake in distress any of our crew during the present voyage."

That sworn, they paddled on, singing their French voyageurs' songs while the Indians watched them from the bank. The last real peril had passed. Climbing the canyon ladders again, reaching the friendly Thompson country, and finding their canoes in perfect condition farther along the river, the expedition pushed upstream with astonishing speed. Though it had to fight the current all the way, it retraced in thirty-four days the steps it had taken downward in thirty-five, a feat almost beyond belief but attested in Fraser's scrupulous record.

On August 5 everyone was safe back at Fort George and the second Great River of the west bore Fraser's name.

5 Gold

FRASER HAD FOUND THE RIVER BUT NOT ITS TREASURE. ANOTHER Scotsman was to hold it when the discovery of treasure suddenly exposed it to siege.

James Douglas was born in Lanarkshire and came out from Scotland at seventeen to work for the Hudson's Bay Company. He was twenty-seven when he reached Fort Vancouver in Oregon Territory as assistant to the famous factor, John McLoughlin. Already McLoughlin saw the American handwriting on the wall. The settlers were trickling in. The United States government was claiming possession of the Columbia and the land northward indefinitely. Manifest Destiny could not be held long on the Columbia line. Perhaps it could be held on the line of the Fraser.

Douglas was ordered by McLoughlin to undertake the holding operation. A British settlement must be built north of Oregon to establish a line which a weak-kneed British government might be willing to support. For this new post Douglas chose the southern tip of Vancouver Island, on a harbor opposite the Indian village of Camosun.

It was a good site, guarding the Strait of Juan de Fuca, the entrance to the Fraser; it was easy to defend and it would provide in time a setting for one of the world's loveliest towns. Fort Victoria was built in 1843, a stockaded village where the wharves of Victoria now stand.

The Hudson's Bay Company had acted just in time. Three

years later the Oregon Territory was yielded to the United States, the forty-ninth parallel was established as the international boundary but Victoria, though south of it, remained British. McLoughlin's tiny anchor was holding so far.

But soon Douglas was hearing strange news from the Fraser. A prospector named James Huston wandered across the border up the fur route of the Okanagan Valley, past Fort Kamloops, at the junction of the Thompson and its north fork, and a few miles farther to Tranquille Creek. Here on a date now lost, but in '56 or '57 he found gold. That was the beginning of America's second big gold rush and the great days of the Fraser.

By 1856 Douglas was writing to the Colonial Office in London that "from successful experiments made in washing gold from the sands of the tributary streams of the Fraser River, there is reason to suppose that the gold region is extensive." This new wealth would bring new dangers—the miner fighting with the Indian and destroying the fur trade, the Yankees pouring in to move the border northward again. The British government was almost alarmed.

A year later Douglas wrote:

It appears . . . that the auriferous character is becoming daily more extensively developed, through the exertions of the native Indian tribes who, having tasted the sweets of gold mining, are devoting much of their time and attention to that pursuit. The reported wealth of the . . . mines is causing much excitement among the population of the United States territory of Washington and Oregon, and I have no doubt that a great number of the people from those territories will be attracted thither with the return of fine weather in the spring.

Even Douglas did not foresee the avalanche ahead.

Already disturbing things had been happening at Fort Victoria. As early as 1849 men with money belts and pistols about their waists, hobnailed boots on their feet, and picks over their shoulders turned up at the company's store to buy tools, iron ladles and wire screens. They paid in gold. Where they got it they would not say, but when a few of them drifted down to San Francisco their news traveled fast. California's rush of '49 was ebbing out, the assorted hordes of Americans, Englishmen, Irishmen, Scotsmen, Chinese and other foreigners who called themselves the Argonauts listened to stories of greater riches to be found farther north, and they moved on.

In the spring of '58 Victoria was besieged. Eight hundred people had spent the previous winter at the little fort. By summer 20,000 miners were camped around the stockade, all clamoring for the chance to reach the Fraser. They had come up from California by steamboats so crowded that the passengers lay on deck in shifts to sleep. They had come in sailboats, rowboats and canoes. What manner of men were they?

Douglas feared them from the start. "They are represented as being with some exceptions," he reported to London, "a specimen of the worst of the population of San Francisco; the very dregs, in fact, of society.

"Their conduct here would have led me to form a very different conclusion."

The foreigners had turned out to be much tamer than he had expected.

He had only a passing view of them. They paused in Victoria long enough to buy provisions and after paying $2,000,000 to Roderick Finlayson, the company's trader, they set out for the mainland in any craft they could find.

Meanwhile the fever had spread up the entire coast. The Argonauts swarmed through Oregon and Washington. They reared tent towns at Whatcom and Steilacoom. Three hundred of them were billeted in a bowling alley in Port Townsend. The miners abandoned the coal mines of Bellingham. The sawmills of Puget Sound were idle. Farmers left their spring plowing. Soldiers deserted the American forts. A navy of rafts and dugouts headed for the Fraser.

This, for Douglas, was not a gold rush. It was an invasion. How many thousands were moving to the river he did not know but he acted quickly to find out. Every miner was ordered to pay a license of 21 shillings a month to the British crown. A fee of $6 was charged for every rowboat and canoe entering British territory and $12 for a decked vessel. These collections provided a rough estimate of the new population.

Such levies were outside Douglas's powers. He had been appointed governor of the colony of Vancouver Island without authority on the mainland, but there was no time to quibble about such technicalities. He alone represented the crown in this wilderness and he proposed to represent it.

His illegal licenses revealed 10,000 men working on the lower reaches of the Fraser early in that summer of '58. The Hudson's Bay post at Fort Langley, near the river's mouth, was crowded with strangers eager for news of the latest discoveries. The store there was taking in $1,500 daily. "Dancing in the most graceful manner" and "rousing balls conducted with the best possible decorum" amused the travelers nightly.

By autumn 33,000 Americans, by the rough estimates of the time, had crossed the border, many returning south. Still there was no violence. The foreigners paid Douglas's illegal taxes without question, thus acknowledging the sovereignty of Britain. The lawlessness of '49 in California was not repeated. This began to look like the most peaceable gold rush in history.

Gold had first been found on the Thompson, the Fraser's great tributary. Now it was being mined on the sand bars from the mouth of the parent river up to the gate of the canyon. Who could tell what lay between the two discoveries, or north of the Thompson's junction with the Fraser? The gold seemed unlimited. It was coarse and easy to extract with a pan, with crude sluice boxes or with a rocker, a cradlelike contrivance in which the gravel was sifted, the nuggets and dust caught on a rough blanket beneath.

Hill's Bar was the first big strike. On March 23, 1858, a

party of half a dozen prospectors stopped to cook lunch beside the river ten miles up from Fort Hope, in the first defiles of the canyon. As they squatted around their fire, one of them, a man named Hill, noticed particles of gold in the moss under his feet. He washed the moss and found nuggets glistening in the bottom of his pan.

They took $2,000,000 out of Hill's Bar that season but their story was almost forgotten until James Moore, one of the men who had been with Hill that day, turned up, at the age of eighty-two, broken and penniless, at the Kamloops old men's home in 1914. The first pan of gold, he said, had been washed on his twenty-sixth birthday. He had lost his share of the proceeds, like all the others.

From Hill's Bar the tide rolled up the river to Yale. Here another town of tents and saloons emerged at the point where the river narrows into the canyon proper. On every bar men were rocking, panning and sluicing. Every creek emptying into the Fraser was explored. Wherever prospectors found a fragment of float, a hunk of gold-bearing sand fallen from some bench above, they followed the lead into the hills.

Douglas reported that three men took out 190 ounces of gold in a week, but most miners averaged from $8 to $13 a day. All the Indians, he complained, had deserted the Hudson's Bay Company and were working for the miners at $4 a day. At Fort Langley the company's factor had 648 ounces of gold in his safe.

Steamboats were moving up to Hope now and beyond it, against the rising current, to Yale. Canoes were lashed together, six abreast, to carry horses and wagons. Many a raft broke in the current and bodies floated down to sea every day or two.

The lower bars were soon washed clean. The gold lay in small pockets. Most of the miners were now making less than their wages as carpenters or clerks back in San Francisco. Yet if gold had been washed down so close to the river's mouth there must be hordes of it farther up, and perhaps the mother lode of ore, lost somewhere in the hills. On foot, since boats could not live in the current of the canyon, the first Argonauts began to move up beyond Yale on the old Indian trail, on the Jacob's ladders. where Fraser and his crew had scaled the slippery cliffs.

The Indians saw what was happening. Their river was being occupied by the ravening whites who ate their salmon. The gold, which they had learned to harvest, was disappearing. In the beginning they had profited by the rush, for they were such skilled thieves that, as the saying went, they could steal a man's dinner after he had eaten it. Every party of miners slept with an armed sentry on guard but still tools, food and clothes disappeared every night. Now the Indians turned hostile.

They tried to stop the white men's progress up the river by pulling the stakes of mining claims and raiding the caches of supplies. Then came news of Indian war in Washington. It soon spread north.

A train of 400 pack horses and 160 men, toiling up through the Okanagan to Kamloops, was ambushed, three men were shot, many horses stolen.

Hearing of this success, the tribes on the Fraser grew bolder and began to pick the miners off one by one. How many died in the canyon no one will ever know, but the bodies floating down the river set the miners organizing the vigilance committees they had known in California. The sale of liquor to the Indians, often the cause of trouble, was suppressed by the miners' own decree.

A rifle company of forty men started up the canyon from Yale when two Frenchmen were found murdered below Lytton. The Indians met the riflemen at Spuzzum. In a scattered fight seven Indians were killed and their ancient village was burned to the ground.

This began to look like war. Many miners retreated out of the canyon. Another company of 160 volunteers was formed at Yale, besieged the Hudson's Bay store, and demanded rifles. The company, whose policy was to placate the Indians, could not resist this demand and armed the miners. The second company joined the first at Spuzzum and both of them advanced up the river.

At China Bar they found five miners hiding in a cave, all of them wounded. They had fled down the river forty miles, pursued by the Indians, under fire all the way. Most of their companions had been killed. At sight of the organized riflemen the Indians raised a white flag of surrender. A truce was patched up for the moment but both sides awaited the coming of Douglas and the law.

The larger danger that Douglas had foreseen now seemed at hand. To the Americans, who had cleaned out the first gold of California, this country looked like Eldorado, and an imaginary boundary line was no obstacle. As they had possessed Oregon Territory despite the British, it should be easy to take over this river land as well.

In January of the new year the cozy fort at Victoria heard the first rumors of real trouble at Yale. Ned McGowan, a deposed judge and badman from California, was leading an insurrection against the British crown. This was "fifty-four forty or fight" again, a challenge which Douglas must meet.

The British government was awaking, late as usual. It had appointed Douglas governor of British Columbia, the whole mainland, and had sent out Judge Matthew Baillie Begbie to enforce the law. In Victoria, on board British warships, were bluejackets who knew how to handle a musket. A contingent of 156 Royal Engineers had come from England to survey the international border. With these forces and his new authority, Douglas decided to make a show of strength in the camps.

He loaded Tom Wright's stern-wheeler with a cannon, a company of engineers, a hundred bluejackets and the new judge. At Fort Hope he landed with a salute of guns, but the rebels seemed to have subsided. Colonel Moody, of the engineers, who had come to fight, found nothing better to do with his Sunday than to preach the first sermon ever heard in this region to forty-five docile miners. Meanwhile Douglas had opened a peace conference with the Indians and assured them of fair treatment. To break a local traders' combine he ordered the price of goods reduced in the company's stores.

The expedition pushed on to Yale, where there had been riots the previous month, but by now the expected insurrection had turned into a comedy.

In the celebrations of Christmas Day a Yale miner had assaulted a Negro, and the Yale magistrate had issued a warrant for the white man's arrest. The offender having fled back to Hill's Bar, the warrant was sent after him to the local peace officer, but that zealous official already had decided that the Negro was the guilty party and ordered him arrested. The law was paralyzed by the quarrel of the two magistrates.

When an officer of the Hill's Bar magistrate tried to arrest the Negro he was jailed for insolence by the magistrate at Yale. At this point McGowan, tired of British bungling, and boasting that he would establish the Yankee miners' law, gathered a posse of twenty men at Hill's Bar and pushed up the river to Yale to arrest the local magistrate. The posse abducted this helpless agent of the queen, took him downstream in a canoe, and fined him $50 "for contempt of court"! McGowan seemed to have taken over the law.

As he was celebrating this moral victory, the stern-wheeler with the cannon at her bow was observed paddling slowly up the river. At first McGowan showed fight, but he cooled off rapidly when he saw the troops disembarked and the cannon put ashore. To Moody he made an apology before the miners and paid a fine for assault. Then he gave a champagne dinner for the officers at Hill's Bar.

A comic incident, the kind of incident that so often deflected the history of Canada when a few men in remote places could decide great issues of power without knowing it. "Fifty-four forty or fight" was heard no more along the Fraser.

The richest strikes were being made now above the canyon and beyond the Thompson. To reach these higher bars a man must crawl along the Indians' canyon trail with infinite toil and constant danger. Somehow a shorter route must be found. It was found on the Harrison River, which enters the Fraser from the north below Hope. By following up this river and a circular chain of lakes, a man could double back upon the Fraser at Lillooet and by-pass the canyon. It was a hard route but not so hard as the original trail.

A man named C. C. Gardiner, from California, was among the first to follow the new trail and he left a written record of the journey. With his partner he purchased an Indian dugout for $135 and filled it with ammunition and provisions. Guided by the Indian, he started up the Harrison.

This, unlike the canyon, was timbered country, covered by a rank coastal jungle where no man could move without a trail or a river. The first forty miles, up Harrison River and Harrison Lake, Gardiner found easy. At the mouth of Lillooet River, where it enters Harrison Lake, he met a party of miners who were waiting for the river to subside.

No Indian would venture on this early summer freshet. The Lillooet was running fifteen miles an hour. But after three days of waiting, Gardiner and his companion decided to push on even though the river was rising still higher. Every day counted. The upper bars were being occupied. A man might lose his chance of fortune by an hour.

Half a dozen impatient men joined Gardiner and began to haul their canoes up the Lillooet. This was work as desperate as Mackenzie or Fraser's.

On the second day Gardiner's canoe overturned, with his meat, sugar, rice, molasses and five revolvers. He and his companions were left with only a little flour and coffee. But "the upsetting of our canoe was nothing more than an accident, which most every company experienced, many not only losing their grub but their lives. We very nearly lost two of our men, but were providentially saved by catching hold of the branches of a leaning tree as the current was taking them swiftly down."

It sounds like Fraser's stilted diary, but the scene can be imagined clearly enough—half a dozen men, soaked to the skin, shivering on the riverbank, a few pounds of wet flour and coffee to live on, an unknown wilderness ahead. But there was gold ahead, too.

After getting our flour ashore and dried, we held a consultation whether we should go on with only our flour and coffee any further, or return; but one moment's thought respecting the new mines being so rich immediately dispersed all fears of trying, which we did after fitting up our canoe.

The Lillooet was only 35 miles long. It took 23 days to reach its end—a mile and a half a day!

Every day of the 23 we were in the cold water most of the time, with our heads out, but very frequently with them under, an unpleasantness which could not be avoided in passing the line outside the trees and brush which grew on the banks of the river, when the water was low, but were now submerged half way to their tops.

They literally waded the river's 35 miles. It might not have been so dangerous but it was harder work than Fraser's. For 23 days no one was dry for an hour. At night the travelers slept in their wet clothes, one man constantly on guard with a revolver against the Indians.

Notwithstanding our guard every few mornings one or the other of the companies would have something missing that the Red Skins had stolen at night. Indeed, it is considered as impossible to keep them from stealing as it is to detect the celebrated Wizard of the North in his tricks of legerdemain.

They reached Little Lillooet Lake at last "and never was the oasis on the sandy desert more welcome to a weary traveller." At the lake's northern end they encountered their first large band of Indians "the most of whom were naked and appeared somewhat hostile." But they told the white men there was an easy trail northeastward to the Fraser. The watershed between the Harrison system, flowing south, and the lake system, draining into the Fraser from the west, had now been reached.

After a recruit of a few days, we, with much difficulty, hired for some clothing a number of Indians to help us pack our stuff across the portage, but had much trouble with them in keeping the villains from stealing their packs and returning home again. I, as well as some of my partners, had the moderate weight of 100 pounds in our packs which we allowed would, at least, be 200 pounds by the time we would have our trip performed, as it kept getting heavier, or we weaker, every hour we travelled. But on the evening of the third day the work was accomplished and we again beheld another beautiful lake [Anderson] which had not a ripple on its surface.

They were over the divide and could paddle most of the way to the Fraser.

The Anderson Lake Indians did not welcome this unexpected invasion. They went through a "great many military evolutions" but allowed the white men to pitch their tents, for a rest of two days.

On the morning of the third the old chief consented, though not without many preliminaries, to take our company across the lake in his canoe, which he did to our satisfaction and where we were met by 200 of the largest and most hostile natives we had yet seen. They were each armed with a musket and knife, besides an innumerable number of bows and arrows; the two former they purchased from the Hudson's Bay Company. Their faces were painted with a red and black substance, always used by them when going to war with another tribe.

They did not intend war, after all. Instead, they agreed to pack the expedition across the two-mile portage to Seton Lake. Arrived at the lake's eastern end, the travelers were only a two-hour pack from the Fraser. They reached the river after 40 days, a longer time than it took Fraser to reach the coast.

Now to reap the reward of these labors.

Some other Americans were there ahead of them, parties that had come overland by the Okanagan trail. These first miners were not doing well. They had killed their horses and mules and lived on them for the past month. Flour, what little there was of it, was selling for $1.25 a pound and beans for $1.

Fraser River was still very high and the miners informed us they could only make from two to five dollars per day, that not being sufficient to grub them, the way provisions sold, and there was not a probability of it getting cheaper for some time.

This was not the opulence Gardiner had expected. Nevertheless,

. . . five of us in company pitched our tent, fixed up our mining tools and went to work. We prospected up and down the river a distance of 40 miles each way and could find gold in small quantities most anywhere on the surface of the bars, which were then getting bare, as the river fell. The gold is much finer than any found in California, and found in a different deposit. On Fraser River what has been dug has been found within three to eighteen inches of the surface, in a kind of sand, being underneath a very pretty gravel, but no gold in it. . . .

We found a bar which prospected better than any other in that section and set in to try our luck. We worked early and late, averaging $3 to $5 a day. . . . Not any one of the miners within fifty miles of us at this time were making grub at the price of provisions. Men began to think it a great humbug and glowing accounts of Fraser River became gradually pronounced a fiction. The natives were all so very troublesome, stealing and pointing guns at men was prominent feature of their character. A few nights before we left the bar one of them entered while five of us were asleep in the tent and stole several pieces of clothing, as well as fifty pounds of flour worth than the sum of $60. One of the boys happened to wake and saw him coming in for another load, but by giving the alarm a little too soon the scamp made good his escape. Next morning we were much amused when the man who detected the thief stated that both pairs of his pants were gone but had a very good idea who had taken them.

The Fraser was a humbug. That word was spreading up and down the river as the water dropped and the sand bars were found empty of gold. Gardiner and his companions gave up.

We packed up our duds and started down the river, by an Indian trail, meeting every day hundreds of men coming up all stating that the mines were of no account. They were all bound for a place called the Fountain [fourteen miles above Lillooet] which they heard was very rich, but to my certain knowledge they could not make a dollar per day within five miles of it. We proceeded onward to Yale, making every inquiry about the mines, the general pay being from one to four dollars per day.

In Yale the frenzy of the early summer had subsided. Everywhere the story was the same—the Fraser was a humbug. Gardiner decided to return to California, convinced that as "the hills are all composed of rock the mines in that country can never be extensive."

While Gardiner and his company were toiling up the Harrison, back in Victoria Douglas was living in dread of the coming winter. Thousands of men had gone up the Fraser. If no winter trail was opened they would be trapped by the snow and must starve before spring. Douglas decided to open up the Harrison trail. But where to find the money to pay for it? The penniless colony of British Columbia assuredly could not undertake such costs. Douglas resolved on another bold stroke.

He called the miners together on the river and persuaded 500 of them to work for nothing. Not only must they offer their summer's labor but $25 per head as well as a guarantee of good conduct! This bond money was to be returned later, not in cash, but in supplies from the company's stores—a good Scottish bargain.

The volunteers divided into companies under captains, marched up the Harrison and set to work. The building of the Harrison trail through the coast forest was the first great construction project in the west but nothing like the greater road to be built four years later along the Fraser. The volunteer workers hacked down the timber, cut ten miles of trail a day, and even built a railway, with a little car pulled by hand, on the portage between Anderson and Seton Lakes. Work started in July. By November freight was rolling into Lillooet on the Fraser and packers' rates fell from $1 to 18 cents a pound. Now the miners could escape from the upper bars when snow blocked the canyon.

By winter this prodigy of labor appeared worthless. All the gold seemed to have been taken from the Fraser. The higher the miners went up the river the poorer their harvest. The great Canadian gold rush was petering out. The Fraser, as all agreed, was a humbug.

In the following year Charles Major wrote from Hope to the Toronto *Globe* that British Columbia was no place for mining or settlement:

> There is no farming land . . . except for a very small portion joining Washington Territory . . . It can never be a place because there is nothing to support it except the mines and just as soon as they are done the place goes down completely, for there is absolutely nothing to keep it up; and I tell you the truth, the mines are falling off very fast. There is nothing in this country but mines and very small pay for that; they are, as you may say, used up. We have been making two, three and four dollars a day but it would not last more than two or three days and so you would spend that before you would find more . . . A party arrived here yesterday from Alexander and they are a pitiful looking lot. They are what the Yankees call dead broke. They have been six hundred miles up the river. When they got down here they had no shoes to their feet. Some had pieces of shirt and trowsers but even these were pinned together with small sharp sticks; and some had the rim of an old hat and some the crown. They had nothing to eat for one week and not one cent of money. This is gold mining for you!

A humbug, and the rush was pouring out of British Columbia as fast as it had poured in. Yale, Hope, Langley were deserted. The merchants of Victoria, who had fattened on the Yankees, "could only stand by their doors and project idle spittle into the streets." If this country was so barren of gold and so useless to settlers, was it worth the British government's struggle to hold it? Was it worth a place in Manifest Destiny? And in far-off Canada, where men now talked of forming a continental nation, what use, they asked, to include this empty shelf on the far side of the Rockies?

Who could imagine by the dismal summer of '59 that the real treasure had yet to be found, that the real rush was still ahead?

6 The Cariboo Road

O N HIS VOYAGE TO THE SEA FRASER NOTED THE FIRST GREAT RIVER flowing from his left and gave it the name of his lieutenant, Quesnel. He did not pause to explore it. In later years the Quesnel lay far off the march of the fur brigades. The miners passed it up, too, in their search for gold in the bars of the upper Fraser. If little gold could be found there, why look for it in the tributaries? On up the Fraser went the Argonauts as far as Prince George and soon retreated, broke and hungry. But there were others, with more imagination and ampler grub stakes. In '59 they pushed toward the Quesnel River country overland from the Fraser.

By the autumn of that year a few of them reached Quesnel Lake, the huge, serrated source of the river. It did not look promising. They made rafts of logs, bound them together with withes, and poled around the lake, testing the sand at the creek mouths. At once they struck pay dirt, in places as much as $200 a day per man. Leaving their rafts, they waded up the creeks and washed the gravel as they went. All these creeks seemed to bear gold. Horse Fly Creek yielded a hundred ounces of nuggets in a week to a party of five men.

Such news could not be suppressed for long. The miners' grapevine quickly carried it down to the Fraser and on to the coast. Within a month a thousand men had tramped to Quesnel Lake. When the spring of '60 opened the trails again the lower Fraser was deserted by everyone except the patient Chinese.

The shores of Quesnel Lake and the bars of the tributary creeks were soon washed clean. Was this to be another humbug?

Doc Keithley, John Rose, Sandy MacDonald and George Weaver reached Cariboo Lake late in the autumn and followed up Keithley Creek into the mountains. Around the campfire they considered their position. They had seen no trace of gold for weeks and soon winter would close the trail. While there was still time they decided to return to the coast.

Next morning, across a deep valley, they saw a stream glistening in the sun. To investigate it would cost only a day. They struggled through the valley, reached the stream and filled a gold pan with gravel. In the bottom of that pan lay an ounce of gold. They filled the pan again, and when they had washed out the gravel they picked up nuggets weighing a quarter of a pound. All that day they worked until their pockets were filled with nuggets and their bodies exhausted. They slept at night beside the stream.

In the morning they awakened to find themselves lying under a foot of snow. Here was gold by the panful but the trail was closing up and their grub was almost gone. Without more supplies they would starve before spring. If they abandoned this creek someone else might find it before they could return. They decided to winter here and each swore to keep the discovery secret. Two of them started to build a cabin and the other two tramped back to Cariboo Lake for food.

No claim on the Fraser River system was ever kept secret for long. When the two partners reached the camp at Cariboo Lake they refused to talk but, to the trained noses of the miners there, they evidently smelled of gold. Why would men winter in the hills unless they had found something too valuable to abandon?

It was easy to follow their trail through the snow as they returned to their claims. Not far behind them marched an eager crowd. That was the beginning of the rush to Antler Creek.

Throughout the winter men poured into the new camp,

dug through the snow, panned the gravel, staked the whole valley (the claims all overlapping), and lived in frozen holes in the ground.

By the spring of '61 the news had traveled down the coast, beyond America, and overseas. The new gold country was called the Cariboo, a curious word, a misspelling, doubtless, by the ignorant miners, and wherever there was a newspaper or men to tell the story that name was known overnight across the world.

Back surged the miners from the coast, and thousands more from California, from the eastern states, from Ontario, from England, Europe and China. Again every ship was overloaded. Victoria was swamped. The Harrison trail was crowded. Bands of feverish lunatics were crossing the plains from the east in bullock carts and drowning in the gorges of the Rockies.

This, Douglas was forced to realize, had become more than a gold rush. It was the beginning of permanent settlement. It required government, roads, public expenditures, and the management of the British crown. Other men in Ontario and Quebec heard the news and evolved larger ideas—this rich western land belonged by rights to Canada.

Many of the miners would remain to people British Columbia. Their gold would build a great province, extending Canada to the western sea. Some of their towns would endure long after them. Their roads would open up the farm lands and the forests. No man but Douglas and a few Canadian politicians back east were thinking of that in the spring of '61. Every eye in Cariboo was staring at the yellow-flecked bottom of a gold pan.

From Antler Creek the rush spilled over the divide and down the creeks running northward into the big bend of the Fraser. At first there seemed to be little gold here.

Ed Stout and Billy Deitz camped on a creek they called Williams after Deitz's Christian name. It looked poor. The other miners tested it and moved on. Williams soon became known as Humbug Creek but Stout, Deitz and a few others stayed with it.

71

Until now the nuggets and dust had been found close to the surface everywhere and no one had thought to dig for them. The two partners knew nothing of geology, of the cosmic heavings that had thrown up the Rocky Mountains, twisted their ore veins, pulverized the gold in forgotten rivers, and heaved the river gravel half way up the hills again. But Stout and Deitz could dig and they burrowed downward beside Williams Creek. It took them only forty-eight hours to sink a hole through the gravel and the blue clay beneath it. They emerged from their shaft with $1,000 worth of gold.

The secret was out at last. Gold lay down deep, close to the bedrock—why, no man could tell and no man stopped to wonder. On seven miles of Williams Creek a furious army of 4,000 men bored into the clay, lifted it in buckets, and washed it in sluices. Some of them took out 40 pounds of gold in a single day. Soon Williams Creek, Lightning Creek nearby, and every brook running into them was honeycombed with shafts. Tunnels were pushed under the creek beds, shored up by timbers, and engulfed by the oozing "slum" before the diggers could escape.

In that summer of '61 $2,500,000 worth of gold was taken out of Cariboo. It sounds like small change now. In those days, when gold was the basis of all money, the source of national power, and had a mystical quality like religion, the news from Cariboo set America crazy.

On the narrow bench where Williams Creek ran close to a sheer hillside Billy Barker sank a shaft—poor Billy, the Cornish sailor who had deserted his ship in Victoria but would return there in the end as penniless as he had set out. It was a rich shaft, so rich that one of Billy's partners could soon lend Cariboo Cameron 50 pounds of gold—and Cameron, luckier than them all, would turn it into $150,000 within three months.

Around Barker's hole in the ground a town sprang up, a wretched hive of log shacks, stores of whipsawed lumber with false fronts, saloons with pianos, mirrors and champagne, packed

72

in from the coast on the backs of mules. They called the town Barkerville after Billy.

It was strung along a single narrow street and wedged tight between the hill and the creek. As the sluice boxes poured gravel down the creek bed, the water rose above the town, was held back by a log dike and, with every rainfall, overflowed down the street. Year after year as the creek rose every building was jacked up higher on stilts until the town listed in all directions and the mud in the street was up to your knees. In Barkerville and on the creek around it 6,000 miners were working by the spring of '62.

Of all the goldtowns in America, Barkerville must have been the maddest. You had to walk 600 miles from the coast to reach it. When you got there you paid $300 a barrel for flour, $2.50 a pound for dried apples, $50 for a pair of boots, and by now you could hardly find a yard of gravel not already staked, washed, and drained of gold.

But still they came up the Fraser on boats to Yale, through the jungle of the Harrison, by the lakes back to the Fraser, then up a mile in the air over Pavilion Mountain, down the other side by a goat track, over the rolling plateau from Clinton to the mouth of the Quesnel and eastward through Devil's Gap, over Lover's Leap, and down into the tortured valley where Williams Creek had once run clearly through the woods and now ran dark and muddy through the miners' tailings.

Not only miners followed that long trail from the sea. There were men in city clothes, top hats and tail coats, who became the merchants and capitalists of Barkerville and took out more gold in the end than the miners who dug it. There were plump, painted German dance hall girls, the "hurdy-gurdies" who demanded pay for every dance. There were escaped criminals from the States who lived on robbery and murder. And right behind them stalked the majestic figure of Judge Begbie, who carried the law in his head.

73

This, as Douglas saw, could not go on. If the new mines were permanent, if this was the beginning of settlement as he hoped (or feared), if the mining camps were to be supplied with food, if government was to be carried on, taxes collected, law enforced, there must be a road to Cariboo.

How to build a road perhaps 500 miles long with only 20,-000 people in British Columbia to pay for it—if you could collect the taxes? Even Douglas hesitated.

He had driven a road of sorts through the Harrison jungle to the Fraser at Lillooet, by-passing the black canyon, but it was a slow, unsatisfactory road at best, broken by four lake voyages. It could carry slow freight by wagon, pack horse and new steamboats. It could not serve the interior if a large population settled there. A more direct and quicker route must be found.

Douglas was not one to trust other men's observations overmuch. He decided to find the new route for himself.

In the summer of 1860 he traveled the Harrison road to Lillooet, turned south on the Fraser, inspected the mines on the Thompson, and headed overland into the Nicola Valley to the southeastward. From there he reached the Okanagan Valley and pushed through the mountains into the Grand Forks country beside the American border. His plans were large—not only a road to Cariboo but also a second road across British Columbia to the prairies through the Crow's Nest Pass.

For the present, however, he had to satisfy himself with a trail which he ordered built from Hope on the Fraser to the Rockies, in itself a formidable project but no part of the Fraser's story. At the end of a summer's exploration he was back on the river at Yale and as he looked at the canyon there he almost concluded that it could never be breached.

Yet somehow men of foot were still moving up the canyon with pack horses and mules. Packing already had become an established and well-organized business to serve the few miners in the canyon and the camps in Cariboo.

The mule trains fed the gold rush. Mules could carry more

than horses, were surer footed on the narrow canyon trail, and wiser. A train included at least sixteen mules and sometimes as many as forty-eight, managed by a boss, a cook, and one man for eight animals. Led, if possible, by a white mare (which seemed to have a curious moral influence on the others because of her sex and color), the mules followed the trail with little guidance

from the men. They were never roped together or kept under any kind of rein. Each carried a rough leather sack called an aparejo in place of the usual packsaddle, and to this 250 pounds of freight was lashed with the essential diamond hitch.

The mule train operated on a regular schedule arranged to bring it every night to some grazing ground. It could cover the distance from Yale to Quesnel in a month, averaging something over ten miles a day, and return, downhill, a little faster. The Harrison road carried the heavy freight but the canyon mule, loaded with mail, newspapers and all kinds of miners' supplies, could earn a dollar a pound for the whole journey. At $250 per mule, with several round trips in the open season, a packer made more money than most miners.

Frank Laumeister was dissatisfied with his mules. Some animal that could carry more freight and live on less water in dry country would increase the profits of the trade. The obvious creature for such work, thought Laumeister, was a camel. Somehow this enterprising freighter acquired twenty-one camels and brought them up the river by boat in the spring of '62. The story of the camels in the jungles of the Harrison spread by the miners' grapevine throughout the Cariboo but at first few believed it. Soon, however, the lumbering beasts, each with 1,000 pounds on its back, became a familiar spectacle not only on the Harrison but also on the trail up to Quesnel. Laumeister, pushing his train along at 30 or 40 miles a day, looked forward to easy wealth.

Unfortunately, he had forgotten that camels have a curious stench. Their owner could endure it but, with one whiff of the approaching camel train, every horse and mule on the trail went crazy. Soon Laumeister found himself involved in lawsuits with other packers whose animals had bolted into the woods or fallen into the river. Besides, the camels' soft feet, made for sand, were wearing out on the Cariboo rock. Laumeister sold a few of his train on the coast and turned the rest out on the Thompson flats east of Cache Creek. They seem to have reared no offspring but the last of them lived on until 1905.

This, then, was the kind of traffic that Douglas saw laboring up the canyon and along the Harrison route. Assuredly it could not support the growing colony that this dull but daring man foresaw. He went back to Victoria for the winter and, thinking the road problem over, decided to study the possibilities of the canyon again.

On May 29, 1861, he set out on horseback from Yale toward Lytton. His impressions, set down in his diary, indicate the dimensions of the task he had set himself—the construction of a road where the Indians had crawled for centuries on their dizzy ladders, where even now a mule traveled with difficulty and danger.

The trail [Douglas writes, with a certain optimism] is very good; grades here and there rather steep. Scenery grand beyond description. Mountains rising to the skies on either side of the narrow pass, and at our foot the Fraser is frantically tearing its way in foaming whirls. Neither is the pass destitute of softer features, every spot of earth is prolifice of vegetation and the mountain sides are covered with beautiful flowers. A rock plant, evidently an evergreen, was covered with clusters of ball-shaped lilac flowers. The trail has given an impulse to settlement; every spot of tillable land has been pre-empted and in process of being cleared and cultivated. Two Frenchmen have selected a beautiful spot at the Falls. They have built a kiosk and laid out the ground with taste. It is planted with native flowers and watered by a brook led from the neighboring hills. They kept refreshments of all kinds, even to a capital good claret.

Douglas had reached the canyon in the first days of spring growth. The air is heavy then with the scent of syringa, its sweetness cut by the clean smell of pine and juniper. The dogwoods on the coastal side of the mountains carry their frail freight of white stars and the maple buds are opening with the color of wine. Between the close canyon walls the spring is held and squeezed of its essence. Even a Scotsman of the Hudson's Bay Company delighted in its strong taste.

Scenery did not concern him long. Of his next observation he wrote:

A party of seven Chinamen are clearing the surface of Spuzzum flats. Having discovered gold on it at a depth varying from 6 to 15 feet, the stripping is heavy but the pay-dirt is rich, yielding from 5 to 10 cents to the pan. The discovery is important and will no doubt lead to other valuable enterprises. The poor Chinamen are elated at their success and promise of protection. Encamped at Chapman's Bar.

Next day Douglas began to realize better the obstacles to be overcome if a road was to be built here. The grades on the trail at the Nicaragua slide, he reports, were too steep for wagon

travel. The route farther on was too dangerous and it ran in
other places "along the face of terrific precipices." Yet he had
no serious trouble in reaching the junction of the Thompson at
Lytton on May 31.

After resting three days, he followed the established trail
on the south bank of the Thompson and crossed it by Cook's
Ferry, doubtless noting that a bridge must be built here to
carry the traffic of a wagon road. He pushed on as far as the Bonaparte Valley, was surprised to find frost here in the first week of
June, and decided that the land was unfit for cultivation. (It
became, a few years later, the richest hay land in British Columbia, and still is today.)

All along the trail Douglas met men bearing gold and fabulous tales of Cariboo. Their stories left him in doubt no longer.
The road must be built. Returning in haste to Yale, he ordered
his local officials to begin construction at once.

Here was a project which a home government in London
must consider quite insane. One imagines the face of the Duke of
Newcastle when he opened Douglas's dispatch of October 24,
1861, and read:

> I therefore propose to push on rapidly with the forma-
> tion of roads during the coming winter, in order to have
> the great thoroughfares leading to the remotest mines, now
> upward of 500 miles from the sea coast, so improved as to
> render travel easy, and to reduce the cost of transport,
> thereby securing the whole trade of the colony for Fraser's
> river and defeating all attempts at competition from
> Oregon.
>
> The only insuperable difficulty which I experience is
> want of funds:—the revenues of the colony will, doubtless,
> in the course of the year, furnish the means, but cannot sup-
> ply the funds that are immediately wanted to carry on
> these works.
>
> I propose as soon as those roads are finished and the cost

of transport reduced to impose an additional tax as a further means of revenue, a generally popular measure and strongly recommended in several petitions . . .

I have in these circumstances come to the resolution of meeting the contingency and raising the necessary funds by effecting a loan of fifteen or twenty thousand pounds in this country. . . .

In taking this decided step, I feel I am assuming an unusual degree of responsibility; but I trust that the urgency of the case will justify the means.

Douglas was exceeding his powers because he had no time to await authority from London. As his dispatch shows, he was still driven by the fear that had sent him to Victoria in the first place—if he did not open up British Columbia and control it, the Americans would. British or Yankee power would fill the vacuum between the coast and the mountains. And, as always, the Fraser was the decisive factor, for it alone could contain the passage to the interior.

The Duke of Newcastle had no time to interfere if he had wished to. Douglas borrowed the money from the local bank, he let contracts for roadwork wherever he could find men to take them, and he turned his Royal Engineers into pick-and-shovel laborers. In that winter of '61-'62, digging through the snow, they began to push the new road from Yale up the river.

This was to be perhaps the largest construction project ever undertaken by a community of some 20,000 people, and most of them temporary visitors from another country. To realize its sweep we must try to grasp the geography with which Douglas was contending.

On the ground, within the jumble of the Fraser canyon, or at any point on the road, the eye is totally confused. But on the map the area chiefly involved lies like a fairly flat oval, its length poised north and south. Its western side is the Harrison route, its eastern the canyon.

From Lillooet, on the Fraser, the Harrison trail toiled a mile into the air over Pavilion Mountain, down to the interior plateau at Clinton, the top of the oval. From Clinton, swinging far east of the river, the trail twisted northward through the country of range and jackpine. It met the river again at Soda Creek, where steamboats carried the traveler north to Quesnel. From there he walked or rode eastward through the mountains to Barkerville.

Douglas's new road would follow the Fraser from Yale halfway along the eastern side of the oval to the junction of the Thompson. On the map it would seem reasonable to continue beside the Fraser to Lillooet, thus completing the oval and joining the Pavilion route, already in use. Above the Thompson on the Fraser, however, the canyon is almost as formidable as below. The early travelers had learned long ago to avoid it. At Lytton they left the Fraser and turned eastward along the easier clay benches of the Thompson, crossed it on Cook's Ferry (now Spences Bridge), followed its northern bank to Ashcroft, and then moved northward along the valley of the Bonaparte to Clinton. At this point, then called the Junction, the Harrison route and the Fraser river trail joined, completing the oval.

Douglas intended to follow the second route, the eastern side of the oval, with little variation from the existing trail. It was a sound, perhaps an inevitable choice. No later engineers have been able to improve on it. The road plan laid down by Douglas, not only in the Cariboo but eastward across British Columbia, is still the basic plan of modern highways. As the chief engineer of British Columbia says, there is hardly a point in the whole existing highway system where it has been possible to vary substantially the locations fixed by Douglas. So far as the Cariboo Road is concerned, the Fraser itself had fixed the plan and neither Douglas nor his sucessors could alter it.

A paper plan thus was easy to lay down, there being no reasonable alternative. But once leaving the map, the engineer faced, first, the appalling obstacle of the canyon, which somehow he bridged at one point; then the deep-cut clay gullies of the Thompson; a second bridge to cross that river; the leagues of high land, with heavy grades, through the jack-pine forests back to the steamboat terminus on the Fraser; and finally the mountain passes between Quesnel and Barkerville.

The thoughts of Douglas as he embarked on the project were conjured up, rather strikingly, sixty years later by Mr. Justice Dennis Murphy, of the British Columbia Supreme Court, who was born and raised on the Cariboo Road in the seventies and knew its every curve and boulder. In the old-fashioned rhetoric appropriate to the unveiling of a monument at Yale in 1925, Mr. Justice Murphy thus pictured Douglas's problem:

> Governor Douglas determined upon a task that, the surrounding circumstances considered, might well have appalled the stoutest heart. He would build a wagon road from Yale, the head of navigation, to Williams Creek, the heart of the gold fields. Through the miles on miles of rock-ribbed Fraser canyons would he drive it, here skirting the river's brink, here perched hundreds of feet above on some jutting cliff, where scarcely could an eagle build its nest; round fearsome Nicaragua Rock would he blast it; over the tremendous ascent of Jackass Mountain would he carry it; then along the sun-baked planes of the Thompson where the bunch grass stood the height of a man's waist; through the lush valley of Bonaparte to Clinton, up and up the steep Clinton hill to the green timber, and straight through this by miles of corduroy down into the smiling Lac La Hache Valley, and along it and over Carpenters Mountain, with its awful beds of miry clay, the terror of all who used the road when built; then down, down the swift descent of Soda Creek hill, to the Fraser once again.

Douglas had no gift or time for speeches of that sort. By the spring the sappers of the Royal Engineers were building the first six miles of road from Yale, hewing it out of the vertical rock cliffs on the north shore of the river. Beyond the sappers, the famous Thomas Spence had taken a contract to carry the road to Spuzzum. At that point the road, like the original trail, would cross to the east bank of the river and the old ferry would be replaced by a bridge.

Joseph Trutch (later lieutenant governor of British Columbia) had undertaken to build this bridge. It was to have a span of 300 feet, the first suspension bridge in the colony. It was impossible to carry steel cables over the mule trail, so Trutch packed in bales of wire which were wrapped together at the bridge site—woven so expertly that no single thread ever snapped. From anchors of rock masonry the cables were stretched over wooden towers and from them the wooden deck was suspended.

The last plank laid, Trutch waited to see whether his bridge, like a tiny spiderweb strung across the bottom of the canyon, would bear weight. A four-horse team with a load of three tons was driven across. The deflection in the deck level was less than a quarter of an inch. For the first time the Fraser had been crossed on foot. Trutch's handmade bridge was used for half a century. The modern engineers could find no better site and built the present steel suspension bridge on it.

Other contractors laid the rest of the road in sections, hiring what men they could find, mostly Chinese who, to increase the difficulties of the project, were decimated by smallpox. In 1864 Spence closed the last gap between Yale and Soda Creek by replacing Cook's Ferry with a wooden bridge across the Thompson. The modern bridge there still carries Spence's name.

In the same year the road was pushed eastward from Quesnel to Cottonwood, and a year later on to Barkerville. At last Douglas's dream of a road from the coast to the interior, with the steamboat passage between Soda Creek and Quesnel, had come to life. The era of wagon travel had begun.

How could men, with no power but dynamite, mules, horses and oxen, and their own hands, carve a road through the sheer rock of the canyon? They succeeded only by taking advantage of every ledge, by curving their road far up side creeks and gullies, by following every flat bench, by avoiding wherever they could the cliffs at the river's edge. But in many places the mountains forced them to the side of the river and here they blasted the bluffs to make a track scarcely wide enough for a wagon's wheels. At the worst points they built cribbing and filled it with stones. Over many a gaping cut they held the road straight above the river on log props and hewn planks.

A fantastic road, hanging like gossamer in the canyon, twisting around every rock of the interior plateau, threading the gorges of the mountains, penetrating the last narrow gut of Devil's Gap, and meandering down at last to the flats by Williams Creek, where the gold lay, built hurriedly in two years, mostly with pick and shovel; supported by innumerable bridges and trestles of wood, which would soon rot out. Yet it carried the whole traffic of the gold fields, the supplies inbound, the leather sacks of treasure out to the mysterious regions of finance, which valued gold above goods, above nationality, and far above the toil of miners who dug it from the earth.

Long after the gold was exhausted, the miners had disappeared, and the gold towns had been deserted, the road carried the travel of the developing ranch lands, of the new towns and the new mines, of a Canadian province which became one of the richest areas of habitation on the map. The same road, rebuilt and widened, but hardly changed in location, carries that traffic still.

When Douglas's work was done the Cariboo Road was 385 miles long and 18 feet wide. It had cost only $1,250,000 and most of that was paid when the work was done. To the contractors Douglas had issued bonds which he redeemed in two or three years. In many places, such as at the two main bridges, he allowed the contractors to levy tolls on all traffic—a plan which increased the cost of freight but enabled the road to pay its way from the beginning. Thus, when Douglas retired in 1864, the total debt of British Columbia was £128,750, less than half the cost of the road. This economical Scot had left his colony in admirable shape. He could hardly imagine that, by 1949, it would be spending on its own account some $75,000,000 a year.

Now that the main road was open, the Harrison route was almost abandoned, the mule trains were replaced by horses and oxen, and the days of freight wagons and fast coaches began, the brief salad days of Cariboo.

Until now the country had been dominated by the sucessful miners, men like Cameron, Barker and Deitz. Now the freighter, the operator of the fast coach, formed the ruling caste. With his drivers, his armed guards, his stablemen, his sleek horses and plodding oxen, he became the most powerful man on the road—a legendary figure who could keep goods moving on schedule in winter snow, in spring mud, year in and year out. You could almost set your watch by the stagecoach in any kind of weather.

Billy Ballou was the first expressman. He had come up from California in 1848, and calculating that there was more money in transportation than in mining, established a fairly regular express service from Victoria to the lower Fraser mines by steamboat, canoe, mule and backpacker. He made most of his money carrying newspapers, the *Chronicle* and the *Colonist* from Victoria, the *Bulletin* from San Francisco, which would be passed eagerly from hand to hand among the miners. There were profits to be earned fast when you could sell a newspaper for a dollar on the river and charge 3 shillings on a letter from the coast to Quesnel.

Soon a man of larger imagination and harder drive than Ballou appeared. F. J. Barnard had first walked into Barkerville carrying mail and small parcels on his back. Then he had established a pony express. When he secured a government mail contract in 1862 he was ready to control most of the freight and passenger traffic. Ballou went broke and Barnard's Express became the first established transportation system west of the Rockies.

As soon as any section of the new road was opened Barnard

covered it with his freight wagons. When the whole road was complete he imported fourteen-passenger, four-horse stages which, from Yale at the south to Soda Creek at the north, made two trips a week between the coast and the interior. They never missed a trip. This is a feat of organization which must have few equals, under such conditions, in the history of the stagecoach.

To make speed Barnard changed horses every thirteen miles. At every stopping place a hotel sprang up, the rude but well-fed mile houses of the Cariboo road, with new hay farms to support the horses. By his unvarying schedule, by hiring the best drivers, by wasting hardly a minute on the whole route, Barnard could carry passengers from Yale to Soda Creek in forty-eight hours— an almost incredible feat when you remember that this is a one day's drive today in an automobile.

On the stagecoach route you started from Yale at dawn after a breakfast of ham, eggs and flapjacks known, for their digestive properties, as "Rocky Mountain deadshot." If you were lucky you got an outside seat with the driver and the armed guards. Then you could listen to the old-timers' stories and get a clear view of the canyon in the moving shadows of the sunrise. If you were inside the coach you were crammed between miners, Chinese and Indians, and perhaps a perfumed dance hall girl on her way to the saloons of Barkerville. The inside seat had one advantage—you could not see the wheels skidding within an inch of the road edge, the sheer drop of hundreds of feet below it, the bridges strung upon jutting fingers of rock, the trestles propped on toothpicks of timber. But you missed the scenery.

At night the coach stopped at a mile house numbered by its distance from Yale. You ate a dinner precisely like your breakfast and slept on a bench surrounded by your fellow passengers. Then, at daylight, on again through the Bonaparte Valley, up the Clinton Hill to the Hundred, down to Lac La Hache and northward through the jack pine to the river at Soda Creek or Alexandria. You traveled in comfort by steamboat to Quesnel.

Another coach took you up over Lover's Leap, through Devil's Gap, along black tarn called Jack of Clubs Lake, over tailings of the Lohee mine, and down the last hill into Barkerville.

There you would shoulder your way through the crowds of high-booted miners on the single street and, in bad weather, wade halfway to your knees in mud. You were unlikely to find gold, but if you did, there was pleasure of a simple kind to be bought in every saloon and dance hall, there were hurdy-gurdies very hospitable at a price, champagne from France, the billiard table in Kelly's Hotel from England, and company from every corner of the earth. And, strangely enough, in this multitude, all gold-crazy, your life was safe, your claim inviolable, and the law enforced.

If you were among the relatively few who found gold you traveled back to the coast without admitting your wealth. Douglas had established a gold escort of Royal Engineers, each man mounted and armed, but, since he could not afford to guarantee the safe delivery of gold at Yale, his experiment proved a failure. Barnard, however, would guarantee you. His guards rode on the coach, every man a dead shot, and you felt safe with a heavy leather bag strapped under your coat.

If you were wise, though, you hired a dance hall girl or an Indian squaw to travel with you and let her carry the gold while you pretended not to know her. At Yale you could deposit your stake at the bank, reward your secret accomplice, and be sure your check would be accepted anywhere.

Actually, travel was suprisingly safe on the BX line. No coach was robbed until 1886, a full generation after the original strike. In that year—the story was so unusual as to be well remembered—Ned Tate, driving a solitary Chinese passenger, was held up by two men near the 82-mile post, north of Clinton. The robbers took the iron safe from the coach. It contained $8,000. Robbers, safe and money were never seen again.

A few similar robberies followed, none of them yielding much to the highwaymen. The only substantial haul was taken by an old man named Rowlands, who held up a coach at the foot of the Bridge Creek Hill, near the 98-mile post, and carried off a safe containing $15,000 in gold. Rowlands settled on the Bonaparte River and pretended to find gold, which he banked at Clinton. When his sudden wealth started a minor rush to Bonaparte and no other miner had any luck, the police became suspicious. Rowlands was arrested as he was about to decamp, served two years in jail, and escaped.

Thanks to Begbie and his police, banditry never became popular in Cariboo. No one like the James Brothers or Billy the Kid appeared there.

The Cariboo, in fact, had settled down after the first feverish years to a routine of hard work. The best ground had soon been occupied by the lucky prospectors and most of the others had straggled back to the States. Though less gold was coming out, a new kind of men was coming in—the cattle rancher, the hay farmer and the homesteader, who would remain. Such men brought wives with them and reared the future stock of British Columbia.

In the first years of the rush the Cariboo had been a man's camp. Nearly all the women who joined it came for man's amusement, diligently earning the profits of their profession. As early as '62 Douglas and the home government realized that a colony could not be built of such material. Through a colonial society in England they arranged to send out a shipload of potential brides. The bishop of Oxford, the bishop of London, and other eminent philanthropists organized this movement with enthusiasm.

Sixty English girls, chaperoned by a clergyman and a matron, reached Victoria in September of '62. As they walked down the gangplank every miner in town crowded the fort to observe the unique spectacle of virginity. No pass was made at these girls—the miner had a strict code in such matters and clearly distinguished the two classes of women—no remark was made as the men watched the procession in wondering silence, but within a few days most of the immigrants had become wives and, in due time, mothers. Altogether nearly a hundred girls came out on the "bride ships" to live at the mines or to manage the first ranch homes in the Cariboo.

But before we leave the rush the most remarkable immigrants of all deserve to be remembered—the Overlanders of '62, the men (and one pregnant woman) who walked to Cariboo across the Rocky Mountains and ran the Fraser on rafts in the strangest movement of those times.

7   The Overlanders

I N THE SPRING OF '62 THE FOLLOWING ADVERTISEMENT APPEARED in the newspapers of London:

British Columbia Overland Transit, via Canada.

The British Columbia Transit Company will punctually despatch on the 21st of May, at 12 noon from Glasgow, in the first class and powerful screw steamship United Kingdom, 1,200 tons burden, 300 horse power, James Clarke commander, a party of first and second class passengers for Quebec, Canada, and over the Grand Trunk Railway and continuous lines of railway to Chicago and St. Paul and via the Red River settlements, in covered wagons, to British Columbia.

This is the speediest, safest and most economical route to the gold diggings. The land transit is through a lovely country unequalled for its beauty and salubrity of climate. More than one half of the distance from Quebec is by railway.

Through fares £42 from England to British Columbia, saloon berths £5 extra.

Letters received from the agents in Canada announce that a first spring party of 52 in number have left for British Columbia by the route. About 1,000 carts annually trade along this line. There are numerous posts, missions and trading stations from the Red River settlements along the Saskatchewan, now discovered to abound in vast gold deposits to the Rocky Mountains. The route is constantly travelled with perfect safety.

The riches of the Fraser River, the golden land of Cariboo (the very spelling of the word sparkled with adventure) and on the way a jolly outing in the Rocky Mountains—all this for £42! The office of the Overland Transit Company at 6 Copthall Court, Throgmorton Street E.C., found itself in happy possession of a minor South Sea Bubble.

The bubble would roll across the prairies through the mountains and down the Fraser to burst unnoticed on the trail to Barkerville. But meanwhile business was brisk at 6 Copthall Court. The forgotten saga of the Overlanders, the maddest chapter in the Fraser's story and the most pitiful, had begun.

Many men, their numbers unknown, had gone to Cariboo from England and the Continent before this. Most of them had traveled to the Panama Isthmus, crossed it, and sailed up, to San Fransisco and thence to Victoria and Yale. In 1859 a few parties actually had walked across the prairies and through the Rockies, but by the southern route of the Vermilion Pass and the Kootenay River, long used by the fur traders. A handful of them worked northward again along the Okanagan fur trail and into Cariboo.

The Overland Transit Company's customers were to cross the mountains by the Yellowhead Pass to the north, hit the headwaters of the Fraser there, and drift pleasantly down to the gold fields. Clerks, apprentices, and the younger sons of the gentry were to undertake, without experience, proper equipment, or even knowledge of the map, an expedition as hard as Mackenzie or Fraser's.

In the first days of May the Overlanders, some English and Scottish, the majority Canadians from Ontario and Quebec, started by railway for St. Paul from Toronto, Queenston, St. Thomas and Huntingdon. They expected to reach Cariboo in sixty days. "The young men composing the [St. Thomas] party," we are assured by their sponsors, "are highly respectable and belong to some of the best families in town."

The first hundred arrivals in St. Paul (among them eighteen bewildered Englishmen) looked in vain for the easy stage route to the Rockies. Only a few turned back. The rest started north by oxcart, luckily discovered a steamboat undertaking its first voyage on the Red River, and reached Fort Garry (Winnipeg) with no worse accident than occasional collisions with floating trees and sand bars. Behind them on foot marched other parties who narrowly escaped massacre by the Sioux.

At Fort Garry the travelers were welcomed by the cannons of the Hudson's Bay fort, dancing, feasting and religious services. Now they felt that the worst was over. Only the easy wagon route lay ahead through the "lovely country unequalled for its beauty and salubrity of climate."

For $40 the travelers could buy a Red River cart made entirely of wood, the creaking of its wheels easily audible for a mile. An ox to pull it cost the same, horses $25, and pemmican, the staple food of buffalo meat and berries, 16 cents a pound. Having bought these essentials from the half-breeds of Fort Garry, the first Overlanders started out across the prairies in early June.

Each party was organized under a captain with a committee to advise him. Discipline was strict, morale high. At dark the carts were arranged in a triangle and scouts were posted against the Indians, who seem to have been entirely uninterested. At two in the morning the camp was broken, the carts strung out in line, and the march began before dawn. It halted for breakfast at six, for dinner at two, and supper at six. By resting only from nine at night until two in the morning even oxen could cover fifty miles in a day. A few weeks should bring them handily to Cariboo. Since there was ample time, the march paused every Sunday for rest and an hour of hymms and prayer.

How many men were straggling across the prairies that summer is not known exactly but the largest party included

150. Among them was one woman, Mrs. August Schubert, who, with her husband, had joined the first party at Fort Garry. She had three children with her in an oxcart and expected a fourth before autumn.

Thus, with mighty creaking of wooden wheels, with bellow of oxen and crack of whip, with men singing as they marched and dreaming at night of gold, with the sound of fiddle around the campfire and the murmur of Sunday prayer, with three babies and a woman far gone in pregnancy, the Overlanders moved west.

At Throgmorton Street, E.C., the Overland Transit Company banked its £42 per head and prepared more exciting advertisements for the newspapers. At Fort Garry the half-breeds gladly sold their carts, oxen and pemmican. And far to the west, past the flat line of the horizon, the Fraser—that route of "perfect safety"—wallowed dark and angry to the sea.

The prairies were soaked that year by heavy rain, the wagon track was deep in mud, the rivers high, the fords dangerous. But at its beginning the route was well marked. The factors of the Hudson's Bay posts sold the travelers supplies and sometimes ferried them across swollen rivers in their barges and big York boats. So far the going was easy.

As the expedition moved out of the flat central plains into the rolling brush country of northern Saskatchewan the trail became harder to follow. Carts bogged down to the wheel hubs, oxen sank to their bellies in muskeg. The pace had dropped to a few miles a day. This was not what the Overland Transit Company had promised, the beautiful and salubrious land, the pleasant outing.

Desperately men chopped down the little poplar trees and laid them in corduroy across the swamps. Where streams were too deep to ford they threw together floating bridges, swam out into the current and anchored them by ropes, and then pulled the lightened carts across by hand, making the oxen swim. Most of these men had been soft when they started out, the Englishmen had never handled an ax or pitched a tent, but they were hardening now under the hot prairie sun, the black flies and the mosquitoes.

Supplies were running short already. A few buffalo were shot but not many, for they ran away at the first sight of man. There were ducks and prairie chickens, curiously tame, and one diary records that a meal of young eagles "tasted delicious." No one starved and when the first party reached the high banks of the North Saskatchewan on July 21, and looked across at the buildings of Fort Edmonton, the worst seemed to be over—an easy pass through the Rockies and then downhill all the way to Cariboo.

The Hudson's Bay men at Edmonton knew better, but as the strangers seemed determined to push on, there was no use discouraging them. At least they could be dissuaded from entering the narrow trails of the Rockies in oxcarts. Most of the Overlanders agreed to trade their oxcarts and oxen for pack horses. A few of them, more stubborn than the rest, kept the beasts that had pulled them thus far. This was their single stroke of good luck from one coast to the other. Without those oxen on the trail ahead everyone would have starved to death.

At the first of August the Overlanders started up the foothills. A few of them, having found faint flecks of yellow in the gravel of the Saskatchewan, stopped there to mine the "vast gold deposits," already noted in the prospectus of the Overland Transit Company. No one made wages.

The prairie trail had seemed hard. It was a paved highway compared with the track winding between the timber of the foothills. Though advance parties cleared away the windfall, the expedition was lucky to make ten miles a day. Summer was waning and the local guides, who knew the Rockies and their early winter, looked westward, where no peaks were yet to be seen, and counted the days left before the first snow. The strangers looked for the mountains, too, but saw only banks of cloud.

On the morning of August 15, as the clouds lifted, a serrated line of rock and snow stood out suddenly against the sky. At this spectacle the travelers burst into cheers, threw their ragged hats into the air, and rejoiced that the Fraser lay just beyond the pass.

The pass—what a word to dream on! Through a valley of wildflowers and rippling streams, such as they had seen pictured on postcards, the Overlanders would stroll blithely to the Fraser and gather the nuggets from its sand. The guides did not pause to argue. They had been paid to lead the party to the source of the Fraser, beyond which they knew no trail, and they would return, if they were lucky, before the pass was blocked. Once over the pass the strangers could look out for themselves.

Now they had reached the gully of the Athabaska and they had to pause here a week, build a great raft with a tree for a rudder, and ferry themselves across the river.

This brought them to Jasper Hawse's ancient trail, the Pass of Yellowhead. Now, surely, their troubles were finished.

Pass there might be, but there was no path. The guides climbed upward on the sheer hills, blazing a trail as they went. The expedition was now strung out ten miles, a long day's march between the guides and the last stragglers. Soon the last oxcart was abandoned. The horses and oxen struggled along ledges so narrow that there was no room for their packs. Many of them slid into the chasms below, taking their loads of food with them. Sometimes the packs were unloaded and the men carried them on their backs.

They were light loads now. The expedition had brought enough food for two months: 168 pounds of flour and 50 pounds of pemmican to the man. Nearly three months had passed already and most of the grub was gone. The travelers shot chipmunks, birds and porcupines. Thomas McMicking, the captain, dined "upon a dish so delicate and rare that it might have tempted the palate of Epicurus himself; so nice, indeed, was it, that I have some hesitation in naming it, lest we might be censured for living too luxuriously by the way." This tidbit was roasted skunk, and McMicking "resolved that his skunkship had been a slandered and much abused individual."

There were no more skunks to be found. The travelers began to kill their starving oxen and horses. One of them stewed his deerskin tumpline. A still more grisly meal lay ahead.

At four o'clock on the afternoon of August 22 the expedition camped on the reedy shore of CowDung Lake and, with a wild surmise, saw that the lake emptied westward. They were over the divide. This little brook, though a man could cross it in one step, was the beginning of the Fraser. The travelers feasted deep on roasted ox that night.

Barkerville was only 400 miles off. Now they had only to follow the river and it would lead them to Cariboo. Their progress was rapid at first but soon the little creek swelled into a torrent, which drove them high up on the hills again. There was no trail, no blaze on any tree, no track or mark. The guides had never been here before, their contract was almost complete and the sharp night frosts told them the mountain autumn was beginning.

West of Moose Lake they found a band of Shuswap Indians, who traded salmon and berries for ammunition, bits of clothing, needles and thread. The salmon had struggled 700 miles from the sea, had eaten nothing on the way, were battered, half rotten and heavy with the spawn which they would lay on the precise creek where they had hatched four years before, but they tasted good to the Overlanders. Dried in the sun, or mixed with berries in the Indians' cakes, they would yet save the expedition from starving.

The Shuswaps were far from home on their annual fishing trek. They knew nothing of the Fraser farther west. On the sand they drew a crude map which seemed to show a white man's road over the next divide but already, they seemed to say, this road was a foot deep in snow. And after two days' march the Fraser was not flowing west. It was flowing north away from Cariboo.

McMicking looked long at the Indian map. If he followed the river he would reach Fort George and the gold fields somehow, but how to navigate a river which, at every mile, widened, deepened and flowed with rising speed? To the south must lie the headwaters of the Thompson and beside it the white man's road. One route or the other must be followed and soon, for winter was in the air.

McMicking left each man to decide for himself. Most of the expedition could bear no more foot travel and elected to run the river. The others, seeing the fury of the water, chose the route overland.

Frantically, with an eye on the weather, the river party cut down cottonwood trees, bound them together with withes to make rafts 40 feet by 20, enclosed the rafts with railing to hold the remaining oxen, and built fireplaces of stone and clay so they would not have to stop even for cooking. Out of the larger cottonwoods crude dugout canoes were hollowed. One man contrived a framework of saplings and stretched green ox skins over it to make a lighter craft.

On September 1 the rafts were ready. Each was placed under the command of a captain with twenty-five men, and each bore the name of the passengers' home town in Canada. First the *Scarborough* was pushed into the current. It spun for a minute and drifted slowly north. The crew cheered, the oxen roped to the railings bellowed, and the Shuswaps, watching from the shore, sadly shook their heads.

Now the *Ottawa* was launched, the *Niagara*, and finally the giant *Huntingdon*, two rafts lashed together, 85 feet long. Beside them floated the dugouts and the ox-skin skiff. The Overlanders, on water at last, lay down on their logs and watched the riverbank glide by. None of them had heard of Mackenzie's voyage and shipwreck on these waters, or Fraser's. No rapids or whirlpools had been mentioned in the prospectus of the Overland Transit Company. Enough that the rafts were moving. The river ahead could not be so bad as the trail behind.

The Fraser, long accustomed to men's folly, was carrying that day a cargo of lunacy and illusion without equal on the rivers of America.

For two days the voyagers floated safely enough. The canyon banks on either side were sheer and unapproachable, but the tree-trunk rudders and the clumsy sweeps of flattened logs kept the rafts offshore. Rain was falling now, the first cold autumn rains that were half snow, and they never ceased to fall for the rest of the voyage. Every man lay soaked across the logs. "Rainy all day," said the diary of John Hunniford, "very uncomfortable, Diarrhoea very bad on board, meat badly tainted—our flour about done."

Still they were making five miles an hour as they guessed, it was delicious to lie on the cottonwood logs after the labor of the trail, and they could drift even in the darkness while they slept. No one asked where they were drifting. Enough that they would drift in the end to Cariboo. But in the meantime they were drifting straight into the maelstrom of the Grand Canyon.

Ahead of them the dugouts moved faster under the pressure of paddles. The first canoe, carrying three men from Toronto, reached the Grand Canyon two days ahead of the first raft. At the sight of the rapids the paddlers beached the canoe and started to lower it on a rope. The canoe bobbed for a moment in the current, was sucked down and swept away. The three men, McKenzie, Carroll and Pattison, were left on the shore for two days without food or shelter in the icy autumn rain. Pattison immediately sickened and was near death when the first raft brought rescue.

Three men from Goderich—Robertson, Warren and Douglas—had lashed two canoes together and tried to run the rapids. At the first riffle the clumsy twin craft capsized and broke

97

apart. Warren and Douglas clung to one of the canoes as it was hurled through the rapids. They had embarked on these waters though they could not swim a stroke! Robertson, a good swimmer, struck out for shore. Looking back, he could see his companions still clutching the canoe as it was dragged under the water. When it emerged again the two figures were still with it. Robertson shouted to them to hang on and he swam toward the bank. By the freaky chances of the river, the canoe was thrown up on a sandbank. When Douglas and Warren crawled out on the sand Robertson had disappeared. He was never seen again.

The two men lay down on the sand bar, exhausted and helpless. They would have died there if the *Huntingdon* raft had not reached the upper end of the canyon a few hours later. Two of the *Huntingdon* crew, Sellar and Fortune, launched a canoe from the raft and somehow ran the rapids to the sand bar. They took off Douglas and Warren, now half dead.

Four canoes had been lost in the rapids. Six more would perish at this spot. Could the rafts survive these waters? The *Queenston*, its crew asleep, was almost into the rapids before the lookout saw them and gave the alarm. McMicking's diary tells, the story better than any secondhand account could:

> At half past five o'clock in the morning of Saturday, the 6th [September] we were suddenly startled by an unusual roaring noise that broke the silence of the morning, the cause and source of which was soon explained by the look-out shouting. "Breakers ahead!" We had reached the big rapids and were already so near them and were being swept toward them by the current so rapidly that we had barely time to row ashore and make fast before we were drawn into them.
>
> After landing we went some distance along the shore to examine the place before we should attempt to run it. We found that the rapids consisted of three distinct stretches, with small bays or eddies of comparatively quiet

water between, which had evidently been formed at some remote period of time, by the breaking through as many parallel ridges. The banks on both sides are very rocky and precipitous and the channel, which is very narrow and obstructed in many places by pointed rocks, contains six sharp angles through which the pent-up and maddened waters rushed with violent and resistless impetuosity.

It seemed like presumption to think of risking our lives through such a perilous place, but we saw no alternative; we had either to run the rapids or starve where we were. We found a passage by which we could make a portage around the first two stretches, but were unable to get over the rocky bluffs of the third.

At length Mr. Harkness decided to try it, if we would lighten the raft by a number of us making the portage, leaving only men enough aboard to man the oars. About ten men remained on the raft, and the balance of us stationed ourselves along the shore where we might possibly be able to render some assistance if it were required. Everything being ready, the ropes were untied and the frail bark pushed into the current.

Onward they sped like an arrow. They seemed to be rushing into the very jaws of death. Before them on the right rose a rocky reef against which the furious flood was lashing itself into foam, threatening instant and unavoidable destruction, and on the other side a seething and eddying whirlpool was ready to engulf in its greedy vortex any mortal who might venture within its reaches. With fearful velocity they were hurried along directly towards the fatal rock. Their ruin seemed inevitable. It was a moment of painful suspense.

Not a word was spoken except the necessary orders of the pilot, which were distinctly heard on shore above the din and tumult of the scene. Now was the critical moment. Every one bent manfully to his oar. The raft shot closely past the rock, tearing away the stern rowlock, and glided safely down the eddy below. The agony was over. The gauntlet had been run and all survived. The issue of the ordeal was announced by an involuntary cheer from the brave hearts aboard the raft, which was heartily responded to by those on shore. The last part of the rapids was less dangerous than what we had already passed and we ran through it safely, all hands being on board.

The *Huntingdon* had been delayed overnight by its rescue of Warren and Douglas. Its crew had no means of knowing whether the *Queenston* had run the rapids or broken up. Next morning the Huntingdon men surveyed the canyon and decided to chance it. A. L. Fortune's diary gives us a second vivid picture:

We thought we might try the run if we lighted the raft, so all stock and idle passengers were put on shore. Eight of the crew with Captain [Sellar] volunteered to risk their lives with the raft. We pushed off and then kept working our sweeps to prevent going to the right side. Down we shot like a cork—a whirl caught the left forward corner of the raft, holding it fast while another terrific eddy below the great rock caught the right after corner of the raft and thus we were anchored for a short time. Although we labored and strained at our sweeps with two men at each handle, we failed to gain upon the power of the eddies. We were tired and troubled in this dilemma when all in a sudden, by some freak of the eddy, we were hoisted past all danger.

In the same fashion all the rafts wallowed through the canyon, and came whole into the calmer waters. The crews, thinking all danger past, flung themselves down on the logs in their soaked blankets.

Thus the twenty-three men on the *Queenston*, except one

man on watch, slept all night while the raft gathered speed. When daylight came they awakened to find themselves in a new series of rapids. For fifteen miles, all hands at the sweeps, the raft was tossed from one side of the river to the other, sank in the whirlpools while the men clung to the railings and the oxen were carried away, but always lurched up to the surface again and moved forward until it stuck fast on a submerged rock. Three men swam ashore with a rope and managed to pull the craft clear. After that it was plain sailing down to Fort George.

The *Queenston* reached the fort at 8:45 on the morning of September 8. The other rafts followed during the next two days.

Back at the headwaters of the Fraser the rest of the Overlanders were still straggling into camp through the mountain pass and building more rafts. How many men reached the river is not known, for the late arrivals were too busy to keep diaries. But they were still trudging through the mountains in the last week of September.

A raft manned by men from Whitby hit a rock seven miles from its starting point. Upended in the current, it dumped all the supplies. The crew clung to it for a day until one man swam ashore and brought rescuers from the camp.

After that the rest of the travelers killed their oxen, dried the meat, bought salmon and dried groundhog from the Indians, and took to canoes. Most parties got through safely but seven men were wrecked in the Grand Canyon and one of them, Philip Leader, was drowned.

On September 30 the last party of five men reached the Grand Canyon, two in one canoe and the other three in two canoes lashed together. The passengers of this ill-fated double craft were named Carpenter, Jones and Alexander.

Carpenter went ahead to reconnoiter and decided to run the rapids. Before returning to his friends he took out his notebook and wrote in it for a moment. The others saw him put it into his coat pocket and hang the coat on a tree branch. They did not know what he had written until they found the coat next day. Then it was too late.

Alexander and Carpenter boarded one of the canoes and, to save weight, left Jones on the shore. What followed is best told in the original version of Alexander's diary:

As we thought it rather dangerous, I took off my boots and buckskin shirt before we started. We went at a tremendous rate for a while, when we got among some big waves and the canoe filled over the stern and went down. When it came to the surface again Carpenter was holding to the stern and I to the bow. Then I let go and swam for it. Carpenter I never saw again, nor yet the canoe. I was carried a long way underwater by the undercurrent but I kept thinking it was not all up yet and resolutely kept my mouth shut till I should come to the surface and get another gulp of air, and down I would go again. Sometimes I would be so long under water that I could scarcely hold my breath.

At last I got down out of the boiling surf and the water, though rapid, was smooth. I then began to keep myself better afloat and began to swim for shore. At first I was under water so much that all my exertions had been to keep my head above water. I was so exhausted that I had to swim on my back and lay gasping for breath, but I was quite cool all the time (the water was remarkably cold) and managed to pull my shirt up out of my pants so as to let the water out. I had on heavy Canadian cloth pants. At last, after swimming a distance of about three-quarters of a mile, I touched shore but was so benumbed with the cold I could not hold on to it but drifted off again. Soon, however, I made the shore again and dug my hands among the pebbles and pulled myself out of the water and lay there.

He had swum the canyon, a feat almost incredible, but he was not safe yet. The bar where he lay gasping was on the edge of an island close to the left of the river. On the right bank he sighted two men who had lined their canoe down thus far. He shouted to them for rescue but they dared not embark on such water. Alexander knew there were no more parties in the river above. He must reach the right bank, starve on the left bank, or die where he lay. Accordingly:

> After running about to try and warm myself a little, I jumped into the water again and swam across. Before swimming the second time I stripped off the remainder of my clothes and left them there. I was so cold that I could not close my fingers and had to swim with my hand open. Oh, I never knew what it was to be thankful to God before as when I tottered up that bank, and ever since in all our troubles and dangers I have been able to place more dependence on Him and leave all to His good pleasure.

Alexander was dragged ashore by the two strangers and Jones, who also had scrambled down the river shore. Carpenter, it was clear, had drowned, but Alexander remembered the coat hanging, with a notebook in its pocket, farther upstream. The coat was retrieved and the notebook read. Just before going to his death Carpenter had written: "Arrived this day at the canyon at 10 a.m. and drowned running the canoe down. God keep my poor wife!"

A message to startle four men huddled alone on the river bank, with no help in sight, most of their provisions gone, and Fort George 130 miles away! Alexander does not try to explain Carpenter's premonition. He says only: "Was it not strange?"

But they had no time to ponder the strangeness of it. The four survivors tried to let the remaining canoe down the river on a line but it broke loose and disappeared. Now it was walk or perish. They started for Fort George on foot with a diet of one groundhog a day between them, "each man getting a piece about the size of your hand. We calculated this would last us eight days in which time we expected to reach Fort George."

Eight days where they had to crawl along the bluffs on hands and knees and wriggle on their bellies through the dense underbrush. The first day they made only a few miles when they saw one of their canoes beached on the opposite side of the river. Here was their last chance. Alexander sat down and wrote in his diary: "If I feel well enough I am to try to swim over for it in the morning which, God grant, I may be able to do. If I fail and am lost, I wish this book to be forwarded to my father in Scotland. The address is on the fly leaf."

Next morning they tied two logs together with rope and on this raft Jones and Alexander crossed the river and secured the canoe. It was too small to hold their supplies and four men, so they took turns riding in it while the fourth man struggled along the bank. They made only seven miles the first day and in two days had covered only thirteen miles from the canyon. The groundhog meat was running short.

At this rate they would starve a long way from the fort. But these were not men to starve so easily. "The canoe," says Alexander, "is a great help, thank God, but we found it so bad walking that we halted, felled a tree and lashed a log on either side of the canoe which by this means we hope to make camp."

They would not have made it if Alexander had not shot a brace of duck and two squirrels. Just as these and the last groundhogs had been eaten, and the first snow dimmed out the banks of the river, the travelers heard voices on shore and, heading in, found a camp of Indians. For the gift of a few shirts and some tobacco the Indians fed the party on beaver and guided it to Fort George.

Everybody save those lost in the river—their number unknown—was safe at the fort now, sheltered, fed and clothed. The sick man, Pattison, who had died on arrival, was well buried under a pile of stones to keep the wolves away.

If the terror of passage down the Fraser does not appear in this narrative—and no words could convey it—one final piece of evidence may be cited:

A few Overlanders, how many will never be known, had straggled so far behind the march that winter caught them in the mountains. Some time before spring they tried to run the river. In the summer their bodies were discovered on the sand bar below the Grand Canyon, where so many Overland canoes had perished. All the bodies save one had been torn and devoured. No wild animal could have reached that bar. The body of one man was fully clothed and untouched.

Fortunately the names of these men were not discovered and the horror of cannibalism died with them.

From Fort George the canoes and rafts drifted safely down to Quesnel, piloted by seasoned river guides past the great canyon where Mackenzie's wild onions grew. At Quesnel the huddle of log cabins on the bank must have appeared to the Overlanders an odd gateway to the land of gold, but a few miles away lay all the glittering promises of the Overland Transit Company. Why, even on the banks of the river by the town a few men were panning and rocking the gravel. With a shout the Overlanders leaped ashore.

That was the last shout. From the townsfolk of Quesnel they soon heard the bad news. There was gold at Barkerville, to be sure, but not enough to go round. For every man who found any, nine found nothing. Even as they listened to these stories the Overlanders saw a steady stream of ragged men walking into Quesnel from Barkerville and hurrying down to the coast before winter blocked the trail. Three thousand miles on foot, on rafts and in canoes, five months of travel and the wastage of their savings, had brought the Overlanders to a country where people "mearly stayed & starved."

A few of the more sanguine spirits walked on to Barkerville and quickly returned. All the rest of the expedition stopped in Quesnel only for a day or two and then floated down the river to Alexandria. There, after selling their rafts, canoes and a few last skinny oxen, they started to walk to the coast by the Harrison trail. A few got work on the new Cariboo Road at $40 a month and board. One party reached the sea by Mackenzie's route westward through the Chilcotin country to Bella Coola.

So far as the scanty records show, few Overlanders left British Columbia. Not one of them had found gold but all had found the "lovely country unequalled for its beauty and salubrity of climate," as promised by the Overland Transit Company. With that they seem to have been well satisfied.

McMicking had set down his expenses in detail. For the trip from Queenston to Quesnel he had spent $97.65. And noting the equipment he had brought with him he added: "Our mining tools were the only articles in the above list that we found to be unnecessary."

8   Down the Thompson

WHILE THE RAFTS AND CANOES WERE RUNNING THE FRASER, thirty-six Overlanders started downward from the base camp for the headwaters of the North Thompson. They included Mrs. Schubert with two small children at her heels and a four-year-old girl on her back. She carried a second child due to be born within the month.

The travelers herded 130 head of horses and cattle before them. They expected to find a route down the North Thompson to Fort Kamloops and would go from there by the long-traveled fur brigade trail westward to the Fraser and up to Barkerville.

Over the height of land separating the headwaters of the Fraser from those of its tributary, the North Thompson, an Indian trail was followed, but after two days it petered out. Now, for the first time, the Overlanders beheld the great timber of British Columbia, nourished in this valley by heavy rain and deep snow. A forest of cedar and fir towered above them, hiding the sky, and at their feet underbrush grew so thick that it must be hacked away before they could penetrate it. Winter was a few weeks off. It would bring six feet of snow, weight down the limbs of trees, and grow into white toadstools three feet wide on every stump. The first snowfall would seal the travelers in the valley. None could hope to be alive by spring.

But, cutting their trail as they went, they could make only five or six miles a day and Kamloops was 200 miles south. The modern train passenger, looking through the window at the dense forest, the fierce and tortuous river, the endless sweep of black hills, will wonder how men on foot, with 130 starving animals to drive, could hope to reach Kamloops before winter. Probably if they had known what lay ahead the Overlanders would not have tried it.

Once over the divide and down to the first trickle of the North Thompson, the expedition was on its own. The Shuswap Indian who had accompanied it thus far from the base camp knew nothing of the country to the south and decided to rejoin his tribe on the Fraser. André Cardinal, the faithful French-Canadian guide who had brought the Overlanders through the Rockies, could be of no further service and was permitted to return to the prairies while there was yet time before the snow. What lay between them and Kamloops none of the travelers knew. Their map showed a river but it did not show the rapids, the canyons and the timber.

The country appeared so forbidding and the daily progress was so slow that an attempt was made to find a short cut westward to Cariboo. The party toiled up a tributary which flowed into the North Thompson from the west but this pass ended in the impassable barriers of the mountains. The main river, whatever its obstacles, must be followed.

For a few days the expedition hacked its way down the west bank, but found this was hopeless. At the rate of sixty miles in seventeen days it would not be halfway to Kamloops when the snow came. And Mrs. Schubert's time was drawing close.

There was nothing for it but to run the North Thompson as the other parties had run the Fraser. This decision made, the expedition halted, cut down trees, built rafts, and slaughtered all the cattle to make jerked beef, the only food left. Some nameless wit found time to scrawl on a blazed tree the legend "Slaughter Camp."

On September 22, abandoning most of the horses, the

expedition launched its rafts. At first progress was safe but slow. The river was blocked with log jams which were cut away to provide a narrow channel. More dangerous work lay immediately ahead. It can be imagined from the experience of seven men who had built two rafts, the first carrying seven horses and one ox and the second the remaining supplies and tools. Archibald Thompson has recorded the ensuing days in a letter to his family in Ontario:

We ran down two days when we ran into a snag in the river with our raft, the other raft out of sight, so I put the horses off in the river and let them swim ashore and tried to get the raft off, but could not, so we tied it up and went down the river by land two miles but could not find the boys [on the other raft] so we built a fire and laid down in the bush without any blankets and it rained all night. We had nothing to eat since breakfast. We stayed there till noon next day and nobody came to our assistance so we went back to the raft and we were pretty hungry by this time. We had a dog with us and were going to kill him.

I said we would go on and hunt up the horses and if we could get the raft off easy we would not kill the dog. We got it off and down the river we went till we overtook the boys, it being dark. We were two days and one night without anything to eat and when we did get our supper it was beef without any bread or salt.

This was only the beginning of bad water. Next morning the first raft lurched without warning into the millrace of Murchison Rapids and would have broken up if it had not been swept against the bank. Two men managed to leap ashore and tried to hold the raft, but it was torn from their grasp and sucked into the main current, with three men aboard. It soon floundered upon a rock, spilling all the horses. Two of its passengers grasped this rock a second before the lightened raft spun into the current again. A third man drowned instantly with the horses.

Two men were clinging to a slippery rock in some of the wildest water in Canada. Their companions, who had escaped to the shore, were powerless to help them. At least they could warn the other parties on the river above. This warning saved the rest of the expedition from the Murchison Rapids. Fortunately one of the rafts carried a dugout, carved at Slaughter Camp, and in this fragile craft the two men on the rock were somehow rescued. The details of that rescue, one of the most extraordinary feats in the story of the Overlanders, are lost.

It was plain now that the upper rapids could not be run. When scouts crawled ahead on the riverbank they found what the rafts had escaped—a sheer canyon, not fifty feet across, through which the river burst suddenly to run at right angles into a spinning whirlpool. Nothing could live through such a passage. Hell's Gate it is called and perhaps it deserves the name even better than the central gate of the Fraser.

The river being plainly impassable, a laborious portage must be undertaken at the waste of much precious time. The rafts were abandoned. Three days on foot were required to cover the nine miles from the head of the rapids down to calm water below—three days spent in continual rain and the first autumn sleet. Among those who labored over that cruel trail were three small children and a woman whose fourth would be born within a fortnight.

Below the rapids new rafts were built. By the first days of October the expedition was afloat again, still 130 miles from Kamloops. Its perils were not quite over.

The first raft soon encountered more rapids, started down a four-foot fall, wedged itself between the rocks, and hung there for several hours as in a sluice. Finally it broke clear and moved down a calm current, only to hit another rock next day. There it stuck fast and the passengers, abandoning it, swam to shore. By rigging a line to the raft they managed to rescue their

belongings which, with the aid of some wandering Indians, were portaged around the last rapids.

As the travelers prepared to build another raft they saw a canoe heading up the river. It carried a party of prospectors, who said that Kamloops was 120 miles to the south. Since the river ran through fairly open country, easy to travel, it was decided to cover this final stage on foot.

Meanwhile the other rafts, with varying fortunes, had passed safely through the last rapids. How many of the Overlanders reached Kamloops by water and how many by land the record does not show. But all were near starvation when a grim piece of luck saved them.

Somewhere along the river they found an Indian village. It appeared deserted and when a score of corpses were seen lying among the empty shacks the mystery was explained—a plague of smallpox had driven the Indians away. Potatoes were growing in a field and the white men dug them and ate them raw, too hungry to wait until they could cook them. Each successive party of Overlanders seems to have found the potato field.

Schubert and the men with him were moving against time, for it was now evident that Mrs. Schubert's fourth child would be born in a day or two. The last potatoes eaten and everyone weak with hunger, the Schubert party came upon another Indian village close to the riverbank. The raft was run ashore and the men hurried to the village to ask the Indians for food. Mrs. Schubert and her children were left on the raft.

While they waited for the men's return an aged squaw, amazed by her first sight of a white woman, came down to the raft to examine this prodigy. Her eye immediately fastened on the rope that tied the raft to the bank—a thong of black oxhide braided from the last of the animals at Slaughter Camp. The squaw had lost a black cow a few days before and immediately concluded that Mrs. Schubert had stolen it. In her anger at this discovery the squaw seized the rope and began to untie it. If she had succeeded, the raft, with a pregnant woman and three children aboard, would have drifted out of control into the current. Mrs. Schubert's shrieks brought the men back to the river just as the raft was unloosed. It was safely tied up again but an hour's argument in sign language was required to pacify the owner of the lost cow. With the scant food secured from the Indians, the Schubert party started down the river again.

By now, the eleventh day of October, the first Overlanders had reached Fort Kamloops, which stood then on the west side of the North Thompson at its confluence with the south branch. In the fort the travelers were fed and clothed by the Hudson's Bay men, who could hardly believe their story of the great trek.

The Schubert raft drifted in to the riverbank just above the fort on October 13. There a tent was thrown up for Mrs. Schubert. She was already in labor. The following morning, with the help of an Indian midwife, the first white girl was born in the interior of British Columbia. The midwife stepped out of the tent, held up the child for all to see, and cried: "It's Kumloops! It's Kumloops!" The parents decided to christen their daughter with this name but, on second thoughts, called her Rose. It seems a pity.

By mid-October the last stragglers were at the fort. Miraculously, considering the dangers of the river, only one man had been lost. With the new Schubert baby, the expedition contained as many souls at Kamloops as at the camp in the mountaain pass.

Kamloops was still far from the gold fields. The nearest point on the Cariboo Road was Cache Creek, some fifty miles to the westward by the Hudson's Bay fur trail. Most of the Overlanders, after recuperating at Kamloops, followed this trail, but few of them turned north at Cache Creek for the Cariboo. They had seen enough of adventure, they had encountered too many disappointed miners, and they were glad enough to make their way down to the coast.

A letter from Archibald Thompson, who had reached Kamloops sick at heart, seems to tell the general story of disillusionment, the end of the Overland Transport Company's high promises. "We came to Yale," Thompson wrote, "and took the steamer for Westminster and there I saw McMicking and Robert making shingles." Making shingles—the men who had crossed a continent on foot and raft to dig the easy treasure of the Fraser!

Six men, too impatient to take the trail to Cache Creek, started down the Thompson from Kamloops in a canoe. In the rapids below Kamloops the canoe capsized, five of the passengers were rescued by Indians, but the sixth, Frank Penwarden, of St. Thomas, was drowned. The second fatality of the trek occurred when all danger seemed past.

None of the Overlanders seems to have found gold, but most of them found a good home in British Columbia, where they remained.

9   Canada from Sea to Sea

FROM THE CURRENT OF EVENTS SWIRLING DOWN THE FRASER TWO
names now emerge. One name is new—Amor de Cosmos. The
other, Manifest Destiny, has long haunted the American border.
The collision between de Cosmos and Manifest Destiny will
greatly affect the future political shape of America.

Amor de Cosmos was born plain Smith. Such a name was
too commonplace for this arrogant, daring and able man. To
proclaim his dream, which ranged far across land and sea, he called
himself the Lover of the World—a man of long, narrow, bearded
face, fierce eye and striking beauty. Though forgotten by most
Canadians and unknown to most Americans, few men have served
Canada better or, on a limited local stage, contended more successfully with American power.

It is de Cosmos who first fights the oligarchy of Douglas
at Victoria, with its clique of Hudson's Bay men and civil servants. In this obscure settlement is repeated in miniature scale,
but with the same objective, the struggle for responsible government which produced the American Revolution, which
flamed briefly in the Canadian Rebellion of 1837, which springs up
where any group of Anglo-Saxons founds a community.

In Victoria the struggle, while bitter, is peaceful, for the
government of Britain has learned something, though not much,
from the experience of the previous century. While it lasts, the
unknown patriots of the colony show the same persistence, the
same understanding of freedom, and the same ingenuity in par-

liamentary maneuver which marked the process of democracy in the east.

De Cosmos and his friends have not proceeded far with their attack on Douglas when they encounter the larger fact of American expansionism, which, as General Cass, of Michigan, says, has "an awful swaller for territory." The United States has just come triumphantly out of the Civil War. Its Northern armies are the greatest military force ever seen upon the earth. Its statesmen, having saved the Union, begin to think far beyond it.

The Canadian-American boundary, after long years of wrangle, has been settled by the treaty of 1846 on the forty-ninth parallel and out through the Gulf of Georgia and the Strait of Juan de Fuca to the sea—a pitiful surrender by Britain, as the Canadians think, of all the land north of the Columbia, to which the American claim is extremely questionable in history.

The boundary is a mere mark on the map, uninhabited, undefended, unexplored. Perhaps it can be moved north? Many Americans are asking that question.

Manifest Destiny has long claimed extension of the continental body of the United States to Russian Alaska. When the United States purchases Alaska in 1867 the demand that it be united with its new owner by a corridor through the intervening British territory revives an old slogan of the original Oregon boundary dispute. It is "Fifty-Four Forty or Fight," watchword of the American election of 1844.. Canadians, who can read the lines of latitude on a map, are quick to understand the meaning of this phrase—the American imperialists, happily a minority, want the whole western sea shelf from the Rockies to the Pacific, an unbroken shore line from the arctic to Mexico.

Standing in the way of Manifest Destiny is a new nation, the Confederation of Canada, a political embryo, scarce born yet in the union of five eastern colonies, under the British North America Act of 1867. Such a group of settlements straggling along the St. Lawrence and bisected by the jungles of New Brunswick is no match for the military colossus produced by the Civil War. Sir John A. Macdonald, the chief architect of the Canadian union, its first prime minister and one of the most practical politicians of the New World, sees this fact without illusion.

"It is quite evident to me," he writes, "that the United States Government are resolved to do all they can short of war to get possession of the western territory and we must take immediate and vigorous steps to counteract them."

Sir John has good reason for alarm. The American House of Representatives already has protested that the Confederation of Canada is a violation of the Monroe Doctrine, even though it has obviously fortified the doctrine by establishing the beginnings of Canadian freedom from Europe. Seward has proposed that Britain hand over Canada to the United States to satisfy the Alabama claims. A Minnesota senator, more modest in his demands, suggest that the claims be settled by the cession of western Canada only. The Americans at large have better sense and deeper generosity than such utterances suggest, but Sir John does not know that yet. Hence "immediate and vigorous steps."

His plan, impractical and rash as it appears, is to join the colony of British Columbia to the new Canadian nation. There is no time to lose. Already the Americans have swarmed over British Columbia in search of gold and have been controlled only by the prompt, unauthorized actions of Douglas. He has managed to hold the boundary for the moment. The great tide of the gold rush has ebbed and has left in Victoria and along the river only 10,000 inhabitants, many of them foreigners. They are cut off from Canada by the Rockies and 2,000 miles of wilderness. They have come here through the United States and they live precariously on trade with their American neighbors.

As Sir John has understood from the beginning, this cannot go on. Either the western colonies must be joined to Canada or they will fall inevitably, of their own weight, by mere gravity, into the larger body to the south.

The fall seems to have begun already. The only articulate group in the frontier politics of Victoria demands union with the United States forthwith. It argues that the British colonies, by the laws of geography, have no future save in the expanding power of the Americans. The British tradition, the nostalgia for the Old Land, the loyalty of the subject to his king, are pleasant sentiments but they will not feed the hungry hamlets left in the wake of the gold rush.

The official coterie does not resist this pressure, can see no hope in union with Canada, and is heartily tired of its genteel poverty. Governor Seymour complains to the British government that his mansion in Victoria is unfurnished and "the walls have no paper to hide the cracks which the settlement of the older parts of the building have entailed upon them." The colony's debt stands at the alarming figure of $1,500,000. The Colonial Office in London sharply reminds the governor that his sinking funds are in worse condition than his sinking residence.

Altogether the union of the colonies and the United States is so logical that only a statesman like Macdonald, steeped in the British theory of politics, where logic is a hateful foreign invention, fit for lesser breeds, could think of preventing this junction.

Logic, of course, has denied the possibility of a Canadian nation from the beginning. The natural geographic lines of the continent running straight north and south; the distribution of America's resources; the very glaciers that have shaved off the topsoil of central Canada and desposited it in the United States, leaving the naked pre-Cambrian Shield lying midway between the Candian east and the western plains; and finally the division of the Canadian race between Anglo-Saxon and French, all point logically to the same conclusion—Canada will break up and slip piecemeal into the American Union in due time. And nowhere is the logic of Canada's future so clear as on the west coast.

In defying it Sir John has three allies, all untested. First, the feeling of the American people, who have invaded Canada twice, in 1775 and 1812, retreated because their heart was never in such adventures, and now have little stomach for conquest. Second, Amor de Cosmos. Third, the Fraser.

De Cosmos already is at work. Rebuffed by the governor, he stumps the country, forms the Confederation League on a policy of union with Canada, and calls a convention. Significantly enough, it is held at Yale, on the Fraser. De Cosmos already has seen that if there is to be union with Canada its only practical avenue lies along the river.

The tiny spark of Canadian sentiment on the west coast Sir John knows how to fan into flame. He is playing a game for high stakes, for control of half a continent, for the last great expansion of power in the final phase of British imperialism. The government in London understands his strategy, spurs it on, and helps him to manipulate his politics at home.

Tired of the shilly-shallying of the Victoria clique, Sir John writes to London:

> It is quite clear that no time should be lost by Lord Granville in putting the screws on Vancouver Island, and the first thing to do is to recall Governor Seymour, if his time is not yet out. We shall then have to fight only the Yankee adventurers and the annexation party proper, which there will be no difficulty doing if we have a good man at the helm.

Opportunely Governor Seymour dies of his troubles in his decaying mansion. The good man picked by Sir John for the screw-tightening process is Anthony Musgrave, a firm but genial figure, with keen eye, massive mustache and bare, aggressive chin. He takes with him to Victoria the instructions of the British government, written in terms more elegant than those used by Sir John but meaning the same thing:

Her Majesty's Government anticipate that the interests of every province of British North America would be more advanced by enabling the wealth, credit and intelligence of the whole to be brought to bear on every part than by encouraging each in the constricted policy of taking care of itself, possibly at the expense of its neighbour.

The screws, therefore, must be applied.

Musgrave moves fast. The Legislative Council, the prelude to full responsible government, is called to meet in the red pagoda-shaped buildings known as the Bird Cages. (The little brown legislative chamber of this session is still preserved behind the modern stone buildings at Victoria and even today it is not too difficult to imagine the scene in that momentous gathering of 1870.)

An hour in advance, says the Victoria *Colonist*, the flimsy public gallery is crowded. On the narrow benches the members of the Council are packed together, beard by beard. The speaker sits on a dais between two wooden pillars. But Musgrave, unfortunately, cannot appear to put the screws on in person. He has fallen off a horse and broken his leg and now lies in the mansion with the cracked walls.

The colonial secretary of the colony, Philip Rankin, reads the governor's speech. When it urges Confederation there is, says the *Colonist*, a round of applause, for public sentiment apparently has been changing. When the governor announces that he will add two elective members to his council and will go no further toward responsible government yet, his words are greeted in "stony silence." When the governor admits another deficit in the year's financing, the *Colonist* reports a "marked sensation."

Then the governor outlines the terms on which British Columbia should enter Confederation. They are his own terms, of course, but plainly written by Sir John. They provide that Canada shall assume the colonial debt, grant the colony an annual subsidy of 80 cents per head, start building a railway to the Pacific coast within three years, finish a transcontinental wagon road in the same time, and pension off the local officials, who are opposed to Confederation if it means the loss of their jobs.

Thus begins the Confederation debate of 1870, among a handful of unknown men in a mean wooden house on the fringe of empty land. In the civilized world few know that the argument is under way, but its outcome will touch the affairs of the greatest empires and round out the foundations of a new nation.

Henry Crease, the attorney general, a gentleman whose sweep of beard exceeds all others, launches the argument for Confederation with the warning that the colonists must join Canada or accept such crumbs of prosperity as their American neighbors will allow them. His vision of a British nation from coast to coast fails to shake the hardheaded leader of the annexation party, Dr. J. S. Helmcken. "However much we are in favor of consolidating British interests," says Helmcken, "our own interests must come first. Imperial interests can afford to wait." Then he repeats the logic that the whole project of a Canadian nation contradicts:

"Whatever may be the result of the present vote, it is impossible to deny the probability of the less being absorbed by the greater, and it cannot be regarded as impossible that ultimately not only this colony, but the whole Dominion of Canada may well be absorbed by the United States."

"No! No!" cries de Cosmos, but Helmcken will not be shouted down. "It is dangerous," he retorts, "to place ourselves at the disposal of superior numbers, who must necessarily legislate for the greater number, the people of the Atlantic provinces. No union on account of love need be looked for."

Before de Cosmos can get in a word Mr. W.T. Drake parades the ultimate horror of Confederation: "We should be transferred from the rule of statesmen at Downing Street to that of politicians at Ottawa!"

"No! no!" cries de Cosmos again, and John Robson, a man

with an eagle's face, begins the Confederationists' reply. He denounces those who imagine that the colony can remain clinging to Britain's skirts "like a mendicant's child." Rather than that he would seek annexation to the Sandwich Islands or Hindustan. British Columbia, after fifteen years of struggle, finds itself worse off than at the beginning. "Her progress has been like that of the crab—backwards." There is nothing for it, then, but Confederation.

De Cosmos, as usual, makes the longest and most ponderous speech. It is a speech of personal triumph, unmarred by any touch of modesty, for he has seen the government at last accepting the ideas he has so long advocated in vain, and he feels that great events are moving with him. "I have assisted to make history," he admits, "and this is a page of it!" No one can question that, and no one grudges him his vindication. In the end the Council accepts his promise: "We are here laying the cornerstone of a great nation on the Pacific Coast."

Almost unanimously the Confederation plan is approved by the same men who had rejected it a year before. Musgrave has put on the screws. But Sir John has supplied the bait. The thing that decides the vote of 1870 is the promise of steel rails down of a great nation on the Pacific Coast."

The Fraser's gold had first peopled British Columbia. Now the Fraser's canyon will provide a railway to bring in more people and prosperity for all. Yet it is not so easy as the men in the Bird Cages imagine.

Delegates from the colony go to Ottawa, they find Sir John eager for an agreement, and they telegraph home: "Terms agreed upon. The delegates are satisfied. Canada is favorable to immediate union and guarantees the railway." That last sentence swells the night's profits of Victoria's saloons.

A railway down the river to the coast—here is a promise which calls for a drink, whether you are on the side of Helmcken or de Cosmos.

Sir John agrees to start building the railway within two

years and complete it within ten. The agreement is ratified by the Canadian Parliament and, unanimously this time, by the Legislative Council in Victoria. On the twentieth day of July, 1871, British Columbia becomes a province of Canada with fully responsible government. The boundary is anchored at last from coast to coast. Manifest Destiny has been outflanked.

Sir John is known to his convivial friends as Old Tomorrow. Better than any of his enemies he knows the value of delay and usually defeats them with that weapon. He cannot get the railway started. Surveyors explore the passes of the Rockies and the Fraser's canyon but at the end of the two agreed years no tie has been laid. British Columbia waits in vain for the sound of the first iron horse around the bend of the river. Old Tomorrow is taking his time.

The new provincial government at Victoria protests to Ottawa, but by now Sir John has larger problems. He is being hurled from office for his dealings with railway contractors. His place is taken by the first Liberal prime minister, Alexander Mackenzie, the second of that name concerned with the Fraser River, and a stone mason who resembles the material of his trade.

To Mackenzie the coastal railway is "a piece of madness." The agreement with British Columbia is "an insane act, a piece of deliberate treachery to the country." Obviously Canada cannot afford such an expenditure. British Columbia or bankruptcy, that is the issue. The Mackenzies were always against bankruptcy.

The new prime minister asks British Columbia for more time. That is reasonable enough, considering that a poverty-stricken six-year-old nation is undertaking one of the largest construction projects in human history. But British Columbia is in no mood to wait.

On Saturday, February 7, 1874, eight hundred citizens of Victoria swarm into the Bird Cages, denounce the members, drive the speaker from the chamber, and find their evening's work recorded in the history books as the "Rebellion." The legislature cannot resist this outcry and protests to Mackenzie at his delay. There is no satisfaction in Ottawa and Premier Walkem, of British Columbia, appeals direct to the British throne.

Britain cannot have the new British nation rent thus with quarrels that threaten the imperial interest. It suggests a compromise between British Columbia and Ottawa on terms framed by Lord Carnarvon, the colonial secretary. Under them the railway is to be completed to the coast by 1890. Mackenzie is ready to accept but the Canadian Senate rejects the whole scheme.

So Lord Dufferin, the Canadian governor general, comes to British Columbia to negotiate a settlement. He finds the streets of Victoria plastered with such mottoes as "United without Union," "Confederated without Confederation," "Our Railway Iron Rusts," and on one street corner stands a stuffed horse wearing the label "Good, but not Iron." These pleasantries the governor general accepts with good humor, but when he sees a triumphal arch bearing the words "Carnarvon Terms or Separation," he refuses to drive under it. With the British Columbians he can reach no agreement and takes a jaunt over the river road in a coach with his lady.

In 1878 the provincial government declares that British Columbia will secede from Canada unless the railway is really under way within two years. Before this ultimatum reaches Ottawa and before the new nation begins to fall apart, Mackenzie has been voted out and Old Tomorrow is back again. This time he does not delay. The railway is pushed forward and on November 7, 1885, just eighteen years after de Cosmos prepared the first Confederation resolution, the last spike is driven by Donald Smith at Craigellachie in the Rockies.

When the first transcontinental train rolls down beside the Fraser to the sea, the Canadian nation, though still a handful of scattered fragments, has been bound together with hoops of steel. Manifest Destiny has subsided. The forty-ninth parallel, an imaginary line, is secured by the river's deep trench of travel where the Indians scrambled on their crazy ladders, where Fraser crawled westward in pursuit of his great illusion, where the miners built their road of sticks and wire, where the trains are now running. Without the Fraser none of these things could have been done.

10   The Hanging Judge

THROUGHOUT THIS ERA OF TUMULT, WHENEVER TROUBLE WAS
afoot, there stalked a figure unique and fantastic—the maker
of laws, the builder of government, the personification of the
Cariboo spirit, the perfect Fraser River man.

His name was Matthew Baillie Begbie. In body he was a
giant with the face, mustache and whiskers of Mephistopheles.
In mind he was brilliant, mercurial, arrogant, yet he had a curious
inner humility. In profession he was supposed to be a lawyer,
though he knew little law. In status he was judge, the first ever
seen in these regions. In the results of his work he qualifies as
one of the molders of the Canadian nation. And in his thirty-
six years of judging, riding, walking, feuding and praying he had
more fun than any other man in British Columbia.

The story of Begbie is largely the story of the river and the
creation of the community that clung to it. Douglas, of course,
was the most powerful figure of the times and no chapter of
early British Columbia history can be written without his name.
But Douglas was generally anchored to his capital, first with the
free hand of beneficent autocrat and then with the growing
irritations of free government, which he deplored and vainly re-
sisted. Begbie roamed at will through the interior, established
the local judiciary and police, made up the law out of his head,
enforced it as he pleased, and built the first structure of government in his own image. Through his lavish life it is possible to
see how, step by step, civilization crept up the river.

Until recent times Begbie was a legend in the west—vague, exciting and incredible. A few old-timers remembered him. Some called him a saint, others a crook. His feats of frontier justice, his quarrels with lawyers and democrats, his brutal treatment of prisoners, and his private peccadilloes are the stuff from which a nation builds its myths, but they were mostly mythical. Not long ago, however, an able young professor at Victoria College, Sydney Pettit, produced a definitive portrait of Begbie and published it in the *British Columbia Historical Quarterly*. In this fine study the man emerges from the myth and loses little in the process.

With the arrival of the miners of '58, Douglas saw at once the peril of his colony.

What he feared most was an Indian war, an appeal by the Americans to their own government, an American push from Oregon into an undefended British Columbia.

If this and other dangers were to be forestalled, he needed a man who would suppress violence before it could spread. He asked the British government to send him a judge, and something more than a judge, a lieutenant who could represent him on the river, a counselor to advise him on the making and administration of law.

The colonial secretary, Edward Bulwer-Lytton, a statesman who had written a library of fiction, looked about him and selected an almost fictional character in Begbie. At the time of his appointment as judge of British Columbia Begbie was a wellbred lawyer without a practise who, after making a mess of his college education had been reduced to reporting the courts for the *Law Times*. Since he had reached the age of thirty-nine and was still without prospects, but with a lusty appetite for travel, he jumped at the chance of a judgeship at £800 a year. Besides, his brother had just stolen his fiancée and he was glad to get out of England.

He left with Lytton's final instruction that a judge in Cariboo must be a man who could truss a murderer and hang him from the nearest tree. Begbie would turn out to be such a judge.

Through the chaotic summer of '58 Douglas made and enforced the law himself, and, so far as the mainland was concerned, without authority. It must have been with relief that the governor watched the tall figure of Begbie walk ashore at Victoria on November 16. The stranger wore his top hat cocked rakishly on the side of his head, his dark mustache was waxed to a fine point, his graying beard was neatly pointed—a man strikingly, almost theatrically handsome and obviously ready for anything.

Next day Douglas took his new colleague up the river to Fort Langley where the new colony of British Columbia was proclaimed. Douglas administered the oath of allegiance to Begbie as judge, and Begbie did the same for Douglas as governor, who now had two colonies under his control. The sappers and bluejackets fired off their muskets, the guns of the little Hudson's Bay ships *Otter* and *Beaver* boomed a frail salute from the river, and the law of England became the law wherever the river ran.

As soon as the trail was open in March Begbie with his clerk, Thomas Bushby, and his high sheriff, Charles Nicol, walked from Yale to the camps along the Fraser. He found the miners strangely peaceable, the Americans, whom he had feared, glad to accept English ways.

The unexpected absence of crime left Begbie ample time to study the land. He examined the mines, tramped over the interior ranges, wrote Douglas enthusiastically about the future of the country and urged him to open it with a road. As a member of the governor's council Begbie was entitled to offer such advice, but it was not welcome to Colonel R. C. Moody, the chief commissioner of lands and works and commander of the Royal Engineers. Moody and his collegues called Begbie the arch-enemy and tried to keep him from meddling in their affairs. The

Judge continued to meddle, outlasting all his enemies in this long feud.

As Mr. Pettit puts it in a happy phrase, Begbie soon became "the government on horseback." He traveled with a string of twelve horses, would turn up anywhere at the first sign of trouble, don his robes and wig and hold court in a settler's cabin, in a barn or, still mounted, in an open field. He slept wherever night found him, often in a tent or without it, winter and summer. In his own account of his life and the hardship of his local officials this English aristocrat says:

At Williams Creek a log house was built by Mr. Elwyn wch being divided across the middle gave accommodation for writing in one half, a space about 12 ft. by 16 ft.—and on the other half, of equal size but possessing the inestimable luxury of a fireplace, Mr. Elwyn, his secretary and 3 constables had bunks piled upon each other in wch each man could spread his blankets separately. At Van Winkle [between Quesnel and Barkerville] Mr. O'Reilly had not found the means of providing himself with any such luxury— and the whole of the business of the district had to be conducted in a tent, wch was the sole protection against the weather for him, and the books and records of the district.

The climate in Cariboo is at times exceedingly wet, as in all high mountanous regions—and it is not unusual to have torrents of rain for a week together almost without intermission. The tent being the same as my own, (a single tent 15 ell size, of the Hudon's Bay Co.) I suppose withstands the weather no better than my own—and although it answers very well in tolerable weather or even for a few days of rain, and where the camp is changed from time to time, I find that my tent becomes occasionally covered with mildew in the inside, while it is impossible to keep books etc. dry, and all writing & recording is carried on at the greatest incon-

venience. Besides, the ground being constantly cold & damp, and there being no opportunity of approaching a fire without going out into the heavy rain, all cooking, or drying any articles of apparel becomes extremely irksome: and all officers who have to remain for any length of time in that district ought to provide at least with one room having a fireplace where they may at least be sure to meet a dry place to lie on, and the means of warming themselves and drying their clothes, keeping their books etc. and placing a table so as to be able to write.

Begbie, accustomed to the cozy bachelor quarters of a London lawyer, seldom found even a roof or a fire in the first years. Often his judgments were written under canvas. Sometimes he would scribble a court order, in his wretched spelling, while in the saddle. But his writ ran through Cariboo and he was seldom far behind it.

Now began the most extraordinary series of trials ever held in British America. Begbie would open court wherever a crime had occurred, hale the prisoner before him, and proceed to act as prosecutor, defense counsel and judge. If the crime was serious, he gathered in anyone who happened to be about and impaneled a jury. Most of the miners being Americans who, up to 1860, had no legal right to act as jurors, the first trials were probably illegal, but they lacked nothing in effectiveness for that.

Begbie, who carried no lawbooks and little law even in his head, proceeded on the simple assumption that if a crime had occurred someone must suffer for it. He cared nothing for law, everything for justice. Several times he refused the verdict of a jury. Once he threatened to hang a man who had been found innocent (a threat never carried out). And in his high, shrill voice, the single defect in an otherwise perfect physique, he would abuse his juries as if they were the criminals.

Since there were no lawyers in the country, an appeal must be taken to England, where no man could afford to go, Begbie could get away with anything. But juries, willing to overlook an occasional killing, frequently dismissed obvious murderers or found that a murdered man had accidentally fallen over a cliff, or died from fever.

The jury was Begbie's bête noire but he could not hang a man without it. When, in a plain case of murder, a jury brought in a verdict of manslaughter, the judge screeched from the bench: "Prisoner, it is far from a pleasant duty for me to have to sentence you only to imprisonment for life. . . . Your crime was unmitigated, diabolical murder. You deserve to be hanged! Had the jury performed their duty I might now have the painful satisfaction of condemning you to death, and you, gentlemen of the jury, you are a pack of Dalles horse thieves, and permit me to say it would give me great pleasure to see you hanged, each and every one of you, for declaring a murderer guilty only of manslaughter."

Another day, the jury having brought in a verdict of not guilty against a man who clearly had sandbagged a companion in a barroom brawl, Begbie looked out coldly from under his massive wig and snarled: "Prisoner at the bar, the jury have said you are not guilty. You can go, and I devoutly hope the next man you sandbag will be one of the jury."

This was the kind of justice that the miners understood. They called Begbie the Hanging Judge, the name still remembered in the Cariboo, and they feared him. The legend is exaggerated. Begbie in fact was a merciful man under all his bluster, always suffered remorse when he sentenced a man to death, and kept a chaplain by his side for moral support when he could not avoid this sentence. Sometimes he secretly advised Douglas to commute it to long imprisonment. In the case of an Indian named Quahook he wrote to the governor:

> The Indian & the murdered man had been getting drunk together; and . . . in this there was some misunderstanding about a female. I am quite aware that if 2 men

engage in a burglary or any other crime, & one kill the other, even by accident, it is murder: but surely, when it is the seducer and the far more guilty party (as to the original crime) who is killed it wod not be irrational to modify the punishment of the murderer.

About another Indian who had been sentenced to die and had been long held in the Lytton jail, Begbie told Douglas:

I am not at all convinced that his execution is necessary, although I am sure that it wod have been just, but after so long reprieve I cannot but think that the sentence ought to be commuted to penal servitude for a term of years. It is scarcely right to keep a poor fellow on the tenterhooks for so long & hang him at last.

Even in the case of the gunman, Gilchrist, where he delivered his famous public dictum that the jury should be hanged, Begbie wrote privately to Douglas:

This wod have been of course "death by misadventure" in California—in British Columbia it is not perhaps an altogether unsatisfactory result that Gilchrist was convicted of manslaughter & sentenced to penal servitude for life, while his friends (who are well known to the police and to me) have left the Colony and are not, I think likely to return.

Begbie's methods achieved precisely the result that Lytton and Douglas wanted. The noisy scenes in the courtrooms, the miners' awe of the judge, and a hanging now and then suggest a reign of crime and disorder like that prevailing in California. Actually little violence of any sort occurred after Begbie's arrival. In the spring of '60, after eighteen months' experience, Begbie could tell Douglas: "There have been 3 murders committed since I first began to hold courts in British Columbia. They were all committed by Indians: in every case the Indians were drunk."

A year and a half later the judge, who hated to write any-

thing, paused long enough in his circuit to pen a report which, in describing the state of justice, is a significant social document of the times:

It is a contined subject of thankfulness that the amount of crime still remains very small in comparison with what might have been anticipated from the amount of population, the extent and difficulty of the country over which the population is scattered, the habits naturally induced by the unsettled and exciting life of a miner, and from the impunity which criminals might hope for, looking to the state of communications and the nature of the country generally, the proximity of a long open Frontier accessible by unfrequented passes, and the necessarily distant and scanty Police Force.

It is clear, however, that the inhabitants almost universally respect and obey the laws, and voluntarily prefer good order and peaceful industry to the violence and bloodshed to which other Gold mining regions have been subjected: and with such dispositions the police force, scanty and scattered as it is, appears to have been hitherto sufficient not only to restrain from crime those who might otherwise have committed deeds of violence, but in general to bring to justice the few persons who have been actually guilty. The exceptions where criminals have evaded Justice during the past year are, I think, only 3 in number, one accused of murder which, from what I have learnt, would probably amount to more than manslaughter, another for shooting with intent to murder, the third for larceny. In these three cases, too, the results prove the general apprehension of criminals that the officers of Justice are not to be trifled with, for there is hardly a doubt but that all these 3 persons quitted the Colony with such speed that pursuit was useless, and the community here are not likely to be troubled with them again.

Three unpunished men throughout a year of the gold rush in an area larger than many nations! This record surely is without parallel on the frontiers of America and it is almost solely the work of Begbie, government and law riding in one saddle.

Behind his word were only fifteen constables, posted from the sea to the mountains—poor Englishmen, wretchedly underpaid, but incorruptible and untiring in their duties. With them Begbie had appointed local magistrates in every camp and county court judges, for minor cases, in the larger centers. The ordinary disputes over mining claims went to the local gold commissioner's court, from which they could be appealed to Begbie as the Supreme Court. Finally the Mining Board, a kind of grand jury of miners, reported grievances, suggested reforms, and helped to frame a growing fabric of mineral law.

In the building of this machinery Begbie showed himself an able administrator, but once out of the criminal court and forced to deal with an increasing body of civil litigation he was a rather grotesque failure.

So long as the river community consisted of a few camps, and the law was needed only to punish criminals, the judge's own version of justice was satisfactory enough. Now towns were springing up—Lytton, which bore the name of Begbie's original patron; Clinton, the junction of the main road and the old Harrison route; the Hundred and Fifty north of Lac La Hache; Soda Creek; and Alexandria, the steamboat terminal; Quesnel, where the road turned east to the mountains, and Barkerville. In these towns there were few people but they were violently litigious, they owned large interests in mining property, and they constantly took their disputes to court.

When Begbie applied to such complex matters the rough-and-ready methods of his criminal courts he got into serious trouble because lawyers had come to the colony at last and knew more law than the judge. When this became obvious he would cover up his own ignorance by abusing the lawyers from the bench. For months he refused to allow George Walkem to practice before him because Walkem was merely a lawyer from Canada, not a "gentleman" from England. Sometimes, sitting in his chancery court, he reversed the decisions he had rendered in the Supreme Court. Once he became so abusive that the three lawyers before him arose with dignity, asked the registrar to strike their names from the official rolls, and stalked out of the court, Begbie still shouting after them.

The miners, too, were becoming restive. After Begbie had rendered an especially perverse decision, five hundred of them held a mass meeting before the Richfield courthouse to resolve "that in the opinion of this meeting the administration of the mining laws by Mr. Justice Begbie in the Supreme Court is partial, dicatatorial and arbitrary in setting aside the verdict of the juries and calculated to create a feeling of distrust in those who have to seek redress through a Court of Justice." Either Begbie should be removed, the resolution said, or an appeal court should be established.

Of such protests Begbie deigned to take no notice. He was used to criticism and to threats against his life. One day, sunning himself on the upper balcony of a hotel, he heard some men on the street below plotting to shoot him. He went to his room, fetched out the chamber pot, emptied its contents on the heads of the plotters, and resumed his siesta.

The anger of litigants and the threats of criminals could not touch him, but something more serious was afoot. The honesty of the great judge at last had been impeached.

On November 26, 1862, a letter signed "A" was published in the *British Columbian*, of New Westminster, at the mouth of the river. In effect, it accused Begbie of accepting a bribe from a man who wanted a questionable pre-emption (homestead) approved by the court. Begbie already had been suspected of dabbling in mining claims, against the specific instructions of the governor to all public servants, but this charge he had quickly refuted. Now in the New Westminster paper he read:

If Judge Begbie could accept 20 acres of land from Dud Moreland, and if the said Moreland could, on appeal to said Judge, procurd *[sic]* a certificate of improvement in opposition to the will of the resident Magistrate, why he, the saie *[sic]* Judge, can hold a claim, or twenty, and feel no qualms of conscience withal.

Begbie saw at once that this charge, unanswered, would ruin him. For some months he had borne in silence the criticism of the New Westminster paper and its famous editor, John Robson, a future British Columbia premier. Now he had Robson where he wanted him—in outright contempt of court.

On December 1, Begbie summoned Robson to appear before him at ten o'clock in the morning at New Westminster. The editor was on hand at the appointed hour but Begbie, with a typical show of arrogance, did not bother to enter the court until half past eleven. Thereupon, speaking from the bench, he said he had constantly disregarded baseless criticism in the press because it was not worth answering. But the letter of "A" accused him of accepting twenty acres of land as an inducement to give a false judgment in mandamus, and hence the publication of the letter was in direct contempt of the Supreme Court of British Columbia.

The charge itself he denied with sufficient detail to show that it seriously worried him. He said he had been taken ill with rheumatism at Cottonwood (the first center east of Quesnel on the Barkerville road) and, being unfit to travel, had decided to erect a cabin where he could rest and recover. A man named Cox, Moreland's partner, occupied the land that Begbie wanted, but Cox was only in process of pre-empting it and could not sell it. Begbie therefore paid Cox 10 shillings an acre to surrender twenty acres of his pre-emption rights and then Begbie pre-empted this area for himself. In ordering the local magistrate to approve Cox's pre-emption of the remaining land the judge strictly observed the law, which he explained exhaustively from the bench.

Robson listened to this lecture respectfully but without the least conviction. He was a grim man, with a hawklike face. He hated Begbie. Like the Canadian rebels of 1837, he was at war with the tight little Family Compact which, under Douglas, ruled the colony, and he would live to see it dislodged.

Begbie concluded by ordering Robson to appear the following day to show cause why he should not be committed to jail. Next morning Robson informed the judge that "A" was not accessible. If the charge was untrue, he regretted its publication. This cool answer threw Begbie into a rage. Shouting at Robson, he declared that the offense had been aggravated by a qualified apology, but Robson would say no more. The judge turned to a constable and ordered him to lock the editor up.

This suited Robson. The cheers of the crowd at the courtroom door told him that his cause was popular, that his martyrdom would forward his struggle against the ruling clique of the colony, and that it would not hurt his political ambitions either.

Robson spent the night in jail and doubtless learned from the jailers that five hundred people had held a public meeting to protest Begbie's sentence, to denounce him as the Tyrant Judge and to send a memorial to the secretary of state in London. Having taken pen and paper into his cell, Robson was not idle on his own behalf. In words of poetic license he wrote an editorial for his paper entitled "A Voice from the Dungeon!" This memorable specimen of frontier journalism began:

Fellow colonists! We greet you from our dungeon. Startled by the wild shrieks of a dying maniac on one hand, and the clanking of the murderer's chains on the other, while the foul and scant atmosphere of our cell, loaded with noxious effluvia from the filthy dens occupied by lunatics, renders life almost intolerable, our readers will overlook any incoherency or want of connected thoughts in our writings.

But his fate, he said, was of small moment, and his readers should not endanger their own freedom by attempting to rescue him. The cause was the thing. And then this fine classical illusion:

The press of British Columbia is virtually enslaved. There are two ways of being enslaved—that of Spartacus and that of Epictetus. The one breaks his chains: the other shows his soul. When the fettered writer cannot have recourse to the first method, the second remains for him. Accept—all of you—our deep feelings of grateful emotion, and, having truth and liberty inscribed on your banner, Heaven will smile upon your path and crown with glorious success your war against oppression and wrong.

These were brave words, but after two days of martyrdom Robson grew tired of Epictetus' method and turned to Spartacus. To break his chains he asked to be taken before the judge again. Begbie listened gravely (and probably with inward relief) as Robson read a second statement of apology. He said he had "only cursorily glanced over" the objectionable letter before printing it and was "not aware that anything it contained could be construed into a contempt of court, otherwise it would not have been inserted in the paper." The letter, he confessed, included a statement not warranted by facts and "I have to express my regret and offer my apology for allowing such statement to be published in the said British Columbian newspaper."

It was not a complete apology by any means, it recanted nothing of Robson's opinion of the judge, but it was good enough to settle an imbroglio which was embarrassing Begbie and the government. Accordingly, the court released Robson, who printed his "Voice from the Dungeon" on the front page and then, in dizzy anticlimax, inserted a note on page three as follows: "Liberated. Since writing the article on our first page we have been discharged from custody. Further particulars in our next."

At this distance the adventure of the dungeon has the look of comic opera. But equally comic was the Canadian Rebellion of 1837, yet it produced the Canadian nation and its original force finally compelled the creation of the British Commonwealth of independent states. The early adventures of Sam Adams, Ben Franklin and the others in the American colonies had not been without comedy either, or serious results.

The Robson trial, though the world took no note of it, was a landmark in the constitutional development of a new state, which presently would stretch from the Atlantic to the Pacific and deeply alter the future of North America. It was always by such minor incidents and fragments of litigation that the Anglo-Saxon system of freedom broadened down from precedent to precedent.

Probably Begbie did not know it, but he represented on his bench, backed by the dictatorial government of Douglas, the last entrenched ruling class of British America, and in Robson he was trying to subdue the new democracy that would soon rule all Canada, as it already ruled the United States. The river community was coming to life, its people were asserting their rights, and the colony, as a colony, was doomed.

As for Begbie, his free and easy days were over and he would carry the cloud of Robson's charges, exaggerated through the years, to his grave. The Voice from the Dungeon, the suspicion that Begbie, for all his pomp, wit and charm, was not above petty graft, is still heard among the old-timers of British Columbia.

But what, in fact, was the truth of these allegations? The verdict of Mr. Pettit, a thoughtful and impartial student of the times, is found in these words:

On the whole, it seems that the evidence for him [Begbie] is stronger than that brought against him. But when circumstantial evidence is involved, and important data is not available, there is in this case, as in all others, a certain residue of uncertainty.

At all events, the dispute did not end with Robson's liberation. The *British Columbian* continued to publish more letters dredging up new evidence on the Cottonwood land deal while other writers tried to vindicate Begbie with much frantic prose. Finally Dud Moreland said he had given Begbie the Cottonwood land for nothing—a shattering repudiation of the judge, who did not attempt to answer it. The controversy died slowly. In later years Begbie, knighted by his king, ceased to be a political issue. He became by general consent the first citizen in the province of British Columbia and Canadian historians would mark him as a great man. Off the bench, Begbie is an exquisite figure in a golden age.

At the edge of Victoria he had built himself a rambling wooden house, with a spacious garden, above the Fairfield marshes (where he shot ducks out of season) and overlooking the Strait of Juan de Fuca, the marching line of the Olympic Mountains in Washington. There he conducted an extraordinary bachelor household.

His tennis parties are still remembered by a few early Victorians, and the cherries his Chinese servant picked from the tree and tied to the shrubbery so that the guests could eat them conveniently. On Saturday nights—for he was an inveterate debater in theology—he entertained the clergymen of the town at dinner to discuss abstract problems of religion over the port, but he ushered the ecclesiastical company out at nine o'clock and ushered in the town bloods to play cards all night. On Sundays he went to church, led the choir in his shrill voice, and invariably ate rice pudding for lunch at the O'Reilly home. Though he never married, he was pre-eminently a ladies' man and was greeted over the teacups everywhere as "Dear Sir Matthew."

A golden age indeed in the new province of British Columbia! The rule of the Family Compact had been dissolved but its aristocracy remained well beyond the end of the century—an aristocracy purely English in breeding and instinct but stubbornly wedded to the soil of the new land, a society of roughly tweeded shooting and fishing men, of horse-driving ladies, of vast and gloomy mansions and unequaled gardens. One can still recall the last remnants of those days in one's boyhood and beside them this age has little to offer.

Of a bright era Begbie was the chief ornament and accepted oracle. A handful of men and women who knew him are still alive and can be found in a few old houses like "Pentrelew," the famous home of the Crease family, or in the Union Club, blinking at the harbor like a cartoon in *Punch*. But their day is long gone. The river, pouring down its wealth to the coast, opening the interior to roads and railways, had made these men and their jolly frontier life, but in the end it had passed them by.

Begbie lived on into the nineties, now chief justice of British Columbia, a belted knight, the leader of church society, a famous breeder of spaniels, which frisked in droves at his feet as he walked the streets. In the spring of 1894 he stopped eating the O'Reilly rice pudding and entertaining the boys at cards. His doctors told him he was dying of cancer. Refusing medical assistance, even drugs because they would dull his mind, he took to his bed. Every night Peter O'Reilly sat with him, talking of better times, but on June 10 Begbie said to his friend: "You must leave me alone tonight, O'Reilly. I must make my peace with God." He died before morning.

When his will was opened a little-known side of this remarkable creature was revealed. His small fortune was bequeathed to a group of poor, unknown men and women whom Begbie had been secretly supporting for years. But none of his friends was forgotten. To each of the clergymen who had dined with him on Saturday nights he left $100 and a case of claret or sauterne "at their choice." To Mrs. Crease and Mrs. Drake he willed "a dozen potted plants and a dozen roses of their choice."

And the Hanging Judge, the Tyrant Judge, showed the inner doubts, which he had so long disguised, by allowing only $200 for his own funeral expenses, forbidding anyone to send flowers, and ordering that his grave be marked by a wooden cross to bear only the inscription: "Lord, be merciful to me a sinner."

Under that cross, it may be said, the great age of the river was buried.

11   The River Pilots

FROM MACKENZIE'S TIME UNTIL THE RUSH, ROUGHLY SEVENTY years, men traveled the Fraser by canoe and raft. With the discovery of gold, the first steamboats appeared on the river. Their brief era of half a century is so little remembered now, though it lasted into World War I, that even the bare facts to be recorded here will come as surprising news to most British Columbians. This is a pity, for essentially the story of the Cariboo is the record of man's attempt to navigate the Fraser, and the supreme navigators were the steamboat pilots.

Steamboating on the Fraser, I suspect, offered higher adventure and more desperate risk than steamboating on the Mississippi, but it had no Mark Twain to make it immortal. If he had taken a leaky tub from the sea to the mouth of the canyon at Yale, or through the still fiercer waters from Boston Bar to Lytton, or past Mackenzie's place of wild onions on the upper river, what a yarn he would have spun! No such tale will ever be written now. As is true of almost everything in Canada's past, the great moments on the river lacked a spectator who could give them permanent life. We have left only some scraps of information, a few names, dates, incidents, and a broken hull here and there on the bank.

As late as 1923 it was possible, with a little imagination, to recapture some faint echo of the steamboat's whistle. In late October of that year I sailed the upper river on its last commercial craft. I say "craft" because it would be difficult to classify the *Circle W* more specifically.

She was perhaps forty feet long, flat-bottomed, square of stern and top-heavy with a superstructure of packing cases nailed together. Her master was Captain Foster, the last and one of the greatest of the river pilots, an aging man now, stout of body, richly colored by sun and storm, saddened by the wreckage of all his hopes.

His crew was a caricature out of a comic strip who wore a cowboy hat, drooping mustaches, a green sweater and a dim view of life; his cook a solemn Chinese, who seemed to hate the river; his power against the current a gasoline engine out of an automobile. Altogether we were a somewhat sober company aboard the *Circle W* as she wallowed into the Fraser at Prince George shortly after dawn.

Quesnel was our destination. It lay only ninety miles downriver and we should reach it by nightfall. In those days there was no road between Prince George and Quesnel but the British Columbia government was building a railway, which it would soon abandon. When a road or a railway was completed there would be no more navigation on the river. This inevitable destruction of his business, and certain events of the immediate past, had given Captain Foster his air of settled melancholy.

Below Prince George the river is broad and smooth. As the captain swung his boat easily from one side of the current to the other, seeking the deepest channel, I began to wonder whether the alarming diaries of Mackenzie and Fraser were perhaps a little exaggerated. Presently the sight of a wrecked skiff on a sand bar and a scow splintered on a rocky island caused me to modify my judgment. The river looked safe only because the captain knew every rock and shoal in it.

He had spent his life, he told me—the two of us wedged in his tiny pilothouse against the biting wind of the river—on a strange variety of ships. He had piloted steamboats on the Yukon in the rush of '98. He had commanded a mine sweeper in the

North Sea in the Great War. He had come to the Fraser and, after learning its tricks as the hired pilot of other owners, had invested his life savings of $20,000 in a handsome stern-wheeler of his own.

On its first voyage that ship shattered itself on a rock. Foster got all his passengers ashore on a plank and even managed to land the freight and an automobile, but the ship was beyond saving. From the bank he watched the river consume it and every dollar he owned.

This last command, the disreputable *Circle W*, with its few parcels of local freight, would support him until automobiles or trains crossed the last gap of Cottonwood Canyon on the river's eastern bank.

The final heir of Fraser and Mackenzie, the last man who knew the river channel, could hardly be cheerful at his prospects. Though he did not know it then, his prospects were good. He was to become a successful automobile freighter on the new road. But the profits of that enterprise, one imagines, would be something of an anticlimax in the life of a river pilot.

By the time the captain's tale was told and we had eaten a hot lunch, magically produced by the Chinese cook among the boxes of freight in the stern, the *Circle W* was entering the first clay canyon. The water here was fast, with occasional rapids. which the captain carefully avoided. The record of Mackenzie and Fraser began to take on a disturbing accuracy. The place of wild onions, as I recalled, must lie not far ahead.

The captain had shut himself in the pilot house and evidently did not wish to be disturbed. From time to time he thrust his head out the window to peer intently at the bank The crew, I noticed, had armed himself with a long boathook. The cook awakened from a nap and, cowering behind his packing cases for warmth, began to show a marked interest in the river The day, opening with autumn sunshine, had turned stormy Leaves of poplar, which had spilled streaks of yellow as far as I could see, were blowing away on a bitter wind, heavy with the first intimations of winter. It was a day made for shipwrecks.

Ahead of us the river seemed to split around a naked island of rock—a spectacle which must have alarmed Mackenzie and Fraser as they beheld it from their canoes, but not so much as it alarmed me. To the left the river flowed into a broad sweep of white water. To the right it swirled through a narrow, twisted gorge. Between the two channels the island cut the current like a crooked finger.

We were now within a hundred feet of the fork. The captain came on deck and studied the river. At his nod the crew stopped the engine and picked up his boathook again. We were slipping down straight for the island. Just as we seemed to head into the rapids at the left, the captain leaped into his pilothouse and spun the steering wheel. At the pull of the rudder the *Circle W* quivered in hesitation and lurched about until she lay crosswise to the current.

With increasing speed she began to drift, rudderless and engineless, into the gorge. The captain apparently had miscalculated. The story of his last wreck occurred to me again with a new clarity. But he seemed calm enough and I asked no questions. The crew made vague motions with his boathook.

We were now in the narrowest part of the gorge, and so close to the rocks on either side that I could have leaped ashore and was inclined for a moment to do so. A twist in the current sucked us to the edge of the island but the crew pushed us off with his long pole. The boat listed to its gunwale, every board creaking, and then slid past the island into calm water.

Such was the place of wild onions.

At dark we reached Quesnel, a row of houses and stores beside the river. Abandoned on the bank lay the last of the steamboats. In the moonlight she glistened like a great white swan.

Within a year after that even the *Circle W* had ceased to trouble the Fraser. The hulk of the steamboat at Quesnel had been burned. Nothing but a shattered scow here and there, a few bleached boards on the bank, remained to testify that the Fraser had once carried a numerous fleet and a race of fabulous sailormen.

The steamboats were carried up the river on the first wave of the gold rush in 1858. All were American, except the Hudson's Bay screw vessel *Otter*, but Douglas compelled them to fly the British flag. By 1859 ships of British registry, though often of American ownership, had almost monopolized the river business.

In that year the first steamboat was built at Victoria, on the Songhees Indian village, across the harbor from the fort. She was a sidewheeler with engines of only 25 horsepower and was called the *Caledonia* or *Caledonian*. Equipped with more powerful engines, she entered the Fraser trade in the following summer. Her owners, a San Francisco firm, expected her to compete with the *Otter* in carrying freight and passengers to Hope but she blew up just outside the river sand heads.

That was the first of several deadly boiler explosions. In the desperate competition for Fraser business the pilots cut corners, pushed their ships through shallow channels, and tied down their safety valves. The *Fort Yale*, the *Cariboo* and the *Emily Harris* all exploded during the next few years, but no accident could discourage the pursuit of freight profits, which often were larger than the profits of most Cariboo mines.

In the definitive work on Fraser steamboating by Norman R. Hacking in the *British Columbia Historical Quarterly* (from which most of the facts stated here are taken) the business ethics of the operators are thus stated:

> The disasters were met with philosophy. The casualties were counted—Indians and Chinese not included—the dead were buried if enough remains could be found and the incident was written off as an act of God. Explosions were considered one of the natural perils of navigation. If the timid wayfarer did not like them he could stay at home.

Lost vessels were quicky replaced. At small cost the builders at Victoria could turn out a flimsy wooden hull in a few
months for a price as low as $15,000. Almost before its paint was
dry it would be scurrying up the river, loaded down with freight
and miners.

American capital was behind many of these ventures but
the House of Assembly at Victoria, an embryonic parliament,
strove by every trick of legislation to keep the business in British hands. Its miniature Navigation Acts were not successful in
barring the enterprising Yankees, who, if they could not secure
incorporation in Victoria, sometimes managed to ram their papers through the less particular government of British Columbia
at Queenborough (New Westminster).

The river business was split by the opening of the Harrison
route to Cariboo. Some steamers ran up the Fraser to Hope and
even to Yale, while others turned from the main stream and ascended the Harrison. The advantages of both routes were vig-
orously advocated by the rival steamboat companies. The operators of the Harrison painted the perils of the Fraser in lurid
hues to terrify the traveler. Their competitors, and the merchants of Yale, exaggerated the inconveniences of the Harrison
portages. A ruinous war of rate cutting soon began.

Most of the trade followed the Harrison at first, for few
ships were powerful enough to buck the Fraser's current above
Hope, and the canyon beyond it, before the Cariboo Road was
built, made travel difficult, even on foot.

The Harrison traffic moved by water from the Fraser up
Harrison River to Port Douglas at the head of Harrison Lake. At
one point known as "The Rapids" Harrison River was so shallow during the season of low water that cargo was landed on the
bank to lighten the steamer and carried upstream, where the
channel deepened.

From Fort Douglas a portage trail of 29 miles led to Lillooet Lake, which was served by the stern-wheeler *Marzelle*. After another portage of 22 miles to Anderson Lake, freight

and passengers were loaded on the *Lady of the Lake*. The gap of a mile and a half between Anderson and Seton Lakes was spanned by wooden rails which bore a horse car of sorts. The *Champion* navigated Seton Lake, from which all travel to Cariboo was by foot and later by wagon.

The little stern-wheelers of the Harrison Lake system were

built locally and equipped with American engines, which were hauled laboriously from the coast.

At Soda Creek, where the Harrison trail ended, another fleet was built to ply the upper Fraser as far as Quesnel. The first of the upriver steamers, the *Enterprise*, was launched at Four Mile Creek, near Fort Alexandria, in 1863. Her engines were hauled over the Harrison route. Other steamers were built in this vicinity and a few continued in operation until World War I.

Thus in the early sixties every navigable stretch of water on the Fraser was served by steamboats. Most of them were slow and many were dangerous. But their accommodation appeared luxurious to the foot traveler. Governor Douglas thought well enough of lake travel to note in his diary of September 3, 1860:

The steamer *Marsella* [*sic*] which plies on Lillooet Lake is 50 tons burthen, 25 horse power. She is hardly finished yet but she is nevertheless a useful boat. The following is a return for her freights from the 24 August, 2 months: 510,246 lbs. or about 8,000 lbs. a day, or 4 tons, which gives at 1¢ a lb. 80 dollars as her daily earnings and 1410 tons transport by this route.

Dr. Cheadle, the observant English traveler, pictures steamboat life with more imagination than Douglas. Under date of October 16, 1863, Cheadle describes in his diary a trip from Soda Creek to Quesnel:

Steamer came in about 2 o'clock bringing a host of miners two of whom were very drunk and continued to imbibe every 5 minutes; during the time we stayed in the house [at Soda Creek] they must have had 20 drinks. The swearing was something fearful. After we had been onboard a short time, the Captain, finding out who we were, gave us the use of his cabin, a comfortable little room & supplied with cigars & a decanter of cocktail, also books & papers. We were fetched out every few minutes to have a drink with some one, the Captain taking the lead by standing champagne all round. We had some dozen to do before supper; no one the least affected, Milton [Cheadle's protégé] & I shirking in quantity. The Capt. told us the boat was built on the river, all the timbers sawn by hand, the shaft in 5 pieces packed up on mule, cylinders in two, boiler plates brought in the same manner.

Saturday, October 17th: As we did not leave Soda Creek until 4 and the boat makes very slow progress against the powerful current, we had to anchor for the night after doing only 10 miles. At daybreak went on 4 or 5 miles & then delayed by the dense fogs which prevail on the river in the early morning at this season. Passed Fort Alexander about 10. Continually called out to have a drink.

Sunday, October 18th: Arrived about 8 at Quesnel mouth, a little collection of about 20 houses, on the wooded banks of the Fraser. Large new stores, & cards all lying about the street. We made up our packs and set out [for Barkerville]. Captain Done [Captain W. G. Doane of the *Enterprise*] met us in street half seas over & insisted to treat us to champagne etc. at every bar in the place. At last escaped . . .

The river pilots, as Cheadle discovered, were a gay, hard-living breed.

The most notable man among them, and a towering figure in those times, was Captain William Irving, who through his skill as navigator and his sure sense of business drove many of his competitors from the river. Irving was not a man to quarrel with. When a scandal sheet called the *Scorpion* attacked him, he refused to carry the *British Columbian*, New Westminster's leading newspaper, on his ship. The *Scorpion*, edited by Wynn Williams, was printed in the *British Columbian's* press room and that was enough to convince Irving that the celebrated editor, John Robson, had a hand in it. Robson (whose feud with Begbie will be remembered) denied responsibility but Irving refused to believe him.

Growing more truculent, Irving banned all publications from his steamboat service by charging $50 for carrying a single paper to Hope. Soon the *Scorpion* ceased to sting and later expired.

Though they respected the criminal laws, as did most British Columbians, the pilots cared little for technical rules of navigation. Captain Alexander Sinclair even defied the edicts of Douglas.

When the governor ordered every person entering or leaving the colony to pay a head tax, Sinclair scoffed at the tax collectors. In New Westminster his ship (ironically enough, it bore the governor's name) was boarded by customs officers and soldiers, but instead of paying the tax as they demanded, Sinclair steamed down the river, followed by frantic police in a rowboat. "Personal violence was offered to Mr. Kirk [a revenue officer] in the execution of his duty" but its nature is not recorded.

Though Sinclair decided to pay the tax on his next call at New Westminster, the public of those backward times, with an old-fashioned prejudice against such levies, supported the captain so strongly that Douglas abandoned his unpopular policy. The tax lapsed and all the money already collected was returned to those who had paid it.

Captain John Deighton was the most picturesque personage on the river. By his endless, boring tales he earned the title of "Gassy Jack" and Gas Town, the embryo of Vancouver, was named after him. But Gassy Jack was much more than a talker. Unbelievable as it seems now, he sailed the *Henrietta*, before her engines arrived from the States, all the way up to Port Douglas, on Harrison Lake.

A still tougher character was Captain Charles Thomas Millard, of the *Hope*. Steaming up Harrison Lake one day, he beheld the *Henrietta* in distress. The *Henrietta* was commanded at that time by Captain Henry Devries, a timid Dutchman. At Port Douglas he had been afraid to resist a gang of a hundred miners who boarded his ship, refused to pay any fare, and insisted on traveling down to New Westminster.

Devries hailed Millard on Harrison Lake and told him what had happened. Millard boarded the *Henrietta* and with his own hands collected $5 from each of the miners. None of them dared to question this forceful shipmaster but tales of his brutality were soon spread on the coast. In a curious letter to the Victoria *Colonist* Millard breathed defiance in these terms: "I am ready to swear neither knives nor pistols were used. . . . When I am afraid to collect the fare from my passengers I will sell out and leave the country." From then on the miners seem to have paid their way.

Captain Billy Moore, a German, was a man of superior intelligence and a sure instinct for gold. Wherever gold was found

Moore would turn up with a ship to carry it. Arriving in British Columbia penniless, he carried freight from Hope to Yale on a barge which the miners called the *Flying Dutchman*. From his profits he built the *Henrietta* and then a famous ship to which he gave the name of his original barge. This new craft drew only five inches of water, could sail "on a heavy dew," and was fitted up "in a plain but substantial manner" (which meant that her amenities were crude even by the standards of those times).

Moore went broke, like many others, by expanding too far, but he followed the discovery of gold to the Thompson, to the Queen Charlotte Islands, and finally to Nome in 1901.

In all the crazy voyages of the Cariboo rush none equaled the feat of Captain G. B. Wright. Business having lagged on the Fraser, he piloted the *Enterprise* to Fort George, through waters south of Soda Creek which were considered impassable and were avoided even by men like Fraser. From Fort George Wright went up the Nechako to Stuart River, up Stuart Lake to Tachie River, into Trembleur Lake and finally up Middle River into Takla Lake.

The new gold rush he had expected in the north failed to pan out, but he had the satisfaction of covering more than half the length of British Columbia by steamboat, far from the sea—a voyage probably without parallel in the fresh-water navigation of Canada.

It was not all steam, adventure and profits on the river. The captains were there to make money, but the traffic was insufficient to support them. The rush had hardly got under way before every shipowner was cutting rates to destroy his competitors. In April, 1859, the *Eliza Anderson* was charging $12 per ton for freight and $10 for passengers from Victoria to New Westminster. By September the rate was down to 50 cents a ton and 50 cents per passenger. Sometimes, to attract business, the steamboats carried passengers free.

The next few years were filled with rate agreements, breach

of agreements, mergers, reorganizations and bankruptcy. Nearly every ship passed through the hands of the sheriff at one time or another.

Every imaginable device was used to attract business—including the hoarse voice of John Butts, the tipsy town crier of Victoria, who paraded the streets to announce the departure of steamers for the river and ended with the prayer: "God save the Queen!" When he slipped one day and cried "God save John Butts" he was clapped into jail.

The real test of a steamboat was not its fare but its speed. The power that a good captain could get out of his crude, wood-burning engines was extraordinary. In the *Alexandra* Captain Billy Moore ran from Yale to New Westminster in six hours, averaging 22½ miles an hour in the fast water from Yale to the Harrison. Between these points I seldom travel much faster than that in an automobile.

Speed, daring and low rates could not save the steamboatmen. One after the other they went broke, with the exception of the redoubtable Irving. But in their time they carried a volume of freight and gold beyond calculation.

According to the *Colonist*, the *Otter* and the *Caledonia* delivered at Victoria more than $1,500,000 in gold dust from the Cariboo mines between August 17 and October 31, 1861. On October 30 the *Caledonia* arrived with $240,000 in bullion, and on November 12 the *Otter* brought $300,000.

For his supplies and for the safety of his treasure the miner was at the mercy of the river captain. No wonder, then, that the arrival of a new steamer on the river was the occasion of public celebration and the excuse for free drinks at the bars. The musty files of the *Colonist* still carry some flavor of these events.

On November 26, 1860, the population of Yale stood on the bank watching the new *Fort Yale* struggle up the river, her big paddles thrashing, her whistle screaming, and her master, Captain Smith Jamieson, at the wheel. She had made the trip from

Hope, 16 miles, against the heavy current and proved that Yale could become the head of navigation even for the large vessels.

She was received by the inhabitants of that flourishing town of Yale with every manifestation of rejoicing [says the *Colonist*, in the upholstered journalism of the day]. Cannons and anvils were fired, the British and American flags hoisted in honor of the event. The Celestial residents came in for their share of fun and set off innumerable packs of Chinese firecrackers. In the evening a dinner was given to the attaches of the boat, and many invited guests, by the inhabitants, at which the humbler classes, ladies and gentlemen mustered in full strength. After the dinner a ball was held and the dancing continued till an early hour in the morning. On Tuesday, at half past eight o'clock, a.m. the Fort Yale took her departure, amid the cheers of the assembled multitude, and made the run to Fort Hope in 54 minutes. . . . The people of Fort Yale are highly delighted with their boat which is a perfect model of beauty and strength.

Their delight was short-lived. In the following April the *Fort Yale* blew up on Union Bar, two miles above Hope, killing some dozen men, among them Captain Jamieson, who was hurrying down to the coast to marry an American actress in New Westminster.

Great days, but brief. The Harrison business was ruined by the opening of the Cariboo Road. After that the traffic from the coast followed the Fraser route up to Yale, but even at the height of the rush most of the boats were losing money. As the first excitement subsided and the luckless miners poured out of Cariboo, the river traffic declined almost overnight, and one by one the steamboats abandoned the lower river.

By 1869 only the *Lillooet* was left to make one trip a week between New Westminster and Yale and soon she, too, was seen no more.

On the upper river, as we have seen, the business lasted longer, briefly stimulated by the discovery of gold in the Omineca country, north of Fort George, in 1869. After the little Omineca rush had played out and even after the road gap between Soda Creek and Quesnel was closed, some steamboat business continued in the isolated country to the north. When it was opened up by the construction of the Grand Trunk Pacific Railway, steamboats were used to move the supplies of the railway construction camps all along the big bend of the river. With the completion of the railway a regular steamboat service linked Quesnel with the new town of Prince George beside the old fort of that name until this traffic dwindled to the occasional voyages of Captain Foster's disreputable *Circle W*.

Meanwhile, in 1866, the steamboats penetrated eastward. Gold had been found on the Big Bend of the Columbia. Miners who had failed in Cariboo marched up the Thompson to the Shuswap country and through the Selkirks. To move supplies to the new camps the colonial government offered a subsidy of $400 a month for the regular operation of a steamboat on the Thompson from Savona's Ferry to the head of the Shuswap Lake at Seymour only 45 miles from the Big Bend mines.

The Hudson's Bay Company finally got the contract and sent James Trahey, the famous boatbuilder of Victoria, to Savona's Ferry with a company of shipwrights. Within two months they launched the stern-wheeler *Marten*, which reached Seymour "City" on May 27, 1866, under the command of Captain W. A. Mouat. The first steamboat to churn the Shuswap waters was greeted at Seymour with a lavish party and a deluge of champagne.

The Big Bend mines were a failure. When they were abandoned after one season's work, the *Marten* was tied up in Kamloops and steamboating on the Thompson, save for a brief interlude in 1875, was at an end.

One final adventure, perhaps the most desperate in the story of the river, should not be forgotten. In 1882 and for two years afterwards the stern-wheeler *Skuzzy* actually ran the Fraser canyon between Boston Bar and Lytton. This, were it not for the reports in the *Colonist*, one could hardly credit. From the road the waters here seem so wild that only a lunatic would venture on them. But without a lot of clear-eyed lunacy among pilots and miners there would have been no Cariboo, no British Columbia and no Canadian nation on the Pacific.

12   On the Old Trail

WHAT IS LEFT OF THE OLD CARIBOO? NOT MUCH, BUT ENOUGH, perhaps, to tell us something of its spirit.

In the dusk of a bitter autumn day, in 1921, I found myself beside the gold creeks of the upper Fraser. I had come here on a fool's errand, to find some trace of the rush, some remnant of its adventure, a touch of the magic that had drawn men from the four corners of the earth. There were still reminders of the rush—the original road, a few decayed cabins, and now and then a grave with a rotting wooden cross at the roadside. But little flavor of the old days, no sense of great events, no feeling of history.

My horse, a hired animal with no stomach for such work, had turned lame. I was hungry, saddlesore, and soaked to the skin by the autumn's first sleet. Barkerville lay 30 miles ahead. I had begun to wonder where I could stop that night, and to remember with a new understanding the labors of other travelers on this road before me, when I saw a light gleaming through the trees. The horse broke into a trot and stopped before the door of a log house. By the oddest chance he had brought me to the one habitation where I could hear the story of the rush at first hand.

Harry Jones lived in that house. I suppose he was over seventy years old then but he looked under sixty—a lean, erect man with a fine weathered face, a plume of white hair and clear, quiet eyes. When he joined the rush of '62 he was a boy just over from Wales, a kind of mascot among the Argonauts. Half a dozen others of that company were still alive then but they were older than Jones and he alone remained beside the Cariboo Road.

He had left it once, after making a stake sufficient to keep him in luxury. He had gone back to Wales, had been a fellow townsman of a youth named Lloyd George, and by his own account had bought all the pleasures of London that gold nuggets could command. But the whole island of Britain, he said, was too small to hold a man who had stretched his muscles in the Cariboo. Jones came back to live beside the old road at Wing Dam on the bank of Lightning Creek. His stake was gone but he did not miss it.

By his fire that night, we could hear the chatter of the creek over gravel, dug and washed and sluiced by a thousand miners. Shivering on the creekbank in the spring of '61, some forgotten prospector looked up at a shattering thunderstorm and shouted to his fellows: "Well, boys, this is lightning!" Lightning Creek it remained, one of the richest and probably the most dangerous in the Cariboo.

Jones worked Lightning with the others. He remembered it as a quiet little river purling westward toward the Fraser. Now its banks were heaped up with the gravel litter of the miners' sluices and rockers. Its current swirled over a broken wing dam of logs thrust out to divert its water from the gold bars. Underneath it a rabbit warren of tunnels, laboriously shored up by wooden cribbing, was filling up with slum.

They could never get to the bottom of Lightning. At the edge of the river they dug down to bedrock and burrowed their tunnels under the stream but always, just as the pay dirt was getting rich, oozing slum drove them back or trapped them like flies. Machinery had been brought in later, more tunnels bored, more gold exposed, but the slum oozed again.

Now Lightning was abandoned and Jones was left alone. He could sit by his window and watch the creek and think about the men who had worked with him here, and of the gold still lying deep down on the bedrock, more gold by far than the miners ever took out. The presence of that hoard, safe from prying hands, seemed to satisfy him.

Most of that night I plied him with questions. Cariboo Cameron, Barker, Stout, Deitz, Begbie and Douglas—he remembered them all as clearly as yesterday's weather, but he had little to say about them. To Jones they were companions of the trail, a few among many who came and went and of no special note.

He finally told me, when I pressed him, how Cameron dug up the bodies of his baby daughter and wife, preserved them in an iron casket full of alcohol, packed them out to the coast on horses, shipped them by way of the Panama all the way to Ontario and buried them at home. This Jones mentioned as a passing incident and seemed surprised at my interest in it. Cameron, he said, had merely made good a promise to his wife. To pack two bodies in alcohol on the backs of horses, he allowed, was a formidable feat. But then, they'd packed pianos from the coast in the same way and even a huge English billiard table for Kelley's Hotel in Barkerville.

Jones knew Barkerville pretty well. A kind of wild town, he said. You had to pay the German hurdy-gurdy girls $10 for a dance and a lot more for larger favors. A respectable woman, he added quickly, was as safe on the Cariboo Road as in God's pocket. A man who looked at her would be run out of camp. But the German girls did all right, for there was plenty of money.

Why, one night Red Jack McMartin brought $44,000 in gold into the Shuniah saloon, set up drinks for everybody, paid for all the glasses in the place, broke them one by one against the wall, danced with hobnail boots on a case of champagne until it all leaked out, smashed a $3,000 mirror behind the bar with a last shower of nuggets, and ended in the street, penniless. McMartin never made another stake.

Billy Barker, who made the first big strike on Williams Creek, took out $600,000, spent it over the bar, got a job as a cook in a road camp, lived his last days in the old men's home in Victoria. Billy Deitz, who gave Williams Creek its name, ended the same way. Even Cameron, the millionaire, set up an estate back east, lost it, returned to the creek, and died a poor man at Barkerville. Jones had been wealthy too, but he had nothing now except the buried treasure of Lightning.

Of the whole story he could give me only such odd fragments and these unwillingly. I was young then or I would have known that to the man who was in it the rush was no adventure but a dull, hard livelihood of toiling, unremembered days. Like most human events, it became an adventure only when the historians put it on paper with an excitement unknown to the men who had made it. Jones had no use for history books and magazine articles that tried to exaggerate the rush into an epic. They were wrong, he said, in most of their facts and in all their explanations.

A few years after this Jones met some of the historians face to face for the first time when, on their invitation, he unveiled a cairn in Barkerville and took the opportunity, in a few well-chosen words, to insult them. Their ceremony, he said, was bunk, their records were distorted, and they had put the cairn in the wrong place. His speech was attributed to his great age and was not reported.

If Jones had known that I would mention him in a book myself, I suppose he would have treated me differently that night. My intentions then were quite innocent. I had come only in the hope of re-discovering the old legends at first hand for myself and, of course, I was bound to fail, for the legends are an afterthought, the legendary figures old men who could give only the facts, never the contents. So I left Jones the next morning in his doorway, peering at Lightning Creek where the gold still lay thick on the bedrock.

It was nightfall again when I rode past the dark, unblinking eye called Jack of Clubs Lake, over the tailings of Lohee that spread for a mile across the valley, and down the last hill into Barkerville.

The town, a double row of shacks along a single street, lay cramped between Williams Creek and a naked hill. The creek had been churned up so long by the miners and so much gravel had flowed into it from the claims farther up the valley that even the log dikes could not keep it out of the town. Most of it seemed to be running down the street that night. Year after year the buildings had been propped higher out of the mud until they reeled on their stilts and seemed held together by two lines of crazy elevated sidewalks.

The stores with their false fronts, the cabins gaping windowless to the weather, had never been painted. They were the same color as the welter of mud and gravel around them and they looked like some fungus growth in the niche of the hills. No, that was too fancy. They looked precisely like a movie set of two dimensions, such a town as a Hollywood director would build overnight for a western picture.

But Barkerville was real. Men had lived in these buildings, miners had walked these sidewalks, girls had danced in these empty barrooms, stagecoaches had clattered down this narrow street, bull teams had toiled through the mud, and in the opera house, with its queer tower, held up now by long props, strolling players had acted Shakespeare and taken their pay in nuggets.

Any ancient ruin has at least a myth about it, a patina, the scent of deeds and the feel of ghosts. Here was nothing but a huddle of shacks, a memorial of cardboard with no relic of life, no sign to stir the blood, or conjure visions. Having read the story of Cariboo and pictured Barkerville when it heaved with life, I was sorry now that I had come.

A few men still lived there, lacking energy to leave, the last dregs of the rush. Of the thousands who had swarmed in this curious nest there were ninety-one in the town and in all the country around it, according to the reliable census kept in the head of Fred Tregillus. None of these inhabitants could be seen out of doors that night, but a light or two flickered in the crooked street. I headed for the nearest one. It shone from the parlor of Kelly's Hotel, which had served the gold rush well and still welcomed the occasional visitor in its old style.

An ancient man with a Santa Claus beard was sitting by the fat belly of the drum stove when I came in. He looked up at me suspiciously. His name was Bill Brown, he was one of the Argonauts, he lived alone in the hills, and he came to town for a bit of excitement now and then. But he would not talk with strangers. This turned out to be a big night in Barkerville, for three other outsiders drove in by automobile—too big a night for Bill Brown. At the sight of this mass invasion he shuffled out of the hotel without a word, mounted a horse almost as old as himself, and rode out of town.

Kelly's Hotel was a friendly, intimate sort of place. Its wooden walls were impregnated with the smell of rich cooking and old liquor, and the smell of good solid mahogany furniture and the smoke of wood fire. The bar (alas, unused under a barbarous prohibition law) still glistened in the lamplight. Nude Turkish ladies, of lavish bosom, smiled down at you with a fixed and sexless smile from heavy gilt frames. Upstairs the bedrooms were richly papered, the beds deep with feather mattresses, the washbasins and jugs of good English porcelain, all packed in by wagon from the coast.

Like every stopping place on the Cariboo Road in those days, Kelly's inundated you with food on heaped-up platters challenging you to deplete them. Also, it followed the fine old Cariboo custom of segregating the sexes at mealtimes. The men ate in the dining room, the women waited on them and then ate the leftovers in the kitchen. This was a man's country still.

How the desolate jumble of shacks and that sterile valley produced our dinner I have never been able to discover—a miracle performed over a stove like a locomotive by a grinning Chinese giant who had walked into Barkerville half a century before and never stopped cooking since. Somehow at Kelly's they had stood the siege and had kept alive a spark of Barkerville's old fire.

Thus warmed and fed, I set out for the Tregillus house, to which I had been directed. It lay at the end of the town, hard by the dike and below the level of the creek beside it. To reach it I had to navigate, by dead reckoning, the stilted sidewalk high above the mud of the street, together with many stairways, creaking bridges and single planks, all invisible in the darkness, and slippery with rain.

It was a strange walk. An imaginative man would have felt the presence of spirits in a place so populous with memories. A nervous man would have imagined all sorts of things writhing in the blackness of those deserted stores, saloons and cabins. As I was neither imaginative nor nervous, I walked on concerned only with keeping upright, but the sound of the creek, of rain hammering on the roof, of water swirling down wooden gutters and gurgling through broken drains was like a sly whispering behind my back. I walked faster.

There were no spirits and no marauders—only four old men playing cards in a dismal room by the light of an old lamp (they played all winter with a few hours out for meals), and a young Chinese reading a newspaper on the counter of his store. A scrawled placard in the window announced that gold was brought here, and the idea of gold still circulating in Barkerville so intrigued me that I opened the door and went inside.

The Chinese—far too young to remember better days—was buying gold as it had been bought here since the sixties—a few tiny nuggets, a handful of dust painfully gathered by a couple of old men out of the tailings. On an antique scale the storekeeper weighed a nugget not much bigger than a pin's head and sold it to me for $3.55, but he had nothing else to offer, no realization that he was the end of a long line, the survivor of an ancient trade, the last gold buyer. So I walked on, as he explained the path, to the Tregillus house.

Fred Tregillus was a black-bearded Cornishman, short, powerful of limb and soft of speech—a hard-rock miner. He had come out from the old country when the placer mines were closing and he had remained in the belief that where gold can be found in the gravel it can be found somewhere in ore. He had spent most of his life looking for the mother lode of the Fraser and year by year he thought he was creeping up on it.

Meanwhile he had mastered geology out of books, and a great many other things as well. In that cabin against the dike there was a better knowledge of world history and current affairs than you would find in most of the houses of Vancouver. I have always contended that men in the wilderness know more about the news of the day than city folk who are close to it and lost in it. Tregillus is the prize exhibit in my case.

His household had been preserved intact from the old days. The furniture was English, substantial and Victorian. The chairs were protected by lace antimacassars. The tiny organ was pumped by foot pedals. While Mrs. Tregillus played this instrument, her husband, the children and I sang hymns, for it was a Sunday night.

The war had just ended in Europe, the world was hysterical, the era of flaming youth and perpetual prosperity had begun. It was hard to believe in such a time that such a house remained at the end of the Cariboo Road, where a Cornish miner, still searching for the ultimate treasure, spent his Sunday evenings singing hymns.

This at least was an unconscious touch of the original Cariboo, the first I had seen, innocent of any pretense. The Tregillus family around the creaky organ was the genuine article, the authentic breed, and quite unaware that they had become obsolete in this new and better world, that they lived in another century and on a worthless hope.

Next morning Tregillus showed me a little burrow in the rocks at the edge of the town, his latest assault on the mother lode, the work of many months, singlehanded. He said it looked promising and held up a sample of ore for my inspection. It meant nothing to me—a chunk of rock, in the hand of a deluded man who, under this calm, outer look, must have turned a little mad. Tregillus evidently saw what I thought, chuckled in the recesses of his beard, and said he would show me something of interest if I came back in a few years.

We met the Pack Rat that morning. His name was Joel Stevens, but it had been forgotten long ago. He was a bent gnome in rags, living amid the accumulation of imaginable junk which he had crammed into his cabin—tin cans, old newspapers, rusty nails, gold pans, broken tools, anything he could lay his hands on. By now there was space left only for his bed and stove and he had begun to heap up his miser's hoard outside. He seemed to value it as the miners had valued gold. Barkerville was always tolerant of idiosyncrasy. The Pack Rat pursued his harmless dream in peace.

Near him lived two old ladies who had been born in Barkerville and had never traveled farther from it than Quesnel. They had gone there to see a railway train. Having seen it, they were glad to come home again. Barkerville, they said, was good enough for them and one of these days it would get lively again. No one could believe such a prophecy on the empty street but, oddly enough, the old ladies were right.

Their snug little house, with potted plants in the windows, stood next to the opera house. We went inside this deserted building but there was little to see. When the rush subsided they had turned the opera house into the town firehall. The leather fire buckets and some axes still hung on the walls. It was here that Barkerville had held its larger celebrations, and here that James Anderson, the civic poet, used to recite his latest verse, in Scottish doggerel. One of them, quoted by Agnes Laut in her excellent *Cariboo Trail*, ran like this:

I ken a body made a strike,
He looked a little lord.
He had a clan o' followers
Amang a needy horde.

Whane'er h'd enter a saloon
You'd see the barkeep smile—
His lordship's humble servant he
Wi'out a thought o' guile!

A twalmonth passed an' a' is gane
Baith freends and brandy bottle!
An' noo the puir soul's left alane
Wi' nocht to weet his throttle!"

Anderson's Highland melancholy shows through all his verses, especially when he considers the price of goods in Barker-ville:

Your letter cam' by the express,
Eight shillin's carriage, naethin' less!
You maybe like to ken what pay
Miners get here for ilka day?
Jus' two poond sterling, sure as death—
It should be four, between us baith—
For gin ye coont the cost o' livin'
There's naethin' left to gang an' come on.

There was more truth here than poetry. Potatoes retailed at $90 a sack, milk (frozen) at $1 a pound, boots $50, champagne 2 ounces of gold per pint, nails $1 a pound, and a stove $700. If you wanted a piano, and a good many people did, you paid $1 a pound to have it packed on mules.

Who cared? There was plenty of gold directly beneath the town. Not far from the opera house Tregillus showed me the entrance to Billy Barker's famous shaft, the first sunk into the clay on what was to be the town's main street. It was only a hole in the ground now, covered over with rotting planks like an abandoned well. But when it was dug the real wealth of Cariboo was uncovered for the first time. Results of surface workings on Williams Creek had been poor at the beginning and few men paused there. When Barker got down fifty feet on August 21, 1862, and came up with the richest pay dirt anybody had ever seen, the camp enjoyed a riot.

Bishop Hills, who had gone up from Victoria to serve the miners' spiritual wants, noted in his diary: "When lead struck on Barker's claim, about August 21st, all went on spree for several days, except one Englishman, well brought up." That Englishman was not Barker. The bars and a widow in Victoria got most of his share of the treasure.

After his shaft many others were sunk beside Williams Creek and tunnels from them were drifted under the creek bed. It was now so honeycombed with timber, the logs all preserved in the slum, that a dredge could not work over the old gravel. How much unfound gold still lay under the tailings of Billy Deitz's creek and far deeper in the gravel and in the blue clay against the bedrock? Tregillus shook his head. He was a hard-rock man.

The placer gold of Cariboo, so unreliable, so unevenly distributed, and so pockety has always been a mystery.

A long time ago, before man appeared on the earth, they say, gold was broken and washed out of its original veins of ore into the beds of rivers, where dinosaurs wallowed among tropical forests. Over these rivers the convulsions of the infant continent carried alluvial deposits, burying the gold under a deep overburden. Then, as the continent heaved again, thrust up its mountains, and established its present land mass, some of these forgotten rivers were pushed up toward the surface.

The process was not finished yet. The glaciers rolled out of the north, shaved off the mountains, and spread another overburden upon the old creeks. New streams, boring their way to the sea, scooped up the exposed gold particles and carried them along, an inch at a time, until they settled in the sand bars of the Fraser. But most of the gold remained at the bottom of the creeks in its hiding place where men like Barker found it.

Meanwhile the original streaks of ore in the heaving igneous rock were twisted, pushed up, and flattened down again into the broken and faulted veins that are mined today.

The Cariboo miner did not find this lode gold. He was too busy sifting out the placer where the gold lay naked. It was not long, however, before others followed up the placer creeks to their headwaters, testing the hunks of float as they went, and began to find on some exposed cliff the outcropping of ore.

On Bridge River, which enters the Fraser above Lillooet, the later prospectors traced the placer into the hills and hit the veins that are now the Pioneer and Bralorne mines—veins narrow, twisted, but so rich that I have seen there a chunk of ore the size of a man's head worth $30,000, almost solid gold.

It was such veins as this that Tregillus sought around Barkerville. The placer of the old days contained fragments only. The real treasure had yet to be found.

The placer was not quite worked out even yet. In the churned and tortured ravine called Stout's Gulch, Tregillus introduced me to Crazy Fraser, an elderly Chinese. He was washing the worked-over gravel in his gold pan and in a tomato can he had two small nuggets. We asked him where he had found them but he only grinned. If he worked hard enough he could find a little gold that the old-timers had missed in their haste but hardly enough to make wages.

It was in Stout's Gulch, by the way, that the Cariboo is said to have found its name. That the miners, who shot and ate this animal, could not spell "caribou" is the obvious explanation —too obvious. Such a ringing name as "Cariboo" surely deserves a better legend. It is supplied in Stout's Gulch by Alex McInnes, the first baby born in Barkerville and now an aged man, who had the story from his father.

In the first years of mining on Williams Creek, Mr. McInnes

says, the resident magistrate was named Cox. Judge Cox, they called him out of courtesy, but the only judge was Begbie. Cox was an Irishman, a gay dog, and an innocent sort of braggart. He bragged one day that he could go out and shoot a caribou at the edge of the town and, being challenged, laid a wager on it.

The boys of the town, entering into the spirit of the thing, went up Stout's Gulch into the hills, killed a caribou bull, propped it up on the hillside, and fastened a rope to the prop. When the judge arrived, the dead caribou presented an easy target. Cox fired, a concealed conspirator jerked the rope and the animal fell down without a tremor. The boys offered to carry it home and Cox hurried back to town to spread the news of his marksmanship.

The joke was told in the barroom that night, it spread up every creek and was repeated all the way down the road to Yale. For weeks after that, before anyone could ask him slyly about his adventure, Cox would take the offensive, shouting! "Boo, Boo, Boo! Cariboo Boo, Boo!" Until people got tired of the thing. But the name stuck and the country is still Cariboo.

This is Mr. McInnes' story, to which he testifies, and it is not for us to question the word of the first child born in Barkerville. Tregillus, when I asked him about it, was noncommittal.

Nor could he remember the revolver duel between Molly Devers and Nellie Bell to decide who should marry Jake Cole, the gambler. The women, it is said, faced each other at dawn before a large crowd gathered in the gulch, and both turned their revolvers the wrong way and simultaneously plugged their fickle suitor, after which they became fast friends.

Tregillus was not given to such legends. He preferred to show me something actual. So I followed him up the gulch to Lohee mine, which has never ceased to yield pay dirt since the rush.

Above Jack of Clubs Lake they started to sluice out a prehistoric creek bed in the hillside. With water shot from a gun they bored a channel into the hill, yard after yard and mile after mile, until they had a canyon a hundred feet deep and a quarter of a mile across.

As we watched from the lip of the canyon, half a dozen men were still burrowing into the gravel with a hydraulic monitor. The monitor looks like a child's toy at the bottom of this huge hole, a frail tube of iron mounted on a swivel, but it has the force of a cannon.

Out of its mouth poured a stream of water so strong that you could not cut it with an ax. Under its impact acres of gravel were sliding down. The monitor swept it into a sluice box as neatly as a housewife sweeps a kitchen.

For miles the sluice wriggled along the bottom of the canyon like a snake. Behind its riffles, settling there because it was heavier than the earth and gravel, lay the particles of gold—not much of it, too little for the single miner to work, but enough to keep Lohee prospering long after the oldest Argonaut was dead.

Tregillus and I stood for a long time watching the miners, no larger from here than insects, and their monitor, the size of a garden sprinkler. You could not believe until you saw it that this frail jet was cutting through a mountain and spreading its refuse over the floor of the valley miles away in a layer so deep that already it had half covered the original telephone poles.

If a single stream of water out of a little gun could alter the shape of a countryside in a few years, it was easy to see how the great rivers, in the first writhings of the young earth, could lift the gold of the Rocky Mountains and carry it to the sea. How did gold get to the bottom of the Lohee gravel, into the central substance of the hills? Where had it come from in the first place? Where was its mother lode of ore? It might be a mile away or a thousand. In this haystack Tregillus hoped to find his needle.

We walked back through Stout's Gulch to Richfield, which used to be a village up Williams Creek a mile or so from Barkerville. Nothing remained of Richfield but the courthouse, a barren structure of clapboard. It was empty now, except for the judge's dais, the jury's bench, and the prisoner's box. The floor was littered with stationery and court documents which bore the royal arms of Queen Victoria.

In this little room, according to the myths that grow thick around his name, Begbie used to sentence men to hanging on a gibbet outside the door. Old-timers still tell stories of five corpses dangling there at once. In fact, a few Indians were hanged in the Richfield jailyard but only one white man—Jim Barry, in July, 1867. He had made the mistake of taking a ring from his victim's finger and giving it to a hurdy-gurdy girl, who talked to other lovers.

Begbie's courthouse was falling down that morning (it has since been repaired and set up as a historic monument), the jailyard behind it was overgrown with brush and the gibbet was gone. The men who died here and the men who watched them die are equally forgotten—all save the Hanging Judge, who is remembered chiefly for the things he never did.

On the hill west of the town some of the Argonauts are buried in Christian graves. Above them, when Tregillus took me to the cemetery, the wooden crosses were rotting and most of the inscriptions were illegible. What matter, so long as the inhabitants still faced the creek where they had worked, and Cariboo Cameron lay directly above his claim? In the crisp autumn breeze the poplar leaves were fluttering down upon the graves like little golden coins, as if to recall the days when gold was free to everybody and valueless in the end.

Tregillus said good-bye to me at the edge of the town. I was sorry for this deluded man who was squandering his life in a hopeless pursuit of the earth's secret. A crank, obviously, as everyone in the town agreed. But the joke was on the town in the end. When I returned to Barkerville ten years later, Tregillus had found his share of the mother lode. He had sold it for more money than he needed. And he had settled down in his house

175

by the dike to raise geraniums in tubs of earth wheelbarrowed out of the hills.

Money had not changed Tregillus but it had changed Barkerville. On the tailings of the Lohee, by Jack of Clubs Lake, the brawling town of Wells had sprung up, the miners were blasting out the veins of ore nearby, and many of them had settled down in Barkerville's empty houses. It was an unconscious act of desecration, an invasion of barbarians who cared nothing for the ruins and the memories around them.

The last man of the rush was gone now and in his place stood only the stone cairn, which Harry Jones had unveiled with contempt and anger, knowing that the Cariboo was beyond the power of later men to imagine, mark or praise.

Barkerville doubtless will sink into the mud someday or burn up like a box of matches, as it burned once before, and nothing but the cairn will remain. But when all the gold has been blasted out of the lode and the valley is deserted, and the rivers and the vegetation have covered all the old scars, historians long hence will pause here, perhaps, to wonder at the heaps of gravel, the Lohee canyon, and Tregillus' little burrows in the rock; or, digging down, they may encounter an inexplicable labyrinth of timbers or some bones on the hillside.

This sentimental journey into Barkerville has interrupted, without greatly illuminating the chronology of men along the river. Returning to that history, we find that as the gold rush began to ebb slowly, even before the end of the sixties, a larger movement was in flow.

13   The River's Mouth

BY THE END OF WORLD WAR I THE LOWER RIVER HAD BEEN doublelined with railways, its tributary waters were making power, and on this backbone the anatomy of British Columbia, with its half million people, had taken on roughly its present form. But the highway that had clung to the river since 1862 had been broken.

Automobiles could drive from the coast into the first defiles of the canyon but there the Cariboo Road had all but disappeared. The vital link of the Spuzzum bridge had been washed out. The coast was joined to the interior by railway only. Across the interior plateau, however, the original road, with an expanding network of side roads, still served the new towns, the mines and ranches. It was not until 1927 that the British Columbia government undertook to close the canyon gap with a new road in some ways more extraordinary and certainly more spectacular than the old.

Since the present road is built, as it were, on the bones of the old, following the Fraser most of the way almost exactly on the route used by Douglas, it offers the traveler at once an easy view of the river and whatever relics, memories and footprints the great days of Cariboo have left behind. In the remainder of this book we shall journey up this road, with a few leisurely digressions and without the speed or strenuous schedule of the modern tourist.

For the sake of clarity in the reader's mind it would have

177

been advantageous to travel the river in one direction, either down or up, from the beginning. But, as we have seen, the first movement to the river came from the sea, eastward, the second down the river from the north with the early explorers, and the third up the river again from the coast in the gold rush. In following this history you could not follow the river in one direction. Today the natural course of travel is from the coast inland and upriver, in the path of the miners. We shall start, therefore, at the river mouth.

The Fraser empties lazily into the sea some twelve miles north of the United States boundary by three channels, meandering through the great delta built by the mud of its waters. Standing on this delta, one surveys on the south the white mountains of Washington, dominated by the sharp, volcanic peak of Mount Baker; on the east the lush river valley; on the north the sprawling metropolis of Vancouver and, beyond it, like a flat backdrop, the blue mountains of the North Shore falling sheer into the ocean; on the west the Gulf of Georgia and the humped line of Vancouver Island.

From this point the Fraser delta reveals itself as a kind of triangular amphitheater, narrowing to the eastward into the only sizable gap through the Coast Range from the United States to Alaska.

The delta is rich and busy.

The gulf, where the muddy river cuts its sharp brown line across the green of sea water, is flecked with liners, ferryboats, fishing craft and tugs with booms of logs in tow. A rusty lightship rides at anchor over the treacherous sand heads. Nearby, the main entrance to the river channel, the southernmost of the three mouths, is marked by parallel lines of piles, on which sea gulls perch with a thoughtful look.

Ships of all sorts, except the largest liners, are constantly moving up and down this channel to the towns and mills along the river.

On both banks, and on the many islands of the delta, every

inch of fertile alluvial soil is under cultivation, crisscrossed by fences, dotted by swelling barns, and thickly inhabited by dairy cattle. Viewed from the air, the entire delta seems to be cultivated down to the edge of the river and the gulf, each island fenced in by mud dikes.

The estuary provides sea transportation for one of Canada's major industrial centers and its silt supports the milkshed of Vancouver. The delta, however, for all its usefulness, is monotonously flat, unlike any other area in British Columbia, and rather drab. The river oozes between brown, muddy banks, cluttered with wharves, small craft and log booms. The land is sodden half the year in the season of coastal rain and only six-foot drainage ditches and the tortuous dikes keep it above water in the summer season of flood. But in the summer the fecundity of this soil, washed down from the interior ranges, is proclaimed in the surging green of the pastures and the resulting flow of milk.

As time is reckoned in a young country, this is old farm land. The first settlers plowed it in the opening days of the gold rush. Many men who had failed at the mines were washed down here like the river silt to find their treasure in the black soil. The Ladners, the Magees and others are names appended to schools, roads, streets and villages on the delta to honor the oldest settlers. Such names are still prominent in the life of Vancouver.

Among all the old-timers the most notable was John Oliver, who deserves to be remembered here as one of the genuine rivermen, as the heir of Douglas, Begbie, de Cosmos, Robson, Helmcken and the other builders of British Columbia.

Oliver was a Derbyshire miner's son, who immigrated to Canada in the days when the C.P.R. was under construction. From San Francisco he beat his way up to Victoria, got a job on the railway and then settled on the delta. There was no Vancouver then and little along the river but jungle and a few settlers' cabins.

Oliver plowed the delta land and tried to drain it, but the

ditches that bore the rain water into the river at low tide poured the salt water back to ruin the crops when the tide changed. He told me once, when he was an old man and full of public honors, that his most satisfactory achievement was the defeat of the river and the purging of salt from his fields. In a dream, he said, he perceived a simple mechanism, a sluice gate which would open as the ditchwater ran outward but would close against the incoming flow. Probably this device had been used in many places long before but Oliver seemed to regard his discovery as a religious experience, a direct revelation from God.

From the delta Oliver—a short man shaped like a barrel with a mane and beard of white—moved into the premiership of British Columbia, stormed across the nation in many stirring campaigns, ruled his province for ten years, and kept its politics in a persistent turmoil. He was unschooled, his Derbyshire accent still clung to him, but he had learned more from books beside an oil lamp than most men learn at university, and he had one of the most powerful minds in the nation.

It was said of him that, given education, he would inevitably have become Canada's prime minister and a world figure. Having interviewed him daily for the newspapers during his whole term of office, I am inclined to think that education might have been the ruin of him. His strength of mind, like the strength of his great shoulders and gnarled hands, was the strength of native intelligence which was never distracted by other men's thoughts. He was wiser for his ignorance of irrelevancies. Here was the product of the delta soil, of long companionship with the river, of a lifetime of struggle against it. It was good that this roughcast creature was never smoothed down by any form of culture.

Oliver died in office and, unlike most of the old-timers, he died wealthy. He was not left to lie in the land he had cleared and worked but in a modern graveyard near Victoria. It is a pity that he could not have returned to the banks of the river, which he hated and loved.

The delta was not allowed to run to seed like so many pioneer farm districts. Its soil was too good and too scarce to be wasted. On it have been built some of Canada's most prosperous farms and finest dairy herds. The barns to house these animals are

shiny white chambers like operating rooms. The farmhouses of Lulu Island (named after Lulu Sweet, an actress who had charmed stern old Colonel Moody) are as good as those in Vancouver across the river. An amateur farmer-editor like Roy Brown, of the Vancouver *Sun*, thought nothing of importing cows from Jersey at thousands of dollars a head.

The final touch of what is called civilization was applied to the delta when Sea Island, fronting on the northern channel, was chosen as the site of the Canadian government's major Pacific airport. Here the planes from eastern Canada, from Seattle and Alaska glide down over the Jersey herds in continuous procession day and night until the murmur of the river is drowned by the sound of motors. Perhaps, after all, Honest John Oliver has found a more peaceful resting place.

To the edge of the river, and spilling beyond into the farm

lands, lies the vast, proliferating body of Vancouver, built upon the rounded heap of gravel which the river laid down here and abandoned long before it built the present delta. Vancouver is essentially the product of the river—physically since it stands upon the river's ancient debris, economically since it lives by the river's transportation, spiritually since its life came out of the first river boom. As truly as the gold bars, the sedimentary rock and the delta, Vancouver is a conglomerate mixed by the Fraser's current.

Of all the river's creations Vancouver is the strángest. It was not intended to be a river town. It began with a sawmill and a few shacks on Burrard Inlet, which cuts into the coast line five miles north of the river, and from its first days it began to spread out. On such a site this growth could not be confined.

The Spanish and British navigators had sailed through the First Narrows, the gate to a harbor some twelve miles long and over two miles wide, one of the most spacious in the world. From the dense forest at the water's edge the first sea captains had chopped down Douglas fir trees for masts, but the possibilities of the inlet were little appreciated then. When the settlers came to British Columbia they moved up the river. Governor Douglas regarded the inlet only as a back door to New Westminster, for use if the river happened to freeze.

When the land along the south shore of the inlet was opened for settlement in 1860 there were few takers. Seven years later the true father of Vancouver arrived in the blustering person of Captain John Deighton, a Yorkshireman. After some experience on the stern-wheelers of the river, he built a hotel, which he called Deighton House, on the inlet, beside a sawmill and a cluster of shacks.

Deighton was a kindly soul beneath his bluster but he talked too much. Folks were soon calling him "Gassy Jack." The captain rather liked that and christened the settlement "Gas Town" in his own honor. Under that name it was recorded for some years in Admiralty charts.

When the sawmill village began to grow, Gassy Jack's name seemed inadequate. Seeking something more dignified, the settlers took the name of Granville from the secretary of state for the colonies. Surveyed and proclaimed, the future Vancouver was a legal entity, but not much more.

The real town on the inlet was to be built at its head and named after Colonel Moody. For a year or so, indeed, Port Moody expected to be the great Canadian port on the Pacific, for here the Canadian Pacific Railway was establishing its western terminus. When that tough old railway builder, William Van Horne, looked over the inlet, however, he quickly saw the advantage of placing his city at the western end of the basin, where there was plenty of elbow room for trains, ships and industries. With his decision to make Granville the terminus, the Port Moody boom collapsed.

The name "Granville" did not suit Van Horne. He wanted something with a grander sound, a name which would stand out among all the place names of the world. "Vancouver," he said, was the name of the great navigator who had explored these regions. It was unique, sonorous and historic. "Vancouver," therefore, despite the resulting confusion between it and the island of the same name, the new city must be. And so Vancouver was incorporated, burned down, quickly rebuilt and, with the coming of the railway, was never allowed to slacken its growth for a moment.

From the edge of the inlet to the mouth of the river stretched a whale's back of alluvial soil, rank with forest growth—ample room here for the expansive ambitions of the Gas Town pioneers. They hacked the forest down. They built wharves and ships. They sent their lumber and fish out to sea. Presently the trails of their logging camps had become wagon roads and then streets, lined by gigantic stumps.

Year by year the village spread southward until, from the houses on the top of the ridge, you could see the hazy waters of the Fraser. The southward momentum did not pause there long.

The city flowed down the slope until it reached the riverbank. Today the entire peninsula, bounded by the inlet and the river, is covered by the sedimentary layers of man's occupation as the shore was once covered by the silt of the river.

The growth of Vancouver has been fast, ferocious and unceasing. An old-timer like Roy Brown can remember when he hired a buggy at the livery stable to spend a day driving out to the river for a picnic, on the same spot where his home stands now. He fished for trout in a stream where the white shaft of the city hall stands. When he began to work for the newspapers the corner of Granville Street and Georgia, the hub of the present city, was a field of stumps.

Even then men of imagination had foreseen what would grow in the carnage left by the loggers. Old Sam Howe, looking at the muddy crossroads of Granville and Georgia, instantly bought all the land he could afford and made himself a millionaire, with a coach-and-four, a few years later. Few places have spawned more millionaires of the same sort in so brief a time.

All this, though few paused to consider it, was the work of the river. It had brought the railway into Vancouver, and Vancouver, like a ripening fruit at the end of a long branch, lived and grew on the business of the railway.

The trains moving from the inlet up the river channel, the only handy passage through the Coast Range, took Vancouver's lumber and fish, and then its manufactures into the markets of the prairies and the East. The trains moving westward brought the minerals, cattle and fruit of the British Columbia interior and the grain of the prairies into Vancouver's port, whence they were shipped abroad. When the Panama Canal was completed and Vancouver could ship prairie grain cheaply to Europe, its future as one of the world's great ports was assured. Soon the circular towers of grain elevators sprouted beside the railway and the harbor was crowded by ships of every flag.

Without the river and its mountain passage there might have been a town on Burrard Inlet, but not Vancouver. For that matter, there could not have been the Canada we know. It was not long, however, before Vancouver, which had lived with its railway indirectly on the river, began to use the river directly in the processes of its industry and commerce.

Though the inlet assuredly was large enough to accommodate a city of any imaginable dimensions and to anchor a navy, Vancouver's plans were not confined to a single port. It would build two—the second by the fresh water of the river mouth, where miles of safe shore line were available for wharves and factories.

Here, centering on Robson's old town of New Westminster, an industrial area developed independently but soon was merged into the bulging business structure of Vancouver. Since the river did not flow to the city, the city flowed out to join the river, until Vancouver is as much a part of the Fraser as Montreal is of the St. Lawrence, as New York of the Hudson, or New Orleans of the Mississippi.

This community of half a million should hold a million not long hence. This third city of Canada, this combination of factories and flowers, of parks and slums, of brazen wealth and socialism, of political corruption and fine scholarship, this awkward, self-conscious, ruthless, generous, half-crazy boy among cities, is the unforeseen legacy left by Indian fishermen, by Mackenzie and Fraser, by the Cariboo miners, by railway builders and unknown valley settlers, all of them creatures of the river.

The Fraser has built more enduring monuments than this. Its canyon will remain long after Vancouver is overgrown again. Hell's Gate will roar when all the factories and streets are silent. The ice will break up in the spring when there are no men to watch it. But, by the little measurement of men's affairs, Vancouver is the river's masterpiece.

Among North American cities it is a masterpiece indeed. In such a place and in such a climate it could hardly be otherwise. All men's efforts to scar and ruin this majestic setting have failed. The city may be ill planned and largely jerry built, its mansions of today may become the tenements of tomorrow as the population surges outward, its arteries may be too narrow to carry their swollen traffic, but you have only to raise your eyes to see the mountains, the ocean, and the ships of the world at the end of the street. You have to walk only half a mile and you are in the untouched forest. You have only to breathe and you will smell the perfume of blossom, of seaweed, fir trees and spicy cargoes.

Vancouver has grown, layer on layer, like the annual growth of trees in its woods. At the north, on the inlet, stand the wharves, elevators and factories. Behind them rises the serrated sky line of the business district—a modest line, compared to the towers of New York or San Francisco, but reaching higher every year. The next layer is a second industrial section, adhering to False Creek, a narrow sea channel which pours its smoke across the city to mix it, at times, with the winter fogs in the texture of London's renowned pea soup. From the south shore of the creek stretches the rich and frosted layer of Shaughnessy Heights, where the rich folks live. Beyond their mansions lie ring after ring of new residential areas, an additional ring almost every year, all the way down to the river, and westward and eastward to cover the entire peninsula.

This rough diagram of two dimensions, length and breadth, omits the third, which gives Vancouver thickness. From the North Shore of the inlet the Coast Range rises straight out of the harbor. Thus the mountains and the sea together seem to penetrate the whole structure of the city, anchoring and elevating it.

To look down Granville Street across the inlet at the mountains is to know at once that Vancouver, for all the bustle of its business and all the frenzy of its wealth, is a frontier town, a camp on the edge of the wilderness, existing only by the grace of ocean, river, mineral and forest. A few minutes from Granville and Georgia take you into country as wild as any on the continent. In spring you may pick roses on the warm riverbank and half an hour later ski in the mountain snow.

As if the presence of mountain and forest at its door were not enough to attach it to the soil, Vancouver has preserved in its heart the jungle of Stanley Park, the dominant physical and, one might say, the dominant spiritual fact of its life.

On the neck of land between the business section and the Gulf of Georgia a thousand acres of the coast woods stand today as they stood when Captain Vancouver sailed past them. Roads have been cut around the perimeter of the park, playgrounds, rose gardens, gushing rockeries and an open-air theater have been built in a few minor clearings, but the central body of the timber has been preserved in its original state, thanks to the foresight of Governor Douglas.

The forest, on which Vancouver has made its living from the first, the gloomy growth of fir, cedar, hemlock, balsam, spruce, maple and alder, with the underbrush of salal, sword fern, devil's club, wild currant, trillium and bleeding heart, stands at Vancouver's elbow, reminding it that it is the child—the very spoiled child—of nature.

With this setting between river, ocean, mountain and snow, another influence, the climate, has shaped Vancouver's life. Perhaps, indeed, the climate is the largest factor of all. Certainly it is the most famous and least understood by Canada at large.

As the Fraser rolls south and west into the Pacific, a greater stream moves north and east across the ocean—the invisible Japanese Current, bearing the warmth of the tropics. Through this genial influence, the only benefaction it has received under a Japanese name, the coast of Washington and British Columbia, though far enough north to expect the temperatures of Quebec, hardly ever experiences the phenomenon of the Canadian winter.

Vancouver is green the year around, with a mean temperature in January of 33 degrees, occasional falls of wet snow and—

its only serious drawback—58.56 inches of rain annually, most of it concentrated in a dark, drenching winter.

Vancouver is used to rain. Its newspapers constantly publish editorials to prove that rain washes away the germs and makes the city healthy. Its people refuse to remain indoors under even the heaviest downpour. Its gardeners dig all winter. There is seldom a day when you cannot pick a few flowers. The golf courses are crowded on Christmas Day. When the citizens of Winnipeg are shivering in a blizzard at the corner of Portage and Main, the old men of Vancouver, not far from Granville and Georgia, will be playing giant checkers in the forest park, on a checkerboard twelve feet square.

Nevertheless, though mild in winter, Vancouver is then cheerless, gray and sometimes choked with fog. Its true glory is its spring, when the rock plants and flowering trees are awash with blossom; its dry summer, when there is never any heat as North America knows it (a July mean temperature of 70); and its autumn, when the maples are turning yellow and the vine maples to the color of claret.

You would think that a climate without extremes, the seasons blending imperceptibly into one another, must make people soft. The first Indian inhabitants of the river region, near the coast, were among the least energetic in America, soft even in their speech and stern only in their aversion to labor. It has always been a favorite theory of mine that in time the coast will make the white man like the Indian. I could point out to any interested investigator a good many specimens to prove my point. In the main, however, the evidence is all the other way so far.

Vancouver is casual, unconventional, untidy, and not too carefully dressed as compared with the older cities of the East, but its energy is appalling to an ancient Victorian like me. A countryman from Vancouver Island finds a day in Vancouver about the most exhausting experience available in Canada. The reason for this bustle is obvious—Vancouver still lives in the atmosphere, the expectation and the exploitation of the camp it once was, which, in its soul, it still is. Here is the perpetual boom town, the irresistible magnet for every footloose Canadian. Here, today, everyone lives in tomorrow.

All this creates a queer, unsettled, rather brash society, in spirit closer to the gold rush than to the settled urban life of older cities.

On the top Vancouver is ruled by the most garish tycoons produced to date in Canada, the owners of the lumber empires, locked in perpetual market feuds; the men who operate the fisheries; the capitalists who draw the dividends of the interior mines; the operators of steamships, factories, sawmills and paper mills up the coast; the entrepreneurs who live in luxury on the toil of countless unknown men in the wilderness.

It is the familiar story of sudden wealth in America. The nouveau riche, the loggers who cut trees with their own hands yesterday and work in skyscrapers today, the financiers, managers, contractors and promoters of sudden eminence form a distinct caste as in every entrepot of commerce. Here they are rather bolder and much franker in their ambition than the same caste in the East.

In the shelter of this mushroom aristocracy, and usually with the aid of its campaign funds, Vancouver has produced some of the worst politics in Canada. The famous machine that has dominated public life almost without interruption for more than thirty years, has appointed its princelings to Senate and bench, has won elections with more money than prayers and always found that investment profitable, is about as efficient and ruthless as any in the nation. Governments, in both Victoria and Ottawa, have often tried to shake it but they have never succeeded, for it can deliver the votes.

At the other extreme Vancouver is a labor town of powerful unions, sometimes controlled by Communist leaders. The Co-operative Commonwealth Federation, Canada's Socialist party, is now better organized, without access to rich donors' campaign funds, than the older parties. As these things are gauged in one of the world's most conservative countries, Vancouver must be considered rather radical. By the standards of other countries, even by the standards of the United States, Vancouver is conservative and safe.

Between the tycoonery and the old party machines on one side and the increasingly vocal proletariat on the other, the mass of Vancouver people is notably uninterested in politics, domesticated, virtuous, quiet and peculiarly provincial.

Less, perhaps, than any other Canadian city Vancouver feels itself a part of Canada. Across all its thoughts, like a prison wall, stands the barrier of the mountains, cutting it off from the rest of the nation. The Fraser is wide enough to carry the physical traffic from the interior to the coast. Its freight of Canadian ideas was remarkably light until, with World War II, all Canada was suddenly knit together in peril. The provincialism of Vancouver, inevitable with a people busy building a city in a forest, is beginning to pass with the stumps. In the past two decades it may be said that Canada, as a civilization, has finally reached the Pacific coast.

No eastern influence, but the presence of the forest and the ocean, has molded the city's character, made its inhabitants an outdoor, athletic, gardening, boat-loving, easygoing people. These qualities in the bulk of Vancouver's population will hardly be noticed by the stranger. He will see only the brassy outside of the city, the brassiness of tycoons, boosters, hucksters, thrusters and politicoes, unequaled in Canada. This is the thin outside. The inner substance of Vancouver is made of simple, homespun stuff.

In modern times Vancouver has paused from its physical labors long enough to develop its mind. The University of British Columbia, on its campus beside the sea, has become one of Canada's chief centers of learning. It has raided eastern colleges to build its competent faculty. Its students have unlocked the chemistry of British Columbia's minerals. Its graduate foresters are beginning to manage the province's depleted forests. The most distinguished figure among its professors, Dr. G. G. Sedgwick, has made Shakespeare one of the popular residents of Vancouver.

Such a recital of facts fails, of course, to convey either the surface or the essence of Vancouver. That is a task outside the scope of this book and the capacity of its writer. But before we leave the fungus growth, monstrous and beautiful, that has sprung up at the lower reaches of the river, we might take a final look at it from above.

By driving through the park and across the First Narrows of the harbor, on a noble suspension bridge, we can reach the North shore a few minutes from the city's center. The narrow bench at the foot of the mountains here has long accommodated the overflow of Vancouver's population in two municipalities, North and West Vancouver. They used to be served by a fleet of cranky, double-ended ferryboats. Since the installation of the bridge more people have moved across the inlet. Every cove along the sea has been occupied. Houses have been pushed far up the hills. Halfway up the slope a residential district, complete with paved streets and golf course, has been hewn out of the rock and timber. Still farther up on Grouse Mountain, at 3,974 feet, stands a massive chalet of logs. From it we may look down on Vancouver as on a contour map.

Spread below is surely one of the three great sights of the world. The other two you can choose for yourself. London? A wilderness of chimney pots bisected by a muddy brook. New York? A narrow checkerboard of steel and brick. Paris? A precious miniature beside a toy stream. Vienna? A flat on the banks of the Danube, which is never blue. San Francisco? Even it is rather flat, for all its storied hills.

But make your second and third choices and then observe this convulsion of forest, sea and mountain; this deep channel of the inlet almost locked together at the Narrows with man's spiderweb thrown across it; this green nose of the park's jungle thrust seaward; this city on its whale's back shrunk to a postage stamp, and beyond it the thin, glittering line of the river, and beyond the river the white cap of Mount Baker, and still beyond, the thousand dotted islands of the gulf and the blue bulk of Vancouver Island, and yet farther on, the line of the ꞏOlympics on the shore of Washington. And at your back, and ever beside every human being who inhabits Vancouver, the jumble of the Coast mountains, a few miles from the pavement, as wild as in their infancy.

Vancouver is large in bulk and always swelling but, from the North Shore, it looks tiny, compressed and lost in the substance of a continent. Its skyscrapers are matchboxes, its deep-sea liners floating matches, its lights a mere wink in the darkness of the ocean's shore. Here, at a glance, is the work of the Fraser's million years, this deep gash in the barricade of the mountains, this flat delta heaped up by the river's silt, this city nourished by its commerce, this nation which the river has carried westward to the Pacific.

14　The Fraser Valley

<hr>

MOST MEN ARE BORN AND DIE IN VANCOUVER WITHOUT ANY
understanding of the Fraser as a major fact in their lives.
The first true river community, where the people see the river
every day as the origin of their past, as their livelihood in the
present and their hope in the future, is New Westminster, fifteen
miles from the river's mouth.

New Westminster, as the reader will recall, was the first
town of importance on the river. As Queenborough it was the
capital of the short-lived mainland colony of British Columbia,
which was soon joined to Vancouver Island. Before Vancouver
was even a gleam in the eye of Gassy Jack, New Westminster
had become the thriving terminus of river navigation, a jumping-off place in the Cariboo rush, a center of violent journalism
and feverish politics. Even when Vancouver overtook it in population and wealth, because the first railway ended there, New
Westminster clung stubbornly to its separate existence and
maintained the special character the river had given it. Some of
this distinction it retains today.

The city, which long claimed that description and now
deserves it, is a northward expansion of the wharves, stores,
saloons and houses that first grew up on the northern bank of
the river. House by house and street by street New Westminster climbed up the steep hill into the forest. The river, which
he could see from his window, continued to supply the living of
every inhabitant, directly or indirectly.

The fisherman who netted the river salmon, the mill hands who sawed the river logs, the stevedores who unloaded ocean ships at the river docks, the workers in manufacturing plants of many sorts, and the middlemen who handled the produce of the river farms all knew, as Vancouver never knew, that the river supported them.

It has supported them generously. New Westminster has a population of 33,000, a port which handles a million tons of freight and five hundred deep-sea vessels a year, some of the largest sawmills in Canada, and assorted industries based on wood and fish.

In building this economy the people of New Westminster have been enterprising and ingenious. They have skillfully attracted shipping and manufacturing. They have developed new processes in their industries to make such things as plywood and new kinds of excellent cheap furniture from the maple trees of the valley, which, up to a few years ago, were considered worthless. They have promoted and financed the clearing of land, the production of farmstuffs in the valley around them. On all these enterprises they have created a comfortable life of substantial homes, abundant gardens, quiet streets, and vigorous civic loyalty.

Their growth from the riverbank outward and the ravenous progress of Vancouver eastward have made them almost a suburb of the metropolis, but only in a physical sense. There is no town in Canada, I dare say, which is so conscious of its separate existence and distinct ways as New Westminster. This local patriotism, of which Robson was the first prophet, is expressed today in the ironclad political clique that isolates itself from the politics of Vancouver, in the constant drive to develop the river port in competition with Vancouver's port on Burrard Inlet, and—most sacred of civic symbols—in the lacrosse team, the immortal Salmonbellies, who took an ancient game from the Iroquois, moved it across a continent, and made it a public passion on the edge of the Pacific.

Such a yeasty climate could not fail to supply figures of

note. Robson was the first, and became premier of British Columbia. In the first days of this century New Westminster gave British Columbia Sir Richard McBride, another premier, who introduced party politics into the province and became a power in national politics. At this writing Byron Johnson, another New Westminster product (though imported from Victoria), is provincial premier, through whom the city's old political talent, the ability of all parties to combine in local defense, is expressed again.

New Westminster is approached directly by ship up the river channel. On this short inland voyage are encountered ships of every nation, most of them loaded with lumber from New Westminster's mills or salmon from its canneries. At times the channel is almost choked with acres of log booms, shepherded by fussy little tugs. When the salmon are running in the late summer, hundreds of fishing boats from the gulf will be hurrying up the river to sell their catch. In the winter, hauled up on the bank, these craft of sundry shapes and colors provide the kind of design that artists like to paint.

By land a network of roads links the river mouth and Vancouver with New Westminster. The original Douglas Road from Burrard Inlet was used in the early days when the river channel sometimes froze and travel from Gas Town had to move to New Westminster by sleigh—a collapse in the coastal climate which the present generation can hardly imagine. The old road and the Grandview Highway are still the main routes out of Vancouver eastward. A third road follows the riverbank from the sea. All roads into the interior of Canada, one of the transcontinental railways, and the highway artery into the United States pass through New Westminster and cross the river there.

Traveling to the interior from Vancouver, your first glimpse of the river will probably be from the crest of the hill now fully occupied by New Westminster. After the forked and rather narrow river mouth you will be surprised at the width of the main channel. It is a calm, straight line of brown 2,200 feet across. The smoky mills, factories and docks of New Westminster crowd the northern bank. The green farm lands flow in neat squares to the south.

At the eastern end of the city two bridges, apparently joined in a tangle of steel, ride high above the river. Around them the rusty tramp steamers, the tugs and fishing fleet, with whistles shrieking, engage in their ceaseless quarrel for passage in the channel.

After dropping down the hill into the main street, the road swings up again to the approaches of the highway bridge past terraces of flowers. The bridge bears the name of Thomas Dufferin Pattullo, another picturesque leader of provincial government. His bridge is a slim, silvery, cantilever span high enough above the water to clear the deep-sea shipping. On closer inspection it is seen to be separate from the Canadian National Railways bridge a few yards upstream. The railway bridge, which once carried highway traffic on an upper deck, later removed, was built at a low level and its center span must be swung open to permit the passage of ships.

It has always seemed to me that these bridges offer the best point from which to gauge the ultimate dimensions of the Fraser. It has now absorbed its last tributaries, reached its maximum volume, and concentrated its waters for the last thrust before its death in the gulf. The current, which a moose could wade in the Rockies, is wide enough to accommodate a liner. The clear mountain water has become so heavy with the freight of Dry Belt clay as to seem almost solid enough to walk on. The river moves so smoothly that its maximum freshet speed of 18 miles an hour is hardly perceptible, except where it lathers the bridge piers, sucks at the wharves, and pushes a white bone of spray into the mouth of every upbound ship.

Downstream from the bridges the river is littered on the north side by its industries and on the south is speckled by fishing boats, by a network of flimsy fishermen's floats, and by their houseboats.

Upstream the river opens into an oval basin about twice the size of the lower channel. Here, too, the north bank is smoky with lumber mills and shipping and is scarred by a hideous square wall of concrete, the penitentiary of British Columbia. How many men within these walls have looked out on the river and envied its carefree journey to sea? How many rivermen from Cariboo, how many Indians who were born beside it, have seen the river here at dawn before the rope was tied around their necks? I have always wished the government had built the penitentiary somewhere else. Its blank stare of concrete on the hillside, its evil towers and false battlements, and its inhuman glitter of light in the darkness seem to pollute the green valley.

The main flow of highway traffic and the Canadian National Railways line cross the bridges to the south bank. Before we follow them it will be convenient to inspect the north bank, so far as the present road system permits.

The Canadian Pacific Railway, as noted already, is built on the south side of Burrard Inlet out of Vancouver. At the end of the inlet it seeks the river channel on the north side. A web of highways leads out of Vancouver and New Westminster to merge into the main north-bank Fraser artery called the Lougheed Highway, after the greathearted and eccentric public works minister who built it.

The Lougheed Highway, after the nature of its builder, is a bold feat of construction. It cuts through massive parapets of rock, rises over high bluffs and looks down through wide vistas upon the calm body of the river. From it the traveler will observe that the Fraser's north bank is much closer to the mountains than its south. The river has piled its silt mainly on the wide south bank and laid out there most of the modern farm area. On the north, for the most part, the valley is narrow and flanked by the Coast Range. The farms here, chiefly notable for their superior berries, lie on the steep side hills, sloping down to the river. These farms, contiguous logging operations, and river sawmills have built a series of prosperous little towns like Mission, where, before they were removed from the coast after Pearl Harbor, the Japanese farmers and millworkers were numerous.

On this north bank the solid wall of mountains is cut in three places within a hundred miles of Vancouver by rivers flowing south into the Fraser out of substantial lakes. The westernmost is the gloomy Pitt, which empties a narrow mountain lake of the same name. The second is the Stave, out of Stave Lake, lying parallel to Pitt Lake. The third lake and river, roughly parallel to the first two, form the Harrison system, which was the first route to Cariboo.

The road crosses all these rather lazy and sullen tributaries without any attempt to penetrate north farther than the extremities of the three lakes. Only Harrison attracts the traveler nowadays.

Few of the thousands of tourists who follow Harrison River to the lake realize, and most British Columbians have never heard, that they are on the original gold trail. The prospectors who struggled up the river at the beginning of the lake chain to Lillooet would find little change in the interior country but they would hardly recognize the fringes of Harrison Lake.

Other British Columbia coastal lakes, whose hillsides could be quickly logged, have been gutted and abandoned in a few years. The southern end of Harrison, at the egress of the river, has been turned into the fanciest hangout for tourists in this part of the world. A palatial hotel, with such adornments as rose gardens, swimming pools, ballrooms and all the other hardships that the richer tourist requires while roughing it in the wilderness, has been built around the hot springs that bubble out of the rocks at the lake shore. A superior clientele swims in hot and sulphurous waters and drinks them for reasons of health, without necessarily confining itself to this therapeutic beverage.

The original Harrison men, bent on the riches of Cariboo, had no time to pause for swimming or drinking, but in modern times the famous Harrison hot springs have provided an industry more profitable than most gold mines and a mountain play-ground within the easy reach, if not within the pocketbook, of Vancouver.

The north-bank Fraser road ends just east of Harrison at Agassiz, where a broad meadow against the mountains supports a Canadian government experimental farm. The traveler, unless he boards the C.P.R. train, can proceed no farther eastward on the north bank. He can cross to the main highway on the south bank by a motor ferry which waddles regularly over to Rosedale and back.

The north bank was once covered by one of the heaviest softwood forests of America. Much of it has been cut out and the rest is disappearing fast before the machine of modern log-ging. This is one of the few places along the Fraser where the coast timber industry still operates on the grand scale—the agile little fallers on their springboards six feet above the ground; the high riggers climbing a hundred feet like monkeys on a stick to top the spar trees; the rigging crew choking the prostrate logs; the donkey engines jerking them up to the sky line and dragging them like marionettes on a string to drop them again on the flat cars; the whole forest, down to the last sapling and sword fern, churned like a battlefield and steaming with the resinous smell of its bloodletting.

The harvest grows faster and fiercer every year with the latest inventions of man and the Fraser still assists the process. Its current carries the great brown booms of logs down to the sawmills at low cost. From the Harrison to the sea the Fraser is a lumber river, smelling of sawdust and wood fire, scarred by the logger's machines, heavy with his freight.

Probably it will always be a lumber river. The new forest is growing again on the hillsides down to the water's edge. A year after the logger's deep layer of slash has been burned off the first green buds emerge from the blackened stumps of maple, wil-low and alder. Fireweed shoots up in a pinkish flame. Blackberries crawl over the charred logs. A few fronds of sword fern uncurl out of the ashes. Under this first shade the tiny seedlings of fir thrust up, stiff and waxy, each bearing a little purple jewel at its tip.

The Fraser's forest, a complex and single organism, which will grow and change by ruthless extermination of the weak over the cycle of centuries, is born again.

Such a forest as lives along the river is insatiable of appetite, ferocious of growth, and jealous of every open foot of earth. Clear a field with years of labor, blast out the stumps, plant a crop, and you will find, if you leave this clearing for a single year, that the forest is reclaiming it.

The bracken and fireweed march over your fences. The maple seeds, each equipped with its own propeller, fly into your field and push down their roots. The alders march like an army. Close behind this advance guard come the first hemlocks, cedars and balsams. In ten years you will have to clear a new forest so thick that you must cut your path through it.

The Fraser's forest, within the range of the coastal rainfall, is a spectacle of energy and power as appalling as the river itself. Mindless, it moves with sure purpose. Voiceless, it murmurs perpetually with the sound of shredded wind in the treetops and the hum of insects in the underbrush. Sightless, it discovers every open space, every cranny between the rocks where it can anchor its roots. Helpless before man's machines, it surges up again the day after he has passed.

So it will always surge—dark at noonday, dank in the rain of winter, dry and crackling in the summer drought, panting under the smoke of autumn fire, forever whispering around you its dismal secrets.

Man cannot live long under its oppression, beside the giant vegetables that reduce him to a creeping pygmy. Wildly he hacks it down to let in the sunlight and restore his own stature. Beleaguered by this numberless army, he fights back the hungry growth at the edge of his little clearing. And when he is buried, as you may see in many an abandoned farmstead, the forest weaves its new roots among his bones.

Yet there is an inner beauty in the forest unnoticed in the green smear of timber on a hillside or in the massive shape of individual trees. The forest should be examined more closely. What can equal the bark of a fir tree when a straight shaft of morning sun reveals its deep wrinkles, like the wrinkles of a friendly face? What palette can duplicate the thousand shades of green under the changing slant of sun on foliage? What painter can convey the gulfs of shadow, the ceaseless movement, the almost liquid quality of the forest's ceiling under the wind?

The minutiae of this growth are complicated beyond description—the maple bud streaked with the color of wine and pouring out its blossom like a handful of green jewels; the tight purple catkin of alder dangling from the bare branch in the first hours of spring; the uncurling frond of maidenhair fern, like a bishop's crosier; the shaggy brown stalks of sword fern, hanging down at first like the trunks of elephants; the yellow violet and the pink bleeding heart beside the swamp; the white fungus growth of Indian pipes, the scarlet trumpets of wild honeysuckle, the white faces of trilliums; and in the autumn the maple leaves tiling the forest floor in yellow.

No painter has caught even its hues and perhaps none will ever convey the overpowering presence of the forest. No writer has recorded the forest's whisper, no poet has written down its song, and no myth, no Paul Bunyan, has emerged from it. It is too big, perhaps, for man's imagination.

The cubic content of matter involved in the chemistry of the forest is difficult to believe until you have seen it. An acre of fir trees perhaps 150 feet high and averaging three or four feet through the butt at a man's height from the ground, will produce 14,000 cubic feet of merchantable timber. Five logs will fill a flatcar. One fir tree will provide enough lumber for a small bungalow. I know a spot where you can touch, without moving, three cedar trees, the smallest 12 feet in diameter at shoulder height. I have seen a hollow cedar stump, burned centuries ago, 25 feet across at ground level.

The forest, and man's instinctive loathing of it, breeds a special human species.

The logger who cuts it and dumps it into the river is dark and desperate of soul like the thing he destroys. From the gloom of the forest he flees to the city's lights and the company of his kind. The retreat out of the woods and into the saloon and brothel is the reaction of men who, without knowing it, are sickened by the proliferation of dumb and senseless life that dwarfs their own and mocks the weak grip of all animals upon the earth.

The logger cuts the forest and moves on, leaving the black mark of progress behind him. The settler clears away the littered debris and plants his seed. But, as the forest grows up again beside his fences, it puts its stamp upon him also.

The pioneers who made the first clearings, and their sons after them—two generations at least to make a farm—are dour men with lean, hard faces, with the unmistakable thin hands of axmen, with eyes ever turning to watch the forest's advance upon their land.

By inherited skill they know how to tame the forest briefly to their purpose. Of logs they build their houses. Of split cedar boards they lay their floors. Of split cedar shakes they make their enduring roofs.

The first man who lived here knew still better the uses of every kind of tree. The Indian made his fish nets of cedar roots, he wove the stringy cedar bark into rope and clothing. He hollowed the cedar bowl into a canoe which could ride the storms of the open sea. He made his bow of the tough yew. He carved logs into totem poles, masks and exquisite images of bird, animal and demon to record his history, to illustrate his myths, and to express his religion in his only form of writing.

Thus, from the beginning, the forest, even more than the river itself, was the great pervasive fact in the life of all men who lived in the lower river valley. It has left its imprint even on the modern British Columbian who lives in cities at the river's mouth. All of us are restless and uneasy when we move away to open country and no longer can see the forest that we love, hate and fear. All of us yearn to enter the forest and lose ourselves in it, but in a little while we rush out of it again to seek the sunlight and the open sky.

The south bank of the river was once covered by the same forest that still remains in patches on the north bank. Stumps which will resist decay for a century still stand in the south-bank hayfields. But most of the forest has been removed, for, as is obvious as soon as you have crossed the New Westminster bridge, the south bank is covered with a soil which must encourage any farmer to clear it.

Another fact immediately reveals itself, a fact of significance all along the border of the two countries that divide most of North America's soil between them: while the south bank is, in most places, many times as wide as the north bank, nature has been niggardly to Canada even here, as in many other border areas.

Washington State possesses a broad plateau of fertile land, large enough for wheat production, but that land ends approximately at the Canadian border in the interior, just as the great American farm belt around the Great Lakes soon peters out, north of the border, in the sterile Pre-Cambrian shield of Canada. Only a small northwest offshoot of the Washington fertile belt pushes northward into British Columbia along the coast and ends in the mountains at Vancouver.

This outshoot, which forms the south bank of the Fraser, extends less than a hundred miles from the sea. It is so small in Canada, and so fertile, that every yard of it will soon be cultivated. This land from the sea to the north-south barrier of the Coast Range we call the Fraser Valley. The Fraser has cut a valley over eight hundred miles long and much of it, in the interior, will produce crops when it is irrigated, but in the vocabulary of

British Columbia the Fraser Valley means only the stretch from the river delta to the mountains.

This arable space of some 550,000 acres, including the north bank, is one of British Columbia's major possessions. It supports about 100,000 people. It provides the milk of Vancouver. It produces vegetables, some meat (especially feeders from the interior ranches), the hops for British Columbia's beer, small fruits, tree fruits, honey, and pelts from the fur farms. About $15,000,000 worth of agricultural products a year come out of the soil the river laid down here in the leisure of aeons.

From the New Westminster bridge the main road of the south bank plunges immediately into the farm country. Your first glance reveals the richness of the river soil. The crops of hay, grain, strawberries, raspberries and vegetables are heavier than in almost any other part of Canada. The herds of Jerseys and Holsteins lie deep in clover like a picture on a calendar.

Unlike the cedar-shake cabins of the new settlers, at the edge of the old forest, the farmhouses and fat barns here are modern and substantial, the people obviously prosperous. They are not so wealthy, say, as the farmers of New York and Pennsylvania, but they have a steady income, mostly from milk, while the cereal industries of the prairies are always at the continual mercy of the weather.

In the valley the rain clouds, moving from the Pacific, deposit enough moisture as they strike the mountains to keep the land green all the year, green even in winter, for snow seldom falls. This idyllic pastoral country resembles the valley of the Hudson or the Susquehanna with one striking difference—here every field and farmhouse is set against a backdrop of high and snowy mountains. On every side, except the west, the lush fields run up to the mountain rim and end there suddenly.

For the most part the valley is flat and low enough to be soaked and sometimes submerged by winter rain and by the river's summer floods, but in places the land rises in gentle hills and changes its loamy quality to gravel. Little space except on these few infertile knobs is left uncultivated. Year by year the latest settlers are clearing and plowing what remains of the good soil at the foot of the mountains. Yet even here, where the conquest of the forest seems complete and permanent, second growth is under way in every spot missed by the plow. On some of the timber limits cut in the first days of settlement and since neglected the trees are now large enough for the saw.

At the Green Timbers—a rather pathetic name which commemorates the forest now gone—the government of British Columbia is using the precious valley soil to produce the future timber crops of the province. In its tree nursery it grows millions of young Douglas fir which will be transplanted to logged-off areas all along the coast where repeated fires have destroyed the natural reproduction. Man is moving the forest of the valley out of this rich earth to mature it in gravel soils on the sea benches.

Many of the older valley farmers of this generation are veterans of the war against the forest. They remember when it cost as much as $500 to clear an acre here. Their sons know this only as an open farm land but are reminded of the harder days by the black and weathered stumps still standing on many farms. Every winter a few more stumps will be blasted out while in the remoter settlements the smoke of clearing fires will hang heavy throughout the autumn.

The valley farmer knows trees and welcomes them, in moderation. He preserves a few choice maples to shade his house. He plants apples, pears, plums, and large orchards of cherries, which specially flourish in this soil. The nakedness of the valley, which followed the first assault on the evergreen forest, has been amply clothed by deciduous growth. For the first time the western coastal land of Canada has been tamed to man's use. The scars of his clearing have finally healed. Within a few years the valley will be as neat, cozy and pampered as the land of Europe, as the farms of the upper Rhine, with the Alps behind them.

The main road runs through the center of the valley and for

some seventy miles the river is out of the traveler's sight. Just east of the New Westminster bridge one branch of the highway turns south to Seattle and the other continues eastward to the British Columbia interior. It passes through half a dozen prosperous-looking villages, each distinguished by the modern kind of schools that the dairy farmers can afford. The roadside has not escaped the universal American blight of hot-dog stands and garish billboards but for the most part the valley is unmarred and every turn in the road presents some new glimpse of crop and orchard against the background of the mountains.

Forty-four miles from Vancouver the road drops down a hillside into the town of Abbotsford, close to the American border (which can be crossed here by a side road), and then runs straight eastward through man's largest feat of reclamation along the length of the Fraser.

The broad expanse of land around Sumas, as flat as the surface of the road, was, until some twenty years ago, the bottom of a shallow lake formed by one of the Fraser's backwaters. Into this lake and on into the Fraser the wild Vedder used to pour its snow water. The lake would rise in winter and flood the valley around it.

A farmer named Edward Barrow, who looked like Lincoln and, like Lincoln, split fence rails by day and read the classics beside his kitchen stove by night, looked out for years on the Sumas floods and coveted the land beneath them. He had a crackbrained scheme for damming back the inflow of the Fraser, which oozed through a narrow channel between the hills of its southern bank. He would also put a strait jacket on the Vedder. Then he would pump out Sumas Lake and farm the lake bottom.

No one would listen to old Ed Barrow until he went into politics, got himself elected to the legislature in Victoria, and, under his friend John Oliver, was promoted to the ministry of agriculture. Then he went to work. The engineers said Barrow's dream was practical enough, but costly. Would the crops of the lake bottom pay the expense of reclamation?

The government was poor in those days, having inherited a gutted treasury and the aftermath of a boom. Why, it asked, should public money be spent to provide a relatively small farm area, however rich, when most of the valley only awaited the settler's ax and plow? But somehow, for he was a persistent man and, in his quiet way, aflame with a vision, Barrow persuaded the government and the legislature.

The backwater of the Fraser was diked. Sumas Lake was drained out as far as possible and the rest of it pumped into the river. The lake bottom emerged into the drying sunshine. The Vedder was imprisoned in a wide canal and, when the rising level required it, was lifted into the Fraser by pumps.

After $1,800,000 had been spent—a large sum for British Columbia then—Barrow could look out from the window of his house and see 20,000 acres of lake bottom ready to be cropped and around it 10,000 acres more which had been flooded by the Vedder every year. That was a great day for Barrow.

His troubles were only beginning, however. Agriculture was not prosperous after World War I, few settlers could pay the price the government must charge for the new land if it was to cover the cost of reclamation. Before the land could be sold it sprouted a forest of willow and a crop of politics at Victoria beyond the reaping of the harried minister of agriculture. Still, through cabinet wrangles and legislative crises, Barrow persisted in his faith. By the time Oliver's government had perished and Barrow had retired to his farm, the settlers were beginning to move into the old lake. Soon all of it was under the plow.

Today, from the white colonial house that he built beside a row of towering cottonwoods at the edge of the old lake, Barrow can look out in his old age on the dream that has become one of British Columbia's proudest possessions. Across the lake bottom sweep the heaviest hay crops in the country, fields of hops, orchards, nurseries of shrubs and roses. Barrow, I suppose, has done more to subdue the Fraser than any other man. He will die beside it, content.

East of Sumas stands Chilliwack, last and largest of the valley towns. It is the ideal farm community. Its main street is wide and modern, its stores substantial, its homes surrounded by flowers. Everybody in Chilliwack's population of 4,000 seems to have a garden heavy with fruit, vegetables and blossom. Around the town the pasture lands are checkerboarded with cherry orchards, the crops from which Chilliwack celebrates in annual festival.

No visitor with a taste for pastoral scenery and fruit will pass by the farmwife's little stand at the edge of the road outside Chilliwack. It is the accepted ritual of the seasoned traveler on his way to Cariboo to stop and buy cherries and strawberries in June, raspberries in July, the first Yellow Transparents in late August, vegetables, keeping apples and honey in the autumn.

Chilliwack is the capital of a culture unknown west of the Rockies in Canada until the present farm generation grew up. From Chilliwack to the sea the Fraser's earth has bred the kind of folk who live in the St. Lawrence Valley and are different in their life and in their ownership of land from the cereal farmers who work the open stretches of the prairies. If the word had not taken on a false implication, it could be said that the Fraser has begun to produce a bold peasantry, their country's pride.

These are peasants in the old-fashioned and best sense of the term—people who love and cling to the soil, and maintain its virtue, asking no more than the fruits of their labor, but people who enjoy a standard of living high among the farmers of America. They have cleared, fertilized and befriended the river soil, the soil has responded, the milk and farmstuffs have flowed into Vancouver, and a species of permanent farmfolk—steady, solid, educated and co-operative in the joint life of the community—has joined in permanent marriage with the river.

15   The Canyon

A T CHILLIWACK THE END OF THE VALLEY AND THE BEGINNING
of the canyon are in sight. The mountains are closing in. The
flat farm land has narrowed into a sharp wedge. The second
growth and a few patches of virgin timber mark the end of the
settler's progress. A few miles eastward the road and the two
railways are squeezed between the mountains and the river edge.

The river is still wide, calm and leisurely after its debouch-
ment from the Coast Range, but it is beginning to twist and
wriggle. The marshy banks of the valley are cut by the first
sharp outthrusts of rock. We are entering the westward reaches
of the canyon.

When the road crosses the little torrent of Silver Creek,
plunges into the last real coastal forest, and emerges on the
riverbank at Hope, a hundred miles from Vancouver, the traveler
looks up suddenly to realize that he is in the mountains, and
that the river channel, after its course east and west, has turned
at right angles and is running straight north and south.

Just beyond Hope the first mountain tributary, the Coquihalla, enters the Fraser from the northeastward and provides
a passage for the Kettle Valley Railway into southern British
Columbia, and the approach of a new highway leading to the
same territory. The angle formed by the junction of the Coquihalla and the Fraser is a bench large enough to accommodate the
old Hudson's Bay fort of Hope and the village that has replaced
it. Standing on the main street, which fronts on the grassy

bank, you have space to perceive the river's first great turn and the increasing power of its current.

Already the mountains are crowding the river. In their confusion they reveal no clear passage upstream or down. A perpetual white cross of snow across the mountain that looms over Hope from the south stands out like a farewell guidepost on the friendly western slope. From here on road, railway and traveler must advance against the western ramparts of the continent.

The old steamboats, as we have seen, paddled upstream beyond Hope, since Douglas's road from the interior did not reach downriver beyond Yale. A few tugs, guiding booms of timber from the tributary valleys, still ply these waters, though the current is increasing its speed with every mile. It is hard to believe that the captains of the gold rush, driving their flimsy craft against the current, considered this easy going.

At the northern side of Hope the modern road crosses on a long bridge to the western bank of the Fraser, where there is ample flat space to carry both the road and the Canadian Pacific Railway's main line. The timbered bench and a few straggling settlers' fields are deceptive, masking the narrowed river gulch.

As the road leaves this brief covert and winds back to the river at Yale, the mask is removed. The canyon stares out in its nakedness. The mountains, deep cut, wrinkled and broken by perpetual slides, stand perpendicular at the water's edge. Only the force of water drunk up from all the moisture of the inland can drive its way through this maze of stone.

Yale squats upon a sloping ridge and looks at the inner gate of the canyon, a gate opened grudgingly in a thin crack. An old town, as towns go in this country, Yale has had a varied fortune. Its single street above the river has known the reeling days of the gold rush, the scream of steamboat whistles, the answering shout from the shore, the majesty of Douglas, the law of Britain in Ned McGowan's comic revolution, and the brawl of the railway builders. Once its name, as the terminus of the Cariboo Road, was known throughout the world. Here men entered the gold lands and here, if they were lucky, emerged from the canyon with their treasure.

Little is left of this history—only the miners' little church, some cherry trees that they planted, a few crumbling chimneys, and the sand bars of the river, where they washed for gold before Cariboo was found. But Yale will always be remembered by every traveler who passes through it as the gate into the canyon.

From here the railways on either side of the river must cling to niches scooped out of the living rock or grope by tunnels through the cliffs. The road must find what space it can beside the tracks of the western bank, must be shored up on walls of masonry, hung over the river on trestles, swung across the railway and back again in the engineer's search for every niggard passage.

Now the real presence of the Fraser is felt. It is so close that an automobile or a locomotive skidding sideways will fall directly into the current, as a locomotive did some years ago. In places only a fragile barricade of dry walling stands between the automobile driver and the river, far below. On many a turn he looks straight down on the swirling water and perceives that it is tearing at the foundations of the road, spreading its bars of sand broadcast against the cliffs, eating them away again, licking at the roots of trees to suck them into its maw, and forever dragging down its slides of rock, earth and vegetation in ceaseless struggle against its prison. And over it, as if they would fall inward at any moment, lean the angry mountains.

We have followed the canyon before in the path of Fraser, the miners and the salmon. It will be unnecessary, and quite futile, to attempt any detailed description of this prodigy. One thing, however, should be understood: no matter how many guidebooks the traveler has read, no matter what photographs he has seen, or how many other rivers he has explored, he will find the Fraser canyon denying all his expectations.

If this book has suggested, for instance, that the Fraser canyon is comparable in size or grandeur to the canyon of the Colorado or the other major wounds cut across the body of the United States, if it has represented the Fraser as one of the largest rivers of the world in volume of water or extent of drainage, it is guilty of exaggeration. If it has seemed to suggest even that the canyon is beautiful, the picture is false.

No, the Fraser is not among the greatest rivers in girth or content, its canyon is a needle's eye between the interior and the coast, and its beauty is imagined only by those who have lived long with it and come to love its ugliness. Not vast as river canyons are measured in America, not beautiful as beauty is usually judged, but certainly unique.

Again and again I have traveled the canyon by train and automobile in all seasons, in the warming days of spring when the flowers are coming out, in the stifling days of summer when the walls are oven-hot under the sun, in the yellow days of autumn, and in the snowbanks of midwinter, and I have asked myself why the canyon invariably staggers the imagination, appals the spirit of man or dazzles it with an instant vision of beauty, according to his individual nature.

I think it is because this canyon, beyond all others, is planless, meaningless and void. In it is no sense of direction or purpose, nothing but the moving current to show that it is carrying the gulped-down waters of a hundred rivers and a thousand lakes in sure passage to the ocean. Between mountains that might have been dumped down like a sack of coal the canyon is all senseless welter, inchoate jumble and blind chaos. Because he loves order, man is fascinated and frightened by this sight.

The mountain barrier was laid here to divide the interior from the coast forever. No passage was to be left. The continent was to be sealed tight. Thus it appears, and the river is an accident only. Somehow, against all nature's arrangements, it has discovered a fault in the dam, has patiently threaded its way, foot by foot, has penetrated the soft rock, searched out the secret gorge, the hidden tunnel, and, in a million years of labor, has finally upset the continental plan.

Man witnesses, therefore, a spectacle of nature which appears unnatural, a convulsion of rock and water which still seems to be in active movement. Not only the river but the mountains have the semblance of motion. To the human eye they are shifting, heaving and bursting into new shapes, as if the whole land mass were yet molten and boiling. And in this endless derangement, viewed from the bottom of the changing trench that divides it, a man feels that he is watching a blind struggle within the very flesh of nature, an aberration of law which must end soon in exhaustion and collapse.

Such feelings, which sound absurd when one attempts to analyze and set them down, but arise inevitably when you are within the canyon beside the dizzy flow of the river, do not make the canyon seem beautiful or grand but only abnormal, shattering and unreal. At any rate, this bewilderment, this sense of witnessing something the eyes of man were not intended to see, drags us back year after year to look upon the thing that delights and terrifies us, and drives us scurrying out again to the genial coast or the open lands of the interior.

But within this mad whirl of rock and water some glimpses of beauty break through the crust of ugliness in defiance of the mountains and the river. A crooked pine tree overhanging the cliff, black against the river like a drawing in pen and ink; the narrow islands in the river channel, carved out in the shape of battleships with trees for smokestacks, forever trying to break their anchors and move upstream; a sand bar deposited at floodtime and laid out flat, smooth and shiny in the sun; a lurch of shadow across the mountains; a green drip of timber down a gulch; the slant of dawn or sunset between the peaks; the glint of moonlight on the metal of the river; a looming face of rock in the dawn—these little moments of beauty punctuate the timeless fury.

When came this canyon, this tumult of rock and water? The geologists hold various theories but they have reached no final conclusions. Much more work must be done before a true geological history of the Fraser can be written. The Colorado presents its detailed record in the visible pageant of successive geological layers along the face of its canyon. No such book lies open on the Fraser.

Having talked to several eminent geologists and come away more confused than ever, I asked Dr. John F. Walker, British Columbia deputy minister of mines, and the most distinguished student of the province's geology, to set down in layman's terms what he knew about the origins of the river. Dr. Walker's account, deliberately written in the simplest, nontechnical terms, shows that the Fraser, like all America's rivers, is the battered creature of the continent's first birth, its emergence from the sea, its subsidence and re-emergence, and the slow erosion of its mountains.

The history of the Fraser [Dr. Walker writes] commences long before the day of man and, perhaps, before mammals first appeared on this world. Somewhere between the time when dinosaurs wallowed in the swamps where the foothills of the Rocky Mountains now are, and the little eohippus, the terrier-sized ancestor of our horse, ran about on toes and not on hoofs, the drainage pattern of the Fraser River began to take shape. The drainage history of the river is thus lost in antiquity and it can only be pieced together bit by bit as we learn more about the drainage pattern of western America in the rocks and rocky structure which have controlled it.

About the close of the Mesozoic, when the dinosaurs were disappearing, the greater part of British Columbia west of where the Rocky Mountains now stand was a land with streams flowing westerly to the ocean and easterly to the Inland Sea. There were mountains where the Coast Mountains, and where the Selkirks and Cariboo Mountains now stand, but they were not as high and rugged. The valleys were wide and the streams had gentle gradients. Between the mountains there was a great rolling plain where the interior plateaux now are.

The building of the Rocky Mountains affected streams that flowed easterly into the old Inland Sea. It altered the courses of many of them and caused them to flow along a trench that developed between the old land mass to the west and the rising land mass to the east. The old land mass was elevated and the streams that flowed westerly to the Pacific Ocean were deeply entrenched.

Some time after the streams entrenched themselves, sediments were deposited in the great valleys so formed in what is now the interior of the province. These sediments, which belonged to the Eocene, when little eohippus appeared, were later disturbed and tilted, and lavas flowed out upon them. In some places later sediments were laid down upon the first lavas, and still later other lavas poured out upon them, filling some of the valleys to great depths.

The drainage of the Fraser River north of the Chilcotin originally appears to have been to the east, to the old Inland Sea, and from south of the Chilcotin it was south and westerly to the ocean. The building of the Rocky Mountains and the warping and uplifting of the old land mass resulted in the capture of the old river that flowed to the Inland Sea by the river that flowed south and west to the ocean. Thus the Fraser now heads in the Rocky Mountains and flows westerly into the Rocky Mountain Trench, thence north-westerly along it to the Big Bend, near Prince George, thence southerly across the interior plateaux and between the Coast Mountains and the Cascade Mountains, where it turns westerly to the ocean.

The outpouring of the lavas has caused minor changes in its course, but the Fraser follows essentially the courses of two very old streams that entrenched themselves deeply, early in the Tertiary period.

When one drives through the Fraser Canyon one gets

the impression of a gorge-like valley, a youthful valley, something quite young. This is true only in part. The upland slopes, away from the valley, are those of a mature valley. The great gorge itself is old. It is only the canyon in the very bottom of the gorge that is young. The canyon would not appear as young were it not for the hard granitic rocks which have confined the river in its lower reaches above Hope.

Few travelers pause to consider this depressing story of agelong change and convulsion, which make the present road and even the present river seem incidental details, soon to be sponged out by some new planetary whim. For the moment the road and the river are wonder enough for brief human eyes.

From Yale the road follows the western bank to Spuzzum, which is halfway between Hope and Lytton. At Spuzzum, as the miners found, there is no further space even for a trail. The river must be bridged to carry the traveler to the broader eastern bank. Here, as we have seen, Trutch built of wood and coiled wire the first suspension bridge west of the Rockies in Canada. Modern engineers could not improve on Trutch's site. On it they built a bridge of concrete and steel which, seen from the hillside above it, lies across the river like a great silvery insect.

While the railways still follow the river's edge, the road winds upward from the bridge, high on the bench of the eastern bank. After the cliffs above Yale the terrain here is relatively easy for a few miles. The road can swing well back from the river on a rolling and timbered ridge.

One realizes all at once—for the transformation has been gradual and nowhere sharply marked—that this is no longer the timber of the coast. The underbrush has disappeared. The trees stand far apart and among them are the first red trunks of bull pine. We are now beyond the reach of the coastal clouds, which have broken on the mountains to pour their moisture on the western slope. This is the westernmost stretch of the interior

Dry Belt, a crooked finger reaching down the channel of the river. But still some of the hills, moistened by winter snow, are clothed with small timber, with the higher mountains bare behind them.

The easy bench above Spuzzum does not last long. Soon, as the canyon narrows again, the road is climbing higher around the cliffs above the river. It pursues many side valleys to find a crossing over the creases of the mountains. It swings far inland and almost loses itself in tortuous zigzags and dark gorges and, still climbing, finally returns to the canyon at a summit of a thousand feet above the river. Here no footing can be found on the cliffs. Like the railways far below, the road must go underground in two tunnels. Between them it rides in several places on wooden stilts.

From this eminence one receives an entirely new impression of the canyon. From the river level it appeared cramped and perpendicular. Now it is seen to be a minor groove lying at the bottom of a vast and open valley, so wide that the river is almost lost in it.

If you had not inspected them at close range, you could not believe that the cliffs stand upright beside the river, that down below you the water is foaming through Hell's Gate, that along its rocks Fraser had to creep on hands and knees and cling to the woven-bark ladders of the Indians.

At this distance the rough spots are smoothed out. The cliffs, the river, the two railway lines and the canyon itself are dwarfed in the immensity of the trench. The convulsion of the mountains and the channel through them have plan, purpose and order after all.

When you were within it, the channel seemed too constricted to carry its cargo of interior waters. Now you see that all the waters of America could flow here without filling the trench. There is room and to spare for every trickle dripping from the snow of the western Rockies, for all the lakes and rivers the Fraser has swallowed across the interior plateau, for all the silt it has sluiced from the clay banks of its upper reaches, for all the rock slides it has scooped out of the mountainsides, for all the burden of earth, rock particles, sand and vegetation it bears westward and dumps into the ocean.

In broad daylight, with the sun straight above, this valley, though garishly colored by green timber, dark rock, and the brown coil of the river, has a flat, monotonous look, like a rather inferior photograph. That is how the photographs usually present it. Only in the early morning or the late evening does its true shape materialize.

At sunrise, when the first light strikes across it, the trench takes on a third dimension. The cliffs rush out between the shadows. The mountains march forward in a single stride. The lower hills are folded like wrinkled cloth. A gigantic design of sharp black and white is pressed down, as it were, from above.

Then, in the evening dusk, when haze is dropped like a thin curtain, the flat, gray surfaces of daylight fade out in a tinge of lingering purple. The cliffs are smoothed off again. The mountains recede. The whole trench turns soft.

In a still night, through a gulch of dark, the sound of the river comes up in a faint insect buzzing. The lights of the trains flicker along the bottom of the trench for an instant and go out. The lights of railway towns like Boston Bar and North Bend are no bigger than pin points.

If there is a moon, the trench takes on shape once more, a vague velvet shape, too spectacular to be quite real, a contrived stage effect. In the middle of it the river lies motionless in a solid glister like ice, like lead which has just hardened in its mold. Presently a new river of mist rolls down to cover the river of water, to blot out the last look of reality, to make the trench a mere daub of dark pigment, laid on lavishly by a reckless hand. But underneath the darkness, deep down below the coiling river of mist, the river of water is still hurrying to sea—as Thomas Wolfe said of the Hudson, "the dark, eternal river, full of strange, secret time."

We have no Wolfe or other poet to sing the song of the Fraser. Until he appears, the river must be presented in engineers' figures, in geologists' maps, and in flat photographs. Perhaps that is no matter. The men who have seen it, from Fraser onward, know what it is and the mystery it holds, without need of poet or painter, and will know as long as memory lasts.

From the heights the road crawls down uncertainly, with many loops, grades and detours; over many green mountain streams; through gullies where, on the hottest days, currents of air blow down in cool puffs from the upper snows; and at last out upon the bare clay benches of the Dry Belt, where the Thompson joins the Fraser at Lytton.

Lytton, 71 miles from Hope, is an ancient town, more ancient than any built by white men in America. Here, it will be recalled, Fraser found a thriving Indian community, centuries old. The confluence of two great rivers and the natural trails of men's travel made this one of the crossways of the continent. The gold rush surged through Lytton and built the white man's town beside the huts of the natives. The two transcontinental railways were pushed together at this point, to intersect and cross from one side of the Fraser to the other. Yet geography, the road, the railways, and the generous flat space of the townsite have never been able to make Lytton more than a huddle of hotels, stores, garages and houses, hardly worthy of the name of the English statesman and romantic author that it bears.

No one will forget Lytton, however. Where the two rivers meet at the north edge of the town the greenish waters of the Thompson, cutting a sharp and solid line across the brown of the Fraser, present an unforgettable conflict of color and force. Two streams of water, which have risen a few miles apart in the mountains and, dividing, have flowed hundreds of miles in diverse directions, join at last to create the full bulk of the Frazer. This is the nexus of the interior drainage system.

The main road to the interior and the railways turn eastward from Lytton along the Thompson. We shall explore that river later. Meanwhile let us follow up the Fraser on the side road north to Lillooet.

It has been my habit to reach Lytton from the coast in darkness and meet the dawn in the canyon beyond the town. In the whole course of the Fraser this has always been my favorite glimpse of morning. The dawn here is stark and violent. It is pungent with the exudation of sagebrush and pine, with the heavy sweetness of syringa and alfalfa in the spring, with the alkali dust of summer, and the smell of dried poplar leaves in autumn. The colors of this dawn are too vivid for the painter. The snow of the peaks turns to orange. The bulk of the mountains floats in blue haze. The walls of the valley glow deep red where the rust of iron has smeared them. Safe from sight, nature can squeeze out the paint tubes, load her brush, and let herself go.

The road from Lytton to Lillooet, 47 miles, was built long after the gold rush. It is narrow, full of sharp curves and dizzy switchbacks. At the Big Slide a mile of broken rock is constantly rolling down upon it. After keeping to a bench above the river, it drops by a steep descent to the water's edge. You can almost dangle your hand in the river as you drive on to Lillooet.

The town of Lillooet, product of the Harrison route, stands on the west bank of the Fraser. To reach it from the Lytton road you cross the river by bridge, and the crossing is worth your while.

Drowsing on the riverbank under its old poplar trees, Lillooet is not much changed from the days of the rush. Among its people you will notice the quality that distinguishes all the people of Cariboo—a complete detachment from the world, a steady feeling of security in good times and bad, and above all, a stubborn will to be let alone.

Though the Pacific Great Eastern Railway runs through Lillooet, the town has been left pretty completely alone up to now. Like every district in British Columbia, the environs of the town are changing under the impact of a growing population. The fertility of Lillooet's soil will change it still more. On both sides of the river here the earth, the summer heat, and the protection of the high mountains produce the finest tree fruit in Canada, better even and earlier than the famous crops of Okanagan. Such an opportunity will not be neglected much longer.

Until recent years fruit and vegetables were grown around Lillooet mostly in small patches for home use, with the aid of a few streams flumed from the hills. Lately more of the benchland has been taken up, mostly by Japanese, who were excluded from the coast during World War II. Already a few fruit farms are irrigated by water pumped out of the river. When cheap electric power is available for the pumps, the entire bench on both sides of the river, from Lytton far up into the Cariboo, should be under crop.

This power will come, presumably, out of the new plant at Bridge River, or from other plants on the Fraser itself. The traveler will waste no time if he turns aside at Lillooet to investigate the Bridge River country.

The road out of Lillooet westward follows the old Harrison route to the western end of Seton Lake. From there on the Pacific Great Eastern Railway is fastened to the lake's precipitous northern bluffs but the road ends. You may take the train or journey down the lake, like the miners, by boat.,

Halfway along the lake shore stands Mission Mountain. Over it an unimaginable road climbs to the headwaters of Bridge River, which, flowing southwestward in a deep valley, empties into the Fraser above Lillooet. This road, presenting Seton and Anderson Lakes as little saucers of deep blue with flecks of purple, is worth pursuing on its own account. Beyond its summit, in the valley of Bridge River, are the mining villages of Pioneer and Bralorne, where deep shafts have carved out the narrow, rich gold veins, some of the original sources of placer gold on the Fraser.

Bridge River has been dammed so that its waters can be diverted by a tunnel through Mission Mountain down to Seton

Lake to turn the power turbines. In the end the expanded power of Bridge River, lighting Vancouver and irrigating the interior benches, should be far more valuable than the Bridge River gold.

This has been a digression from our main route. Instead of crossing the Fraser into Lillooet we could have kept to the eastern bank and followed it northward for 21 miles over a high bench, which is eroded by gullies and cut by queer rock outcroppings in colors of crimson, magenta, yellow and orange.

This land, like all the Fraser bench in the Dry Belt, is filled with the chemicals of growth but needs water to bring them to life. Every trickle running out of the mountains has been guided down to some tiny farm on the lip of the river, some square of green on the brown range about the size of this book, as it seems, in the compass of the valley. Such a farm is just large enough to grow winter hay for a few cattle, which graze in summer on the bunch grass. It is enough to support a poor family of whites or Indians, who seem to live abundantly on nothing.

Ancient log houses, a few adobe ruins, lopsided log barns, scowling, white-faced cattle by the roadside, an Indian family perpetually on the move in its wagon or dilapidated automobile, hayfields which puff up sudden spurts of alfalfa perfume in your nostrils, miles of the cracked range, behind them the low, rolling hills of sage and bunch grass, and always below you, in a gut of brown clay, the oily substance of the river, hardly recognizable as the same river of the lower canyon—this is the Fraser trench in the Dry Belt. It stretches on, with very little change, into the first ranks of the Rockies.

Now look back, downriver, for I have always supposed this to be one of the great views of the world. The highest Rockies are more awesome, but the Lillooet mountains, at dawn or in the evening dusk, have the texture and the wonder of a dream. They hang like draperies of soft, flimsy stuff, almost transparent and deep azure. Woven through this cloth is the gleaming thread of the river.

225

No photograph can ever catch this translucence, nor have I seen any study in oils which conveys its look of unreality. A ten-minute water-color daub, executed by old George Southwell from a bluff beside the road, and now hanging before me, somehow has affixed a brief memory of the river and the mountains in the shadow time of twilight. It is fixed forever in the eye of the beholder and in the life of every man who has lived here.

So chaotic are these mountains, so wide the trench where the river can cut its way at will through soft clay, that the geography of the country is never clear to the traveler. Ernest Carson, who has driven this road all his life, perhaps more often than any other man, was amazed not long ago when he saw an aerial photograph taken directly above Lillooet. For the first time he realized that from the town northward the river curves in a perfect letter S to the ramparts of Pavilion Mountain. I doubt that many of the men who live along the riverbanks have noted that fact. All sense of direction is obscured among the clay hills, the deep gullies, and the windings of the river.

By an up-and-down road, past the mouth of Bridge River on the left, through the old Fountain ranch, where gold was found in '58, and among open stands of bull pine, you turn inland at last from the Fraser up a narrow draw to the hamlet of Pavilion. It is not much to look at—a gaunt store, a railway shed, and a cluster of cottages so deep in the draw that the sun cannot touch them in winter—but this is the center of the river community, the natural crossroads between the Fraser and the interior.

Since the farms from here south toward Lillooet were far from the main road, they depended upon the Pavilion store for outside supplies, and on the flour mill nearby, where their wheat was ground by stones imported from England. The still more isolated farmers on the west bank of the Fraser, lacking any road, also traded at Pavilion, as they trade today, crossing the river by rowboat and sometimes swimming their horses.

Several stores have stood on this site but all of them contained the same goods, the same customers, and the same splendid odors. What a smell of leather chaps, bridles and harness, of cotton bolts, bacon, coal oil, sweet biscuits, Indian buckskin gloves, and of Indians themselves emerge from the store's dark cavern, mixed with the smell of sweet peas, poppies and marigolds growing in the little garden beside—a garden planted by a beautiful woman, who hated ugliness!

What a brave illusion, under this nostalgic flavor, that you are living in the safer and more spacious days of your grandfather! With what unfailing excitement, twice a week, the train climbed the hill from the river and, with a last long gasp of relief, wriggled triumphantly up to the platform! How earnestly we waited for the Coast papers in the days before the radio and read them, every line, until we knew more about the world than the city folks! How lonely it seemed in the draw when the train labored out of it again and began the desperate climb around the edge of Pavilion Mountain!

The Indians' trail from the river to the Bonaparte Valley ran here and their village still stands, a rather pathetic company of log shacks around a church with a white wooden tower.

As I drove past the village in the first hours of daylight, an aged Indian woman, Annie, invariably would open the door of her cabin and stare out with amazement as if no traveler had ever come this way before. (She usually had a calf, which she kept in her house or in a structure of packing cases, and fattened on grain which she swept off the platform of the railway.) But in the home of the Pavilion Indians, who used to war with the tribes from the interior in the Marble Canyon and left their sign writings on the rocks there, little life stirs today. These people are content to work for a few weeks in the hay harvest, to grow a few sacks of potatoes and shoot a few deer and doze in the sun. Their placid faces, like every Indian face along the Fraser, disclose the deep wisdom of the child.

From the Indian village—since the river canyon affords no

practical alternative—the road climbs straight up Pavilion Mountain on the old Harrison route. Halfway up you can toss a stone directly on the white Indian church. Eastward from the village, between cliffs of granite and marble, lies the entrance to Marble Canyon. And above looms the ragged top of Pavilion, hiding its secret.

This is the border of Carson's kingdom. To understand the Fraser country better, and the kind of rivermen who live in it, let us pause here and look back some ninety years.

16   Carson's Kingdom

IN 1858 A YOUTH OF NINETEEN, WHO HAD BEEN BORN IN
Edinburgh and taken to Ohio by his parents, joined one of the
immigrant trains moving westward to Oregon by wagon. He
was powerful in build, handsome in countenance, quiet in speech,
somber in mind. His name was Robert Corson, but as no one
would pronounce or spell it that way, he accepted the more
common name of Carson. In this version it was to become
famous and honorable in British Columbia.

Young Carson did not reach the Oregon seacoast. Somewhere along the trail Indians massacred everyone else in the
immigrant train. He alone escaped, under circumstances so desperate that he would never talk about them afterwards.

In the mixture of recklessness and caution that divided this
remarkable character, the first, for the moment, prevailed.
Hearing of gold on the Fraser, he turned north and made his way
by the Hudson's Bay trail through the Okanagan Valley to
Fort Kamloops, then up the North Thompson and westward
through the mountains to the Bonaparte Valley.

This route had long been used by the fur brigades and
already miners were following it, in advance of the men who
were pushing up the Fraser from its mouth. Carson does not
seem to have been much attracted by gold, probably because
few miners were then making wages. He collected a string of
horses and began packing supplies between the miners' camps.

From the Clinton country he moved westward into the

Kelly Creek pass and found himself on the bank of the Fraser. Already a trail of sorts had been cut by the miners from Kelly Creek southward beside the Fraser, over the bluffs of Pavilion Mountain, and thence down to Lillooet. The Pavilion trail had become part of the Harrison route to the interior, now being used for the first time.

When Carson reached the summit of Pavilion a mile above sea level and 4,500 feet straight above the Fraser, an extraordinary spectacle greeted him. Instead of the rocky ledge he had expected, he found a rolling green tableland which, being circled by distant peaks, seemed to be a deep cup within the Coast Range. Here was bunch grass such as he had never seen, back of it forests of immense fir trees and red-barked bull pine, bluffs of poplar and, beside a clear stream, shady groves of cottonwood—a little kingdom high in the air, immediately surrounded on all sides by deep gorges, separated from the world as by a moat.

This plateau, which looked like a valley, was about ten miles in diameter. To the south Carson looked down on the winding chasm of Marble Canyon with its three lakes, the size of teardrops. To the west he could stand on a wall of clay and see the Fraser, straight below, no wider from here than his hand. To the north lay the Kelly Creek valley, Kelly Lake itself like a glistening blob of ink, and beside it a smaller blob called Pear Lake. To the east, at the far side of the plateau, rose a gray ridge of granite which dropped down into the central rangeland of British Columbia.

This little kingdom in the clouds Carson resolved to make his own. The others could search for gold farther up the river and in the mountains around Barkerville. He wintered his horses on the luxuriant bunch grass of Pavilion and prepared to stay here and farm this land. Caution had now triumphed over recklessness.

Yet his plan seems reckless enough at this distance. By geography, which he had yet to grasp, he was totally isolated from any market or source of supplies. The miners, it was true, had begun to move up the Harrison trail from the coast and they skirted the west side of Pavilion as they pushed on north, but they brought no supplies. Traveling on foot or grazing their horses by the trail, they would not buy the hay that Carson proposed to grow on his plateau. There was talk of a road, someday, to Cariboo but it would follow the fur brigade route and would not pass this way.

Nevertheless, Carson settled down to farm. The ditches that some forgotten miners had dug to carry water across the plateau and down to their diggings in the canyon of the Fraser Carson used to irrigate a little patch of the parched range. On this he planted his first crop.

With logs hauled out of the woods by horses and squared by his ax he built a cabin and barn. From Marble Canyon he brought limestone to make mortar for his stone chimneys. From the canyon lakes he took ice in the winter and stored it to cool his meat in summer. The fir trees, so dry that they could be burned as soon as they were cut, fed his stove and kept his house warm when the mountain was swept by blizzard and snow blacked the trail. Split jack pine built his fences and some of them stand today as he left them.

The kingdom, except for clothes, a few tools and luxuries like tea, coffee and salt, was self-supporting.

Within a few years Carson was driving swine and freighting hay northward to Clinton to feed the passengers and the stage-coach horses of the new Cariboo Road. He even drove a band of cattle down the Harrison route as far as Lillooet Lake, thence southwesterly to the coast on Howe Sound, and finally—an almost unbelievable feat—through the mountains and forests on the north side of Burrard Inlet. By now his cattle, the few that had survived the journey, were so poor that he had to ferry them across the Inlet and drive them from Gas Town (which was to be Vancouver) to the Fraser Delta.

Here he fattened them for market and here he met the

lady whom he took back to Pavilion as his wife. She was one of the Magees whose farm, on the north bank of the Fraser at its mouth, covers the present Kerrisdale district of Vancouver.

With his increasing herds, the green smear of his alfalfa fields across the brown range, his family of nine boys and girls, Carson was considered one of the most substantial men in the Cariboo. The whole plateau was his and he never left it.

He died in 1911, when his younger children were in their teens. Neither he nor his wife, who survived him for some years, lived to see one son, Robert, become the speaker of the British Columbia legislature and the youngest, Ernest, the provincial minister of public works, the most respected public figure in the province, a man who rebuilt the provincial road system on a scale which Douglas could never have imagined.

The older maps of British Columbia printed Carson's name at a point just north of Pavilion village on the road over the mountain. The newer maps omit this notation, since the original ranch is no longer a stopping place on the main highway. The unique triangle based on the Fraser at the west, with its apex in Marble Canyon to the east, has been by-passed by modern traffic. Few travelers to British Columbia ever see what is, at least to this traveler, its rarest jewel. Nor will they ever see there again, all the Carsons having left the plateau, the kind of family which, ignoring the pursuit of easy money in the gold fields, built British Columbia. These were the authentic folk of the river.

The triangle and the people who first subdued it to their use should be worth the study of anyone who tries to understand the agricultural community of the river today. Each of a hundred other families on the riverbank or in the adjoining valleys could tell its own story, equally remarkable, but the Carson ranch will serve as a good sample of this local river civilization.

It has been my custom, as I have said, to drive the river road in darkness and meet the dawn, head on, in the defiles around Lillooet. This would bring me to the crest of Pavilion

at sunrise. The sun and I would burst upon the plateau together. Burst is the exact word for the sun and the human
traveler. Each arrives suddenly, unexpectedly and with amazement (even the sun must be a little amazed) at the edge of
Carson's Cup among the hills.

The sun shoots his first rays between the peaks and across
the open range and rises steadily, as is his wont, in the course of
the day's work.

The human traveler, climbing through a mountain gorge
and instantly, in a few yards, finding himself no longer in the
mountains but in a lowland valley, pauses to gasp. This mountain which turns into a cavity, this broad sweep of arable land
which somehow has escaped the erosion of wind, rain and glacier,
is one of geography's strangest pranks. How wide must Carson's
eyes have opened at the sight of it!

But, bursting out of the ravine into the circular depression
of the plateau, I never paused long, not at breakfasttime. Ahead
lay the rolling brown range, the green sweep of alfalfa; behind it
the gray hills of granite; and midway the huddle of log barns
and corrals, the great sprawling house that Carson built, all
weathered like the range and seeming to sprout in a dusty
vegetation from the soil. For this habitation, after a hungry
night, a man headed with speed.

A few ranch hands were probably stirring already. The old
Indian stableman would stand grinning at the horse trough
(with a solid bar of silver, a country dentist's masterpiece,
taking the place of his teeth). There would be the usual early-
morning commotion in the corrals, hog pens and chicken yards.
If I was lucky, the cook would have a fire going and coffee brew-
ing on the kitchen stove.

Once I crossed the threshold of this gigantic house I was
back by this single step into Robert Carson's time. The world
was well lost.

Carson's signature was legible in his house. The beams
showed the scars of his broadax. The boards were marked by his

hand saw, which had cut them from the logs. On the floor were two grooves made by the legs of his chair as he pushed it from the table after meals. The ceiling was smudged by the lamp when he read in the winter nights.

Under his hand the house had never ceased to grow. From the original two rooms others continued to sprout as the family increased, so many galleries, stairways and passages that the house was no longer a creation of architecture but a problem in geography. The logs weathered under sun and snow, the pitch oozed out of the boards, the outside of the house took on the color of the land and seemed part of its living substance. Long habitation, birth, death and toil, the adventures of many sons and daughters, the strangers constantly stopping here and moving up the road, gave the house a palpable feeling of life, carved it with wrinkles and proclaimed it a sanctuary in the silence and loneliness of the mountaintop.

All travelers found refuge there on the long road from Lillooet to Clinton. The stagecoaches and freight wagons stopped at this door, their passengers slept in the proliferating rooms, their horses were housed in the gigantic barns and fed on the best alfalfa hay in British Columbia. They left their relics in the rutted road, in the grooved thresholds, in antique saddles, bits of harness, rawhide lariats, dusty bottles of horse liniment and forgotten six-shooters, still cluttering the stables, awaiting the return of their owners.

Here the Indians gathered for spring plowing and summer harvest, were plied with mighty meals in the kitchen, and were paid their wages in the little office room where all the records of the ranch from its first days were heaped on bulging shelves. And at Christmastime the whole tribe from Pavilion village, braves, squaws and papooses, rode up to the ranch, were given presents, with toys and bags of candy for each child, shyly left their own gifts of beaded gloves and buckskin coats, and rode away on their horses through the snow.

The Carsons were used to strangers. They were far from

the main road but every day, except when it was blocked in winter, the road carried its slow laborious traffic. Sometimes politicians from the coast, in search of votes, came this way and argued the public issues of the times with the head of the house. Loaded down with maps of new railways, bluebooks and printed acts of the legislature, John Oliver would try to persuade Carson from his stern conservatism, but he never succeeded.

Thus the Carsons, out of long experience, took the invasion of my family in their stride.

After a Cariboo breakfast of beefsteak and fried potatoes, topped off with a few dozen flapjacks, we would sit a while to consider the latest news.

There was always news on the plateau. A new horse had been acquired in a barter lasting half a day and seemed likely to win the races at the Green Lake stampede. A coyote had been snared in the gully below the sheep pen. The lambing season was under way with half a dozen motherless lambs cradled by the kitchen stove and fed from a bottle. The swallows were back and busy plastering their mud nests in the eaves of the barn. The bluebird family had built again on the post of the main gate and the gate could not be closed, lest it crush the nest, until the birdlings were able to fly. The water supply from the mountain sloughs was ample or scarce—the important news of the year, on which the prospects of the crop depended. Or the price of beef was up or down—news of equal weight in a cattle country.

Up here, a mile above the sea and a million miles from the frenzy of the city, all such news fell into its true perspective as reality and what you had left behind in Vancouver appeared as empty folly, which most of it actually was. Even in the bitter years of the depression, when cattle sold at three cents a pound on the hoof in the Williams Lake auction and grim ranchers returned home with less than the cost of production, everything went on as usual. The plateau seemed invulnerable to the world's shocks.

When war came, Cariboo's sons marched off to Europe but

on their return resumed the life their fathers had led. Save for automobiles, tractors and telephones, life was essentially the same as in Robert Carson's day. In depression and in war, you had the feeling here that you had found the only safe spot left in the world, whose echoes died in the mountains and seldom reached the plateau.

After digesting the breakfast and the news—one never needed sleep in this upland air even after a night's driving—we would saddle up horses in the barn, safe horses like old Sox and Bluebell, for indifferent city riders. Then, if there were cattle to be herded, we could play at cowboy on the range and help the hired hands with branding, dehorning and surgical operations in the corral behind the house. Or, at harvest time, ride on the mountainous hay wagons and explore the enduring mystery of the hayloft.

We were always impatient to see our own special view of the river. Over the slope to the west of the ranch we headed into the timber, past the clay mound with its single pine tree where Carson, his wife and two sons lay. The timber on the western fringe of the plateau is surprisingly large, fir three feet in girth, gnarled by the wind, slow and hard of growth. No underbrush lives in this open park land. We could ride anywhere. In half an hour we were through the timber and out on the lip of the canyon.

Now, for the first time, a man could see the full size of the river trench. It was so wide and deep from the water's long battering against earth and rock that the current below us seemed like a piece of brown string. It was so steep that one leap would carry you to the bottom.

To the north the river was lost in the curve around Pavilion. To the south it coiled, with a greasy look, into the Lillooet mountains. Above it, on both sides, a few clay bluffs hung perilously, cut by shadowed gullies, and on the bluffs of the western bank little dots of green marked the settlers' hayfields.

This brown gash through the earth's surface encourages the

beholder to let himself go with adjective and simile but they are useless. The word "Fraser" is enough to convey the picture to any man who has seen it; to those who have not, it can never be conveyed.

The river and its trench change with every season.

In the first days of spring the bunch grass on the southern slopes surges up overnight in a faint green water-color wash. The irrigation ditches on the bench farms glow red with the new color of the willow bark and lie like full veins across the yellow stubble fields. Day by day, almost hour by hour as the colors deepen, you can see the spring marching up the canyon from the south.

Soon the pink pentstemons will gush out of the clay, with them the first yellow sunflowers, and then the pink and yellow of the cactus blossom. And as the warming air rises from the river up the side of the plateau all the perfume vials of the woods are opened at once—stinging smell of sagebrush, acid smell of pine, and clean medicinal smell from the crawling junipers.

In the spring the river is as green from here as the sea. Its frozen banks ceased at the first touch of winter to pour their mud into the water, but they will thaw out overnight and the current will take on its summer brown again. A little rime of ice still clings to the banks in sheltered places but it will be gone tomorrow.

A man could ride out to this pinnacle every day and seldom see the same view. Behind the river trench the Coast mountains are in constant flux of color. The little farms on the bench turn from the first faint green of spring to the deep green of summer, to the gold of stubble. The bare poplars take on their round, fluttering leaves and, when the frost touches them, daub all the hills with miles of yellow. The dead, dun-colored clay of the range comes briefly to life with the green of bunch grass and seems to die again before summer. But always, in the movement of the river, the canyon is alive.

To learn the geography of the plateau and realize its isolation we must ride east from the ranch house across the fenced hayfields and the pasture beyond them. There sheep are grazing and some lonely shepherd is living with his dog in a covered wagon. To him the cluster of houses and barns at the ranch are a small dot on the sweep of range. To the eastward another mile of range lies between him and the granite mountains.

At the sheep camp we wheel to the right on a flat ridge and, breaking out of a timber bluff, stand on the southern edge of the plateau. Below lies the floor of Marble Canyon, hardly wider than the Fraser, and in this floor are inserted three brightly colored tiles, the chain of little canyon lakes.

A poet might find a better description for them. He might call them a string of jewels thrown down carelessly among the dark hills. He could never define their color.

For lack of better definition, it may be said that the first and largest lake is metallic blue and, at close sight, from its banks, is the most beautiful stretch of water in British Columbia. Into it the granite bluffs fall headlong, with white spurts of mountain rills in springtime, with deep splashes of yellow foliage in autumn.

But metallic blue is a vague adjective. This blue has a dozen different colors in it, depending on the sun and season—greenish blue at the edges above the shallow bars of limestone; dark blue, the color of a cowboys's overalls, in the shadows of the bluffs; and in between, every other blue on the palette.

A few yards away, across a barrier of rock and timber, lies the perfect circle of the second lake. Even from the plateau you can see that it is of an entirely different hue. Green it certainly is but not the green of sea water; not a clear and glittering green, but an opaque green, rather like asparagus soup.

The third lake, still smaller, hardly larger than a good-sized puddle, is green also but deep, clear green that shimmers in the sun.

Each is lovely in its own way. Each has its passing moods and varying colors. Each contains gigantic trout which leap high at dusk but seldom take your fly, the most intelligent, baffling, maddening trout in these parts.

From the plateau edge the course of the three lakes indicates the Marble Canyon passage from the Fraser on the west to the central range of Cariboo in the east—the old Indian route and battlefield, the source of limestone for Carson's chimneys, and the watershed between the drainage basin of the Fraser and the Thompson.

The canyon is narrow, walled on both sides by eroded cliffs of gray tone, but pleasantly shaded by bull pine, which flourishes in safety from mountain storm. To the westward—that is, directly below us as we stand on the plateau—it opens out to provide a few acres of irrigated land, through which a team of horses and mower move, to our sight, like a minor insect. This oasis is small. Beyond it, toward the river, the valley is roughly pebbled by rounded hummocks of dull-red stone, rolled there, no doubt, from the hills long ago. Among them a white spot marks the tower of the Indian church at Pavilion. To the west, spread perfectly flat like stage scenery and vague in blue haze, are the hills behind the Fraser. The river itself lies too deep to be seen from here.

All the snow and rain of this valley and all the water of the Pavilion lakes are sucked toward the river in flood season, but in the summer they are guided by ditches—each under ancient government water license—across the bench farms. Every drop is used in the dry season here, as all along the river, and this supply limits absolutely the area of arable land.

Until Fraser water itself can be lifted, perhaps by power of its own creation, most of the bench will remain under bunch grass and sagebrush, richest of soil, only waiting for irrigation. In time, when power is available for pumping, the entire bench and all the valleys running into it will be cropped, and in a province where only one acre in a hundred is fit for the plow, this empty country will support a substantial production, a population of many thousands. In this Dry Belt water is the central fact of human life but the farmer, hoarding like a miser every trickle out of the hills, must stand on the river's brink and watch its unused cargo moving in prodigal flood to the sea.

Riding north from the bluff above Marble Canyon, we used to follow up the little creek that Carson harnessed to irrigate the plateau (not without long and costly lawsuits to determine the scope of the original water licenses). The creek rises in the granite hills on the eastern fringe of the plateau. A few tiny puddles among the dark spruce forests, some potholes on the range where the ducks breed and the cattle drink, somehow supply a continual flow even in midsummer.

By long, circuitous ditches and wooden flumes, all contrived to divert the natural course of the stream, the water is led down to the fields. A seasoned irrigator, usually an old Chinese or Indian who has spent his life in such work and can gauge the exact slope of the land by eye, opens this ditch or that, closes another with a shovelful of earth and thus patiently soaks every inch of hay land. As he distributes the water, as he keeps it all flowing on the land and prevents it from leaving the plateau unused, this ranch, like all others in the Dry Belt, prospers or fails.

North of the hayfields the plateau rises slowly, almost imperceptibly, through the open pine woods. When you look back from the summit you are amazed to find the ranch a thousand feet below you and five miles to the south. The distant peaks of the Coast Range have risen suddenly and stand in points of blue and white like the Rockies. More than ever the top of Pavilion Mountain resembles a deep, circular valley, its brown summer floor crisscrossed by streaks of green along the irrigation ditches. This wide sweep of open land seems large enough to hold a hundred farms but it supports one house and a few barns. Only water can change the brown to green and all the water from the hills is being used already.

From the summit the plateau drops off, on the north, as steeply as on the south. Since they could find no other passage, the miners of the Harrison route built a trail down this precipice into the Kelly Creek valley and gradually widened it into a road.

The road has been little changed since their day. It is carved in such sharp zigzags, one directly below the other, that until recent times you had to back your car up at every curve. The freighter in the old days never dared to start down the hill without chopping a tree and' tying it to the back of his wagon as an extra brake. The first automobile drivers took the same precaution and their trees can still be seen lying in the bottom of the valley.

I suppose this must be one of the most dangerous roads in Canada. It is hardly wide enough for a car. From its edges the precipice falls in drops of a thousand feet. Its grade calls for low gear, either up or down, in the most powerful car. Somehow freight wagons were slid down this wooded slope and hauled up again even on the glare ice of spring and autumn.

In summer any experienced driver can travel it if he takes his time. In freezing weather no one but a madman or an old hand like Ernest Carson will risk it. For several winter months it is blocked by five or six feet of snowdrifts. In spring I have driven it with Carson when every curve was a skating rink and every bluff seemed likely to be my last sight of this world. Yet such roads actually are safer than the best highways because even the most reckless driver travels them at a snail's pace.

From the top of the road the isolation of the plateau is finally revealed. The northern moat, like the southern, is cut in from the Fraser, which is the western and the deepest moat of all. Kelly Lake and Pear Lake—two glittering lenses in a pair of dark spectacles—drain into the river. In their valley the road and the railway (which has descended from the west slope of Pavilion Mountain) turn eastward by an easy grade to Clinton, the old junction with the Cariboo Road. This valley is well watered by drainage from the vertical mountains that flank it on both sides. It supports a few acres of farm land, a heavy forest growth, some trout of superior flavor and energy in Kelly Lake, and a grove of tart wild raspberries that were always picked and made into jam at the ranch.

Our ride has divulged in a rough way the geography of the plateau, but to understand its life, or the life of any river ranch, a man must work here upon the land, at all seasons, with the rough yet complex techniques invented by the first settlers.

He must cut wood and feed cattle from a sleigh in winter, when the plateau is swept by cruel winds, when the old house trembles and creaks at every joint, when the stoves must be stoked with pine knots all through the night. He must ride through snowdrifts up to his horse's belly in search of some stray steer, and head into a blizzard which almost peels the skin from his face and blots out the nearest hills. He must know the welcome wink of a distant light and the sanctuary of the ranch kitchen at nightfall.

In spring he must trudge the miles of irrigation ditches, clearing them with a shovel. He must herd the cattle onto the upper ranges and feed the sick lambs around the stove from a baby's bottle. He must plow the heavy, sodden soil before it cakes. He must watch the first bunch grass turning green, the first swallows nesting in the stable eaves, and he must smell the warm south wind from the Fraser.

In summer he must cock the hay behind the mower and pitch it up on the high hay wagons and into the gaping lofts. He must smell the heavy perfume of the alfalfa fields in the twilight and listen to the chuckle of the irrigation ditches, the munch of cattle on the bunch grass, and the distant murmur of the river. He must see the plateau in the summer nights, lying like folded velvet close, so very close, to the stars.

In autumn he must harvest the grain and bale the straw and drive the cattle down out of the hills. He must witness the sudden miracle of the frost when the poplars turn to yellow and the plateau is colored like a Turkish carpet and the sun is still hot at noonday and the horse trough is covered with ice in the morning.

And at every season a man must learn that all life, animal and vegetable, clings to the river, nourishes itself on the drainage waters of the river's trench, travels by the passage that the river has cut through the hills and soon dies, while the river lives and moves and wears away the land perpetually.

The seasons and their toil are not enough to root a man in the ways of this land. He must know the people who have lived here from the beginning—the quiet, slow people who never seem to hurry, to whom there is always another day, another year, another harvest, in unchanging procession.

With the climate of the plateau, he must learn the climate of these people's minds. He must sit for hours on a shady porch while the rancher swaps a twenty-dollar pony with a neighbor, or loll in the store through a lazy afternoon arguing crops and politics. He must listen to a local politican in the schoolhouse at election time and drink coffee and eat sandwiches with the Conservative or the Liberal ladies afterwards. He must follow the coffin of some old-timer as it is carried in a truck down to the little church in Lillooet and buried in some remote graveyard. He must learn to talk to the Indians in a mixture of English and Chinook and wait for a week perhaps before they turn up for work.

He must learn that nothing happens, nothing ever changes, that water will always trickle from the hills upon the hay lands, crops will always grow and cattle fatten, that the river flows forever to the sea.

17   To the River's End

THE RIVER TRENCH HAS BEEN WIDENING GRADUALLY FROM
Lytton northward, but in places, as at the base of Pavilion
Mountain, it closes in to form those rapids which Fraser found
so difficult. The rapids above Lillooet, indeed, are some of the
worst on the whole river and potentially, for power purposes,
the most valuable. But, running straight north, the trench soon
angles out of the diagonal of the Coast Range and gives the river
ample space to flow quietly through an easy region of clay. The
Fraser is now bisecting the plateau of Cariboo.

The Cariboo plateau, unique in the topography of Canada,
is an oval about 125 miles across and 160 miles long. While its
boundaries are vague, it may be said to lie between the Coast
mountains on the west and the outer fringes of the Rocky system on the east. It stretches northward from the Thompson
to latitude 56, even beyond the first sources of the arctic
drainage system.

On average the plateau is 4,000 feet above the ocean—a fact
which makes the Fraser and its tributaries a gigantic source of
electrical power. But the term "plateau," though well understood by the natives, appears as a misnomer to the stranger. Instead of a flat space which that word may imply, he finds a region of rolling range, low-lying meadows, a confusing skeleton of
mountains sprawled in all directions, a maze of deep river gullies
finally joining the central gully of the Fraser, and everywhere
the unexpected bodies of upland lakes.

The Cariboo actually is less a plateau than a saucer between the mountains, and the saucer is almost an island. The Thompson on the south, the lake system tucked into the eastern foothills of the Coast Range on the west, the Nechako River and its multitude of lakes on the north, and the rivers and lakes on the western flank of the Rockies to the east almost surround the largest part of the plateau with water.

Curiously enough, the plateau itself contributes little water to its single drainpipe, the Fraser. The water flowing across the plateau into the Fraser comes mainly from the snow of the two mountain ranges. The plateau lakes, 850 square miles in all, act as a catch basin for a runoff which, for the whole Fraser drainage area, moves at the average rate of one cubic foot a second for every square mile. Hence even the driest sections of the plateau contain large bodies of water in lake and river, nearly all of it borrowed from the mountains.

The Cariboo is so large in compass and so varied in appearance that the stranger cannot possibly grasp its general plan. It appears to him as an endless and almost empty wilderness of clay, timber, rock and water, one of the loneliest stretches of settled country in America and, in our eyes, one of the most beautiful.

That beauty is impossible to describe and, at first sight, perhaps hard to catch. The charm of the Cariboo for dwellers on the narrow coastal shelf is, I suppose, its feeling of unlimited open space, its clear skies, its clean upland air, its careless life. No explorers' maps, no meteorological tables, no written word can hope to convey the presence of the plateau. One can only record that the people who settle here rarely leave, that the people of the coast return again and again with the sensation of breaking out of a prison into the daylight, that to all British Columbians, from the days of the first gold miners, Cariboo has been a magic word. More than any other place in Canada it seems to offer sanctuary from the world. In it even the Fraser is at peace.

The Cariboo Road and the Pacific Great Eastern Railway provide the only two routes across the plateau, north and south.

With ample elbowroom, they swing far east of the Fraser to avoid its side valleys and shifting gullies. The traveler, therefore, cannot follow the riverbank. Usually he turns eastward from the Fraser at Lytton on the main road along the Thompson, leaves the Thompson at Ashcroft, and goes north by the Cariboo Road.

We shall inspect that road later. Meanwhile, after crossing Pavilion Mountain, we reach Clinton, the old junction point between the Harrison route and the later gold route built by Governor Douglas. (If all this sounds confusing to the reader, he might glance at the map, remembering that, after the narrow mountain gorges of the lower river, we have entered a big, confusing country, where the roads of men hardly make an imprint on the substance of the plateau.)

From Clinton, instead of going north on the Cariboo Road, we can turn off westward by a winding side road with the lovely name of Jesmond and, after traversing a stretch of meadow and jack pine, head back to the Fraser again. We reach it at the Canoe Creek bridge and realize at once that this is not the river we have known in the canyons of the Coast Range. It is still moving through a canyon, but this is a canyon of clay, which the current has cut to its own requirements. It coils peacefully at the bottom of a deep, brown groove. With this single cut down its center the land rolls out on either side.

Zigzagging down the clay cliffs and crossing the Canoe Creek bridge, we reach an area which, by British Columbia standards, is remarkably open and regular. This is roughly the southern boundary of the Chilcotin country on the Fraser's west bank (or the Chilacootin as the Indians and old-timers call it), a plateau within the greater plateau of Cariboo.

In the Chilcotin you can see farther in every direction than in any part of Canada west of the Rockies. The open range supports such huge cattle ranches as the Gang, but even the irrigated fields of the Gang, seen from the hills behind them, are a tiny green square. The Fraser itself shrinks into a trickle. Across the face of this countryside the river trench becomes a wiggling pencil line.

The Chilcotin seems to have been designed by nature for the nourishment of beef. It has range running all the way from the river westward to the outcroppings of the Coast mountains. It has succulent bunch grass to feed the grazing herds and bluffs of timber to shelter them from the winds of spring and autumn.

For the production of beef, however, something more is required. In the winter the cattle must be driven down from the upper ranges and fed around the home ranch. Every herd is strictly limited by the amount of hay that can be grown for this winter feeding and the hay crop is limited by the amount of water that can be poured upon the earth.

While there is water in the Cariboo plateau to irrigate every arable acre, it seldom lies at a level to serve the adjoining country. Only a lake or river here and there can be tapped by the rancher and carried by gravity to his meadow. Yet of British Columbia's 150,000 irrigated acres the Fraser's tributaries water 100,000, most of them in the isolated hayfields of the Cariboo.

By such irrigation and the abundance of bunch grass the Chilcotin has built an economy based entirely on beef for the Vancouver market. But you may drive all day without seeing a single steer. The ranches, depending on some local creek for irrigation, are far apart, lost in some inland valley at the end of a nameless road or wedged into the foothills of the Coast Range.

For the most part cattle ranching is not a poor man's game. Many of the ranches are large, often owned by powerful business syndicates and conducted on a lavish scale. Big houses, hundreds of miles of barbed wire and rail fence, cattle grazing on every hillside, bands of wild horses on the upper range, cowboys everywhere make the typical Chilcotin ranch the closest replica of Hollywood's wild West that Canada affords.

Here and there a poor man has found a convenient lake or river, has flumed it down upon the dry range, grown a few acres of hay, and started to raise cattle. He is not so poor as he looks, though. His house may be a log cabin, his barn may be falling down, his dress may be a faded shirt and patched overalls, but if he owns a hundred beef animals today he is worth $12,000 at least in ready cash. Most ranchers, who count themselves poor, own many more than that. The investment of the big ranches runs into millions.

Times have not always been so good. One remembers the days of the depression when the ranchers drove their cattle in from the Chilcotin to the auction at Williams Lake, drove them sometimes as far as 250 miles and lost much of their meat by shrinkage on the way, and then sold them for three cents a pound on the hoof, less than the cost of raising them. Such times may come again, but since the beginning of World War II every cattleman has been a capitalist, whether he knows it or not.

Good times or bad don't seem to make much difference in the Chilcotin. In war, peace, depression, boom, drought, flood, heat and cold everything goes on without perceptible change. Nowhere in America, I dare say, does life beat with a slower and steadier pulse. Nowhere on earth, I am certain, are people so contented and secure. It may be a false security, but in this immense land, without a single town from one side of it to the other, no man can take the troubles of civilization very seriously. So long as rivers run and grass grows and cattle fatten, the Chilcotin expects to live as it has always lived in the best of all possible worlds. All it asks is a reasonable price for beef.

The main ingredient of this life is the Chilcotin River, since its tributaries provide the essential water of irrigation. The source of the Chilcotin is a complex of lakes lying on the eastward slope of the Coast Range. Chief of these are Chilko and Taseko. Their outlets, which bear their names, together with many smaller neighbors around them, flow north to join the Chilcotin proper, which flows down from the northwest. To the west other tributaries of the Chilcotin drain an area of range, meadow, forest, lake and marsh narrowly separated by the coastal mountains from the rivers flowing westward to the sea. In places the ridge between the westward and eastward drainage systems is less than ten miles wide.

In general the Chilcotin river system, draining 1,600 square miles and providing over 5 per cent of the Fraser's total volume, lies across the plateau like the shoe of a giant horse facing northward. Enough subsidiary streams run into the horseshoe to serve the territory within and without it.

The Chilcotin is a muddy river and its silt helps to color the Fraser. In most places it is quiet, one of the best behaved of the Fraser's larger children, but it rouses itself in occasional rapids. Economically it is one of the most important branches of the whole system, since it hatches out about a third of the salmon run. As a power river, diverted through the mountains directly to the coast, it will be one of the most productive in the world.

The Chilcotin country is served by two roads which join the main Cariboo Road on the Fraser's east bank. The southernmost road we followed out of Clinton. After crossing the Fraser at Canoe Creek it leaves the river and seeks a parklike ridge where the fir trees in places are almost as large as those on the coast. Bearing northeastward, it meets the other road, which has followed the main course of the Chilcotin from the Fraser and goes westward to the sea. When you have traveled all these main roads and the innumerable sidetracks of the cattle ranches you have still not begun to see the Chilcotin. You would need a lifetime on horseback to explore it.

While the term "Cariboo" has no precise geographical meaning, and even old-timers quarrel about its boundaries, Clinton may be regarded as its southern gateway. This old town must have been a lively spot when the gold rush was going through. Even after the rush had died, Clinton remained a freighting center in the days of wagon and stagecoach. Hugging either side of the Cariboo Road, it occupied one long, muddy street.

Today the street is paved, the town is neatly kept under the shade of trees planted at the beginning, but otherwise it has changed little since then. The elongated wooden hotel, flush with the road, is the same that accommodated miner, freighter and stage driver, though its interior (to the regret of old-timers) has been modernized, and I am even told that the mighty drum stove made by a local blacksmith in the sixties has lately been removed. I hope that rumor will turn out to be false.

Clinton lies within the fat, open ranch land of the Bonaparte Valley. A few miles north the road ascends, through an unbroken forest of dwarf jack pine, to a higher layer in the Cariboo plateau. This is not apparent from the road, but westward toward the Fraser and eastward toward the Clearwater Mountains many cozy ranches nestle in open meadows beside quiet lakes. The high ridge that the road follows is dismal and useless.

Ernest Carson, whose father freighted on it ninety years ago, has been relocating the Cariboo Road and gradually making it into a modern highway. In general it follows the original route. Until recent times it followed every twist and turn where the first builders could not stop to blast a rock or dig out a stump.

In those days a mile meant something and every mile was marked. Starting first from Lillooet, as the jumping-off place of the Harrison route, and then from Ashcroft when Douglas's road was built, every stopping place along the way was called a "mile house." It had no name but its number. Even now you speak of stopping at the Seventy, or the Hundred, or the Hundred and Fifty. Since the old houses were measured from Lillooet and the later settlements from Ashcroft, a number is no guide to distance. The complete jumble of mileage never mattered in the least. Every house along the road was known, every bed and meal had its own special reputation with the freighters.

In my young days, for example, we always tried to stop at the Hundred and Twenty-two, where I have seen such meals, such gargantuan breakfasts and steak dinners, such pies of wild raspberries, such lavish hosts and such red-faced cooks as a civilized man never encounters. Those days, alas, are gone. Many of the old stopping houses are closed (though the 50-cent meal at the Seventy is still on the old scale), modern hotels have opened here and there, and even that final North American horror, the chromium coffee bar, in the middle of the wilderness.

But the road remains, and all human life clings to it as children cling to the skirts of their mother, for the road, indeed, is the mother of Cariboo. Freight trucks have replaced the ox teams, automobiles the saddle horses, and airplanes fly over here on their way to Alaska. They cannot alter the loneliness of the country or the knowledge of every man that the road is the frail foundation of his life.

After you have been here a little while you come to think of the road as a living creature. You listen for the latest news of ruts and snow. You wait eagerly for the traveler from the coast as if he came from some land across the sea. You eavesdrop on every telephone conversation along the road by means of a primitive but convenient loud-speaker, known locally as a hooter. You follow every curve and dip in the road with the sense of going on forever to nowhere. You recognize every bump and chuckhole in it, every landmark, every ranch, and almost every cayuse. You love and hate the road by turns as the weather changes. Never for a moment do you forget the road, which alone links you precariously with the rest of humankind.

Up and up by toiling curves the road climbs over the hill of the Hundred (where an English lord is dressed like a cowboy and the walls of his stopping house are covered by the portraits of his Elizabethan ancestors), down through the pleasant meadowland beside Lac La Hache and westward past the Hundred and Fifty to the cattle town of Williams Lake, close to the Fraser.

Williams Lake is a fairly modern product of the railway and lacks the patina of the gold-rush towns. Here the cattle from most of Cariboo are assembled at roundup season for shipment to the coast. Here the ranchers and Indians gather once a year for the innocent fun of the stampede. Here dwells a fabulous Scottish merchant, Roderick Mackenzie, who got his start selling billiard tables to Boer farmers on the African veld, having ordered them from England by a mistake in a cable.

And here a still more fabulous character, the late Benny Nicholas, editor of the Victoria *Times*, once set the whole Cariboo country on fire by whispering confidentially to a town character named Benjamin Franklin that he was John D. Rockefeller, Jr. in disguise, was secretly buying the railway from the government, and would make Williams Lake a second Chicago. (The price of real estate went up overnight and it was years before the government could dispel the rumor of impending opulence.)

From Williams Lake the northern Chilcotin road runs westward across the Fraser on the Chimney Creek bridge. The main road swings northward on the bluffs above the river. (You can by-pass this section and Williams Lake altogether by going straight north on the alternative route from the Hundred and Fifty.)

The river route passes through Soda Creek, the old southern terminus of steamboating on the upper Fraser, of which no visible evidence is left. The Fraser from here northward is quiet and mannerly, easy for the navigator, between its eroded clay banks. Its open, wriggling course is visible for miles in either direction. The road rides on its bluffs most of the way until it curves into the jack pine, leaves the last of the Dry Belt behind, and drops at last down a long hill into the valley of the Quesnel and the town of the same name.

It was a great name in the days of the rush. Quesnel became the northern terminus of the steamboats, the outfitting point for the last dash eastward to Barkerville. Today it is the northern terminus of the Pacific Great Eastern Railway and the shipping point of northern Cariboo. Strung along the grassy banks of the Fraser, it looks, despite a few new store fronts and modern hotels, very much as it must have looked to the miners who came north on the steamboats, to the Overlanders who drifted down on rafts. It carries an air of age about it in log houses, in ancient trees, and in grizzled old men who used to mine gold and now sit staring across the river. Being well north of the Dry Belt and amply watered, Quesnel is a green and shady town, wrinkled by a long and comfortable life. Its people see no reason to move. Among them the most notable, until his untimely death, was Louis Le Bourdais, the telegraph operator, who became the painstaking and unpaid historian of Cariboo. He gathered at first hand all the lore of the gold rush but, being elected to the legislature, was too busy to write down what he knew before he died. When they buried poor Louis, the band playing "Don't Fence Me In" at his last request, they buried much of the most exciting history of western Canada. While he lived every sensible traveler stopped at his telegraph office on the riverbank to listen to his stories. Now they are lost beyond recapture, since the men who gave them to him are long dead.

In search of gold, the miners tracked straight east of Quesnel into the mountains. The natural course of travel, however, leads southeastward up the Quesnel River to the two-forked, fifty-mile lake of the same name. It was in the tributary creeks of Quesnel Lake, as the reader may recall, that the first gold of Cariboo was discovered. For years afterwards, though the rush went overland to Barkerville, someone was always finding a pocket of gold in the original field. Names like Hydraulic, Likely, Horsefly and Bullion record the adventures of mining camps which, until recent years, continually sprang up and were as quickly deserted. No records remain except a few decayed cabins and broken flumes.

The permanent riches of this lake region have still to be tapped. The spruce forests and waterpowers of the Quesnel will be combined someday in a major pulp industry. Great as are the forests of the Canadian coast, the largest timber area left in Canada stretches from the general vicinity of Quesnel northward to the arctic drainage basin, most of it tributary to the Fraser system. Its exploitation is still ahead. Meanwhile the

Quesnel Lake country, with its trout and game, contributes heavily to the tourist industry.

The confusions of the Rocky chain (which bears many names and is divided into many distinguishable ranges) narrowly divide the Quesnel Lake area from another of similar character to the east and south. The latter contains Canim, Mahood, Clearwater, Azure, Hobson and Murtle Lakes, all of which, by a freak of topography, flow eastward into the North Thompson, even though they seem, on the map, to be direct tributaries of the Fraser and almost touch it, in places, on the west. The gap of the Clearwater River, through the Clearwater Mountains on the west bank of the North Thompson, draws all these lakes away from the Cariboo plateau but they are part of the plateau for the uses of men. The most notable and spectacular feature of this eastward-flowing chain is the falls of the Mahood, which joins Canim and Mahood Lakes and which we shall inspect later in the pursuit of trout.

North of Quesnel the Fraser remains generally peaceful though, as Mackenzie and Fraser found at the place of wild onions, a few dangerous rapids are formed where rock bluffs break through the edges of the clay canyon. These places are not seen from the road, which lies well east of the river.

The road, like the old navigation system, has its troubles. Not far beyond Quesnel it plunges into the gigantic gulf of Cottonwood Canyon, the drainage channel of the westernmost creeks of the Barkerville country. By laborious zigzags the road can crawl down the clay wall of the canyon and up the other side, but for many years it was the terror of all northern drivers. Countless tons of gravel were poured upon the gumbo but always disappeared. In wet weather automobiles sank to the hubs and a figure as eminent as the late Lord Bennett, prime minister of Canada, was once forced like everybody else to dig himself out with a shovel.

The road at last has been made safe and sound. Within the gulch of Cottonwood the Pacific Great Eastern Railway gave up the ghost. When the provincial government finally surveyed this dizzy space it scrapped the bridge it had already fabricated and decided not to carry the railway past Quesnel, even though tracks had been laid north of Cottonwood. No bridge will ever be built here. If the railway ever goes beyond Quesnel it will swing eastward to hit the Cottonwood at a narrower spot. So far, one of the Fraser's smallest tributaries, a mere creek, because it has hollowed out such a gap in the yielding clay, has defeated the public treasury, defied the engineers and kept governments constantly in political hot water.

The Fraser is tortuous in this region but the road (following the abandoned railway grade in places) is notably straight. In some eighty miles of jack pine, cleared meadows of excellent mixed farming land and stark promontories of clay, it drops down suddeny to the river again and crosses it into Fraser's trading post of Fort George.

In some ways Fort George was the most notable white man's habitation on the river. From it Fraser started for the river's mouth and the fur brigades moved southward out of the northern trapping areas down to Kamloops and the Columbia. Steamboats plied from the fort up and down the river. Finally the Grand Trunk Pacific Railway reached here from the Rockies and made a town.

Or rather three towns, for it took Fort George a long time to settle down. The original fort lay on the west bank of the Fraser south of the present town and called itself South Fort George. The speculators planned a town to the northwest. The railway fixed the townsite finally at the junction of the Nechako and the Fraser and called it Prince George.

It has seen a lot of life. The railway builders floated down here, like the Overlanders, on rafts and scows around the Fraser's big bend, hundreds of them—no one will ever know how many—drowning in the Grand Canyon when the life of an unskilled bohunk laborer was cheap, his death unrecorded. The trappers made Prince George their headquarters for the annual sale of furs and for riotous refreshment. The speculators drew a townsite large enough for a metropolis, sold their lots, and waited for population to appear.

The local board of trade, aflame with visions of private enterprise, persuaded the madam who conducted the red-light district of South Fort George to move her ladies to the new town and build the finest palace of entertainment ever seen in the north. But on the official opening night, with all the leading citizens in attendance, and now aflame with champagne, the police raided the resort, influenced, it is said, by the jealous burghers of the old town.

Insulted at this churlish reception to a promising new business, the proprietress shook the dust of Prince George from her silver slippers and so did her employees. The palace on the outskirts of the town was deserted until some man of imagination persuaded the city council to use it as a city hall in which, as the malicious local editor observed in print, the mayor and aldermen could find accommodation exactly suited to their character, with the Christian name of some fancy lady painted on each office door.

Prince George never captured the red-light industry from the old town but it managed to get along all right. Those were spacious days in the river town when everybody expected to be a millionaire before next week, when the railway builders filled every bar and cash register, when the first trains were coming in from the prairies and the coast, when the steamboats were still puffing north from Soda Creek and far up the big bend, when the first sawmills began to cut spruce along the river, and Canada discovered its northern frontier.

The Canadian boom collapsed in World War I and Prince George realized that it was not to be a city after all. The townsite grew up in brush, the railway builders moved on, the steamboats were beached on the riverbank. Even in the depth of the last depression, however, when many townspeople were on relief and a new thing called communism made its first appearance in this part of the world, Prince George somehow maintained a spirit of hilarity, a night life of whisky and poker, and a boundless hope. It knew it was was only midway between the forty-ninth parallel and the northern boundary of British Columbia, that half the province lay to its north, with undiscovered wealth of timber, mineral, fir and farm land, that someday this rich vacuum would be filled.

If Prince George ever weakened in its hopes, its leading citizen, Harry Perry (an English tailor's apprentice who had become a provincial statesman), reminded it of the high destiny just over the horizon. In speeches to the legislature, in blazing editorials, Perry kept the old vision alive.

World War II began to confirm his judgment. Prince George became a vital point on the air route to Alaska. Its population grew to 5,500. The tributary sawmill industry of the river boomed. Old-timers like Pete Wilson, the town's perennial lawyer and advocate, felt that they were living in the first careless rapture of railway construction again.

The exploitation of the unequaled northern forest for pulp, with the river to carry the logs, should make Prince George a substantial community someday. In the meantime it still retains, in its broad streets of the land boom, its false store fronts, its insatiable ambition, the reckless, pioneer character of its people, a look and a feeling of the frontier, not to be found anywhere else in British Columbia. This, after all, is the gateway of the north and the north is the only frontier left in America.

The Nechako, joining the Fraser at Prince George, drains perhaps the most beautiful lake area west of the Rockies. Only a map can indicate the complicated pattern of water that lies on the eastern flank of the Coast mountains and pours down the Nechako, and only a surveyor can fix the line that divides the lakes of the eastern flow from those which, a few miles off, empty westward into the ocean.

The lake country is reached by the railway and the main road running west from Prince George to the coast at Prince

Rupert. At first the Nechako Valley appears barren and monotonous, a waste of jack pine. At the village of Vanderhoof it changes suddenly into a spacious flat, heavy with grain and so wide that you can imagine you are on the Canadian prairies. Through this prosperous farming belt a side road swings northwestward to Stuart Lake, which the first Hudson's Bay men, under Fraser, found so enchanting.

Their opinion was sound. Stuart Lake is the intermediate reservoir for a series of lakes and rivers all emptying through the Nechako into the Fraser. On them the explorers' canoes could travel without a portage for a hundred and fifty miles through Trembleur Lake to Takla Lake and thence strike over the divide to the headwaters of the westward-moving rivers and the first creeks that feed the Mackenzie and pour into the Arctic Sea. This route is still traveled every week by old Dave Hoy, pushing two scows before his gas boat, and carrying trappers, Indians, hunters, horses and freight for the remote settlers.

The last traces of civilization disappear at Fort St. James, which the Hudson's Bay Company established on the northern shore of Stuart Lake even before it built Fort George. You are now in virgin country, among wilderness people.

A few traces of the wilderness, in the days when white men first saw it, still remain.

Some of the squared-log buildings of Fraser's fort still stand, neatly whitewashed and red roofed, just as the great Governor Simpson must have seen them when he paddled up here every summer from Montreal, with Scottish pipers in the bow of his canoe.

The Indians who trade at the old post and live in a picturesque village around a steepled church are still Indian in their crafts, their woodlore and their habits.

I remember going to Fort St. James with a junket of Canadian and American stuffed shirts, among them a lieutenant governor of British Columbia, an amiable figurehead without constitutional power or political influence. When the Indians heard that the great white father was among them they sought his attendance in the spotless little house of their chief and there, as if addressing Champlain, Frontenac or Simpson, petitioned the helpless representative of the King to give them back all their hunting grounds and expel the whites.

The innocence of this request, translated with unction by a young interpreter, would have embarrassed a man of feeling, but the viceregal personage solemnly promised to consider the tribe's request among his braves at Victoria. And when the Indians gave him a ceremonial pair of beadwork gloves he thought quickly and handed his walking stick over to the chief, who seemed to consider it a rather inadequate gift on such an occasion.

The peculiar magic of this northern lake country, quite different from that of the central Cariboo, is difficult to define. One remembers only the shattering skies, the massed clouds and the snow-lined mountains reflected in the clean lake water; Indian women cross legged on the beach mending fish nets and making baskets of birchbark as they have done since remote time; a procession of Indians chanting a hymn as they carried the tiny coffin of a child to a grave beside the old church; the memories of Fraser and Simpson and their adventures on this shore; and on all sides the sense of limitless and uninhabited land from here to the Arctic Sea.

Stuart and its tributary lakes form only the northern arc of the great circle of water that spills down the eastern slope of the Coast Range. South of Stuart lie Fraser Lake and, directly to the west of it, the long, crooked body of François. Then, to the southwest, Ootsa, Whitesail, Eutsuk, Tetachuk, Euchu (reading anticlockwise), many minor lakes and a complicated veining of rivers form an almost unbroken moat of water around Tweedsmuir Park, one of America's loveliest habitations of fish and game.

All this water flows through the Nechako to the Fraser. Cheek by jowl with the Fraser tributaries—and seeming on the map to be part of the Fraser system—is another chain of lakes like Babine, the largest of all, draining north and then west to the ocean by the Skeena's pass through the mountains.

The western lake country, though strictly speaking a part of it, bears little resemblance to the rest of the Cariboo plateau. It is far outside the Dry Belt, is green with lush meadows and broken by high mountains, the eastward thrust of the Coast Range. Its lakes, unlike many in Cariboo, are clear and deep, its rivers generally clean. Its valleys, watered by the adjacent mountains, require little irrigation to produce crops.

Up to now its remoter stretches have been little traveled and hardly settled but they contain many sizable pockets of rich land. Edging out from the Nechako and the railway that runs westward to Prince Rupert, settlement is slowly moving into the valleys and building a mixed farming industry which produces milk and profitable clover seed and which lives, in its first stages, on the cutting of timber for lumber, ties and poles.

Some impression of this country's distinctive aspect is suggested by the little colony of Swiss settlers who have come here because, they say, it reminds them of home. Its green bottom land, its timbered hillsides, and the white peaks above them are, in fact, rather Alpine. There used to be a wonderful old Scottish innkeeper at Endako, just west of Fraser Lake, whose favorite roost was a barber's chair in his parlor. Safe in this comfortable refuge, he would tell me that, given a hundred years or so, the farmers would have every valley under cultivation and herds of milk cows grazing on every hillside to the timberline as in Switzerland. Better still, the country might even look someday like the highlands of Scotland.

In these pioneering days the wilderness is hardly scarred by a few lonely little towns and the first penetration of settlement. Only Indians, trappers, sportsmen and government surveyors go far beyond the road and the railway into a fastness where a man can travel for weeks by canoe, seldom portaging, and where he will see no other man. The world has yet to discover the Alpine lake region.

To return to the Fraser itself: At Prince George the big bend begins. Its most northern point, just before it arcs southeastward, lies within eight miles of arctic drainage, the farthest tributaries of the Peace and the Mackenzie. No mountain range divides the ultimate springs of these two great currents, which between them cover a large part of North America. If the little flat between the Fraser and the dark puddle of Summit Lake, headwaters of the Crooked, were tilted a few feet one way or the other, most of the north would drain into the Fraser or the Fraser might flow to the arctic. A man can almost stand with one foot in the drainage of the Pacific and the other in the drainage of the arctic—a fact which enabled Mackenzie, Fraser and their successors to travel, with a small portage, from the prairies up the Peace and thence down the Fraser to the western ocean.

The winding bend of the Fraser is uninteresting and weary, useful to man chiefly as a water grade for the transcontinental railway and as a convenient carrier of spruce logs to the sawmills on the riverbank. As was noted in the record of the first explorers and of the Overlanders, the river is generally peaceful between banks of clay but broken, especially in the Grand Canyon, by some of its worst rapids. It is shrinking all the time as the mountains close in on it, and becomes cleaner as the clay canyon is left behind. Presently it is a minor mountain stream, milky from the ooze of glaciers, and now lying at the bottom of the intermontane valley that stretches all the way south into the United States.

At the point where the railway from Prince Rupert joins the North Thompson railway from the coast to run eastward through the Rockies I have often looked down on these upper reaches of the Fraser, on this clear, babbling creek, and tried to imagine how such beginnings could make the river that stains the waters of the Pacific; and how the main party of the Over-landers could make rafts move on such a boulder-strewn trickle.

Over the valley that starts the Fraser on its journey to the west and opens the Yellowhead Pass through the Rockies to the east looms the lonely monument of Mount Robson, layer on layer of rock and snow, in sharp bands of blue and white, its top sheared off flat, like a damaged wedding cake.

Robson's roof is 12,972 feet above the sea, the highest peak in the Canadian Rockies, but no giant among the mountains of the world. Height is not everything, even in a mountain. Robson has a special nobility because it stands alone and dwarfs all its brothers. Whether such a bulk of stone, circled like a barrel by bands of snow, is beautiful I cannot say. Assuredly it is appalling and, at a glance, cuts the beholder down to proper size. I have never looked at this grisly titan without pulling down the blind after a few minutes and wishing the train would hurry through the mountains to the open prairie. Such a spectacle of ageless and sterile rock was never intended for a self-important creature like man.

We are now at the source of the river. It rises in the glacial brooks and spruce swamps of Fraser Pass. These empty into Moose Lake, a narrow splinter, eight miles long, lying from southeast to northwest in the tight grip of the central Rockies. A few miles eastward the creeks and marshes are draining imperceptibly down the eastern slope into the Athabaska, the Mackenzie and the Arctic Ocean. A few miles to the south they are flowing into the Columbia and, by it, through the United States.

Precisely where the divide between these three river systems lies it would be difficult to say, for it is marked by nothing more than some nameless dribble, hardly bigger than a garden hose. Here a moose stands knee deep in the swamp that is the beginning of the Fraser, too preoccupied to turn his head at the train's approach. But the Fraser's seaward flow has begun. The Overlanders saw its tiny current, saw the water moving northwestward into the big bend, and knew they were on the western slope, beside a current which would take them to Cariboo. Its widening trench has carried much larger freight—four railways, the interior highway system, the traffic of steamboats, the march of gold miner and settler, the ceaseless autumn migration of the salmon, the destiny of two great nations.

18　The Thompson

THE THOMPSON, WHOSE CONFLUENCE WITH THE FRASER WE passed at Lytton, is a formidable river, though the tributary of a greater.

In its lower reaches, just before joining its parent, it has bored a channel through the inner rank of the Coast Range, just as the Fraser bores through the outer in the final passage to the sea. The Thompson's gorge is hardly less spectacular than the Fraser canyon, but it is more naked.

The sterile banks of the Thompson nourish only sagebrush, dwarf jack pine, some bull pine and poplar. The mountains around the river in most places are as clean and barren as if they had been hewn out yesterday. But they are incomparably rich in coloring. They ooze in stains of crimson, yellow and purple. Their deep clefts seem to change in depth and contour with the daily progress of sun and shadow. The Fraser canyon lies in a dark and narrow jumble of wooded rock; the Thompson is a wide and empty trench, burning under the sun.

In the ample width of the Thompson's course travel is not difficult. A man or a horse never had any trouble moving into the interior once he reached Lytton. This was the route of the original Cariboo Road and is the route of the new road that has replaced it.

From Lytton the road climbs the bench above the south bank of the river among the jack pines, drops down to the water's edge and climbs again, giving you alternating bird's-eye views of the canyon and close-ups of the current. Whereas on the Fraser you feel at once the dimensions of a continent.

The road crosses from the left to the right bank at Spences Bridge where, it will be recalled, a thrifty pioneer of that name operated a ferry in the first days of the gold road and replaced it later with a toll bridge. The modern bridge, on Spence's site, carries no toll and no gold. Around it sprawls a dusty little village and, it is said, a thriving population of rattlesnakes.

At Spences Bridge the pretty little Nicola River enters from the south, draining Nicola Lake and several others. Probably I am prejudiced, having spent part of my boyhood here on the back of an Indian pony, but the Nicola country has always appeared especially pleasant to me. The lake was good for swimming, fishing and boating, the river gave me my first Rainbow trout (on a caddis worm), at Douglas Lake, not far off, was the largest cattle ranch in Canada, the cowtown of Merritt in my time was taken out of a western movie and Coutlee's livery stable was inhabited by an old and gaudy Texan, named Texas, a train robber and bandit, who reputedly had killed thirteen men in the States.

A boy brought up in such surroundings, the intimate of cowpunchers, coal miners, badmen, Indians and horses, will always think of himself, in his old age, as a relic of the lost West. But when he returns to Merritt today, finding it a huddle of mean stores and houses, seeing the glamorous hotel, with its barroom full of chaps and spurs of a Saturday night, now pitifully squalid, then he mourns his lost illusions and does not wish to come here again.

At Spences Bridge you are out of the mountains and into the real Dry Belt. No crop will grow without irrigation water and, since only a few trickles come out of the parched Thompson hills, the farms are small and scattered. Under this baking sun, with alkali dust and the smell of sagebrush in your nostrils, it is pleasant, on crossing the bridge, to find yourself in one of those long avenues of giant poplars which the old-timers planted so hopefully long ago and nurtured with their precious water. After this momentary shade you are on the bald range again, high above the river.

The old road here, which was used long after Douglas's route was abandoned in the Fraser canyon, was hung on wooden stilts and fastened to the hillside gullies with hay wire. To drive it required a sure eye and a sober head. The present road is wide and safe and allows you almost any speed. It zigzags down presently to the river at Ashcroft, though you can go north, by a short cut, without pausing to inspect this curious old town.

Ashcroft was a child of the gold rush, and long after the rush remained as the entrepot of the whole Cariboo country. When goods were brought by rail from the East and from the coast they were transferred at Ashcroft to the freight wagons, which carried them northward to the ranches and dwindling mines. The town swarmed with packers, drivers, gamblers, fancy ladies, horses and oxen.

Since then the physical content of Ashcroft, though emptied of its old population, has not changed much. The inevitable Chinese maintain two or three grimy stores and restaurants. Before the hotel old men still doze on their tilted chairs under the poplars. An ancient green parrot, older than sin, still clucked and swore in his cage outside the hotel door when I was last there. The transcontinental trains, on either side of the river, wake you with their hootings in the middle of the night. At harvest season the town is red with spilled tomatoes on their way to the cannery and odorous with the fumes of boiling ketchup. Down by the river the last freight wagon slowly molders, a frail monument to the days when the wealth of Cariboo poured through Ashcroft.

This is hot country, about as hot as any in Canada. Combine the heat imprisoned in the oven of the Thompson Valley with water from its upland lakes and you can make the caked Dry Belt soil produce Canada's finest potatoes and tomatoes. The irrigated farms around the town are not large but the quality of their products has made them known throughout the nation. The Ashcroft potato is as famous in Canada as the Georgia peach in the United States or the wines of Champagne in France.

At first sight the Dry Belt of the Thompson Valley, as viewed from the vantage point of Ashcroft, is only a depressing waste of rounded hills and dull cliffs. On closer inspection its beauty begins to emerge—not the conventional beauty of colored photographs, calendars and Christmas cards, but a hard, stark beauty offering no concession to man's sense of comfort. It is hard in its staring rock faces, its deep ravines of clay, its criss-crossed gullies and arid range. Hard in texture but strangely softened at dawn and dusk with a haze of purple in which hill, cliff, rock and distant mountain peak seem almost to float.

The over-all design is fantastic and opulent. The tool that cut the pattern is erosion. Rain, snow and ice, though scarce, have slowly carved off the soft clay, leaving the rocks outthrust. They have leached the minerals to smear the cliffs in the color of the spectrum. They have cut the valley of the Thompson and the honeycomb of side canyons running into it. They have rounded off the foothills like loaves of dough, with the finger marks still visible.

The scenery from Ashcroft, looking north across the valley of the Bonaparte, is for the strong eye only. Perhaps it is never understood without years of observation. When you have seen it often enough in its different seasons—in the pale spring wash of bunch grass, in the yellow of autumn and the patchy white of winter—you grow to love it for its clean lines and violent coloring, for its dry air which makes you feel young again, for its biting smell of sage, pine and juniper, and for its loneliness.

At Ashcroft the Thompson, after running almost north and south, is bending eastward. The road goes north along the little creek that proudly calls itself the Bonaparte River, detouring around the Thompson canyon. At Cache Creek, in days of Indian and white the crossroads of travel, the road forks. The northern fork follows the lush Bonaparte Valley to Clinton, where we arrived by the old Pavilion route on the journey up the Fraser. The eastern fork cuts across the bench and back to the Thompson.

For half an hour or so on this eastward journey the river is hidden behind the hills to the right. We are clear of the high mountains altogether and on the rolling interior plateau, a country as friendly to man and his animals as the lower Fraser is hostile.

Men have farmed and cattle have grazed here since the first settlement came in with the gold rush. Every creek, where water is rare and priceless, supports its few acres of green hay land, its ranch house and a bluff of poplars. Every hill is grooved by the long-worn grazing trails of cattle, in parallel lines, one above the other, like a circular staircase, so regular and invariable that the stranger takes them for the original work of nature. And every turn in the road opens some new view eastward across the generous valley of the Thompson.

One always thinks of this as fat country—fat in the anatomy of undulating hills, fat, too, in its yield of bunch grass, in its heavy, irrigated fields, and in its product, the white-faced beef steer and the black-faced sheep. Fat and friendly, after the niggard channel of the Fraser, and wide open under the sky. The Fraser is harshly male; the Thompson softly female.

In summer the Thompson Valley lies in drab grays and browns which, at sunrise and again in the evening dusk, are cut with broad splashes of purple shadow. In autumn it is pure gold—gold dust sprinkled across the hills by the poplars, little golden nuggets of stubble fields, and at every season the gold of that peculiar sunlight which sifts through the Dry Belt atmosphere.

Except for the ranches, miles apart, a steer or two, some stray horses, a coyote or a family of pheasants, the valley is empty of animal life. It will not remain so much longer. When cheap power can lift the water of the Thompson upon these benches they will support a hundred miles of cultivation on both sides of the river, from Spences Bridge eastward. This will be another Okanagan fruit valley, a farm area as rich as any in Canada.

Where the road curves a little southward, revealing the Thompson and the two railway lines almost lost in its wide ditch, you may see what this gray land can yield when water turns it into a black muck. Beside the road, and sloping down to the distant river, stands the proof of the land's fertility and the futility of men. Note it well and weep for the folly of your species.

There is little enough to see now, only a few miles of dead apple trees, black skeletons in well-ordered rows, but this was once a young man's dream.

Before World War I a colony of Englishmen planted this hillside in orchard, brought water in long flumes from the hills to the north, built houses, founded a town and called it Wallachin.

That very name, when it is rolled over the tongue in the Indian fashion and pronounced as Wallasheen, has in it the music of running water, the most beautiful name, I think, in Canada. Here is the sound of tinkling bells, of Indian campfires long ago—a name to be placed with Saguenay, with Miramichi, Lachine, Okanagan, Assiniboine, Medicine Hat, Montreal, with the drumbeat of Fundy and Nipigon, with the trumpet blast of Yoho, with the thunder of Kootenay and Cariboo, with the wild bird cry of Canada itself, with all the diapason of sound in the heavy-freighted names that tell the story of the Canadian people.

The young men heard the music of Wallachin, they saw the fertility of the Thompson soil, and they planted their trees. The trees were starting to bear apples when the first war came. Every man marched off to Europe, the houses were deserted, the irrigation flumes rotted in the hills, the earth dried up, and the trees withered of thirst.

When the soldiers came home there was nothing left of Wallachin but its name and the long lines of skeletons. The government of British Columbia pronounced the whole project uneconomic and would advance no money to salvage it. Wallachin was surrendered to the sagebrush and the tumbleweed, but for twenty years a few trees somehow survived the drought, half dead, yielding apples which you could pick from the roadside.

Finally even these relics of the young men's dream no longer could push out a single leaf. Wallachin returned to the days of the Indians who had named it.

Another town will rise here someday when the river is pumped and greater orchards will grow in straight lines up the hillside. Then, perhaps, the people living in a green valley will remember the soldiers who left all they owned to fight for this country, and came back to find their fields turned brown.

From the Wallachin ridge the Thompson does not appear green as at its junction with the Fraser. Only the heavier sediment of its parent stream could give this river by comparison a look of clarity. Now it is seen to be brown, too, or a lifeless gray. It lies perfectly still, without visible movement, more solid than liquid. But when the road swings down to the Savona bridge you discover again the volume and power of the current.

I have fished hereabouts and found it dangerous to wade more than a few feet into the water. Every mile or so the smooth and oily surface is broken by the white froth of rapids. It is no wonder that the Overlanders' canoe capsized in such a torrent and smashed upon the boulders at its edge.

At Savona, however, the river widens into a basin eighteen miles long and over a mile across and now bears the name of Kamloops Lake. The high and reddish bluffs of the lake are impassable on the south shore. After crossing the Savona bridge, the road must climb behind the bluffs and wind through the ranch lands of Cherry Creek, some of the best in British Columbia. Broad hayfields are spread here to support the lurching log barns and ranch houses. Farther up the slopes the herds of sheep graze to the edge of the timber.

You can hardly fail to stop at Henry Cornwall's by the roadside. His towering row of poplars, his trim stone fence, his cozy house and the massive figure of Henry himself, inevitably sitting under the trees and watching the world go by with a look of motionless immortality, will certainly invite you in. And the cooking of his table will discourage you from going further.

Henry (he will insist that you call him by his Christian name at first sight) is of the famous Ashcroft family, the English aristocrats who brought the first fox hounds to British Columbia and helped to rule it in the early days. Henry is pure Canadian, as indigenous to this country as the tumbleweed and as tenacious, and he is wise with the wisdom of more than seventy summers, seventy harvests, and seventy years of brooding under his cool trees.

In their shade it is pleasant and profitable to listen to Henry's stories, which come out slowly, with many pauses, as he decides whether you are worthy to hear them.

I have listened to him there, the breeze rumpling the poplar leaves, the irrigation ditches chuckling, the apples reddening almost visibly in the orchard, while he told me how Bill Miner held up the main-line train of the C.P.R. east of Kamloops in the fashion of the James brothers, and how this most notable of our Canadian bandits, a peaceful soul beloved of his jailers, always kept an egg in his pocket for good luck, and took it out and peered at it thoughtfully during his trial.

In these same agreeable surroundings (for Henry always talks best out of doors) he told me the true story of the Cornwall fox hounds, a special gem in our western folklore.

According to Henry, who had it direct from his father, the celebrated event did not take place at Ashcroft, as is generally supposed, but in the Nicola Valley. There the elder Cornwall took his hounds and, dressed in the scarlet hunting habit of England, set out in pursuit of coyotes, there being no foxes handy.

With him went a wild, irreverent company of cowboys, unschooled in the sacrament of the English hunt. Each of these amateur gentlemen was instructed to shout "Tallyho!" at the first sight of a coyote. With a fine dignity, with the flash of scarlet coats, the immemorial sound of the huntsman's horn, and the baying of English hounds, the hunt moved majestically across the range. Every cowboy rehearsed his part in the ritual, muttering the mystic word "Tallyho!" to himself.

But at the critical moment, when a coyote at last was sighted, the ritual was forgotten. The first cowboy let out a whoop, screamed, "There goes the son of a——!" and, with all the others echoing the cry, almost rode the hounds underfoot.

At this act of desecration Mr. Cornwall called off the hunt and never wore scarlet again. That is why, as Henry says, the sacred call of "Tallyho!" has not sounded yet on the ranges of British Columbia.

Henry prefers to sit and talk. His brother, Gilly, though no longer young, will take you up to his camp in the hills. In his dark little lakes among the spruce the trout are sometimes almost too easy to catch, but a pack-horse trip with Gilly, even if you are not a fisherman, is certain to be memorable.

This lean, hard woodsman, who has had more than his fill of life, knows every animal and bird. His stories around the campfire, of traplines, grizzlies, blizzards and sudden death, are still remembered in detail by my children, though they were barely seven years old when they rode into the mountains with Gilly.

Next to Pavilion the Thompson Valley around Cornwall's offers the best riding and the loveliest open scenery I have found west of the Rockies. Between the ranch house and the river stands a steep ridge which you can reach in an hour on a surefooted horse. From the top you look out northward on the basin of Kamloops Lake, backed by the Clearwater Range, which divides the North Thompson from the Fraser; westward upon the green specks of the Cherry Creek ranches; southward on Cornwall's clump of poplars; eastward to the Thompson at Kamloops. The panorama reveals the Thompson's valley as hardly smaller than the Fraser's. Indeed, as between the two, now that you have had a good look at both, you almost wonder which is the main river and which the tributary.

For twelve miles eastward beyond Cornwall's the road keeps inland, then suddenly, in a single swoop, debouches upon the high banks of the river, as if it had been constructed to command the broadest vista of the whole interior.

Between a brown flat on the west and the bare mound of Mount Paul on the east, the two Thompsons come together in peaceful confluence, very different from the violent, two-colored union of the Thompson and the Fraser. The north branch meanders down a wide valley, which closes northwards into the blue defiles of the Clearwater Range. The Thompson itself, the larger stream, runs in from the east between dusty, rolling hills. Nowhere is the desolate beauty of the Dry Belt presented on such a gigantic scale or in such hues of blue, brown and burning ocher.

Two rivers, linking the lake country of the Selkirks to the east and the timbered valleys of the Rockies to the north, must always bring travelers to this natural meeting place where the waters join.

In the early days the fur brigades moved out of Oregon Territory, through the Okanagan Valley and, leaving the watershed of the Columbia, reached the Fraser system at Kamloops. Here they paused before moving on to the Fraser or, ascending the North Thompson, crossed westward into the Cariboo country on their way to Fort George and the lake posts farther west. Inevitably the junction of the two Thompsons was chosen as the site of the first Hudson's Bay post in this part of the interior. The fort was built in 1812 on the north bank of the Thompson and on the west bank of its northern tributary. The modern town of Kamloops has spread across this flat where the fort stood.

Inevitably also the two transcontinental railways—the Canadian Pacific out of the high Selkirk passes to the east and the Canadian National out of the Yellowhead at the headwaters of the Fraser—met at Kamloops to follow the Thompson and the

Fraser out to sea. Just as the furs moved through Fort Kamloops in the old days, every ounce of freight hauled in and out of Vancouver must move through the town today.

Kamloops stands on the south bank of the main stream, directly facing the rivers' confluence. From the high vantage point on this last turn of the road you can look down directly on the roof of the town and realize at once what skill and imagination went into its construction. All around it, to the edge of the last back yard, the range is parched and bare, but within the circle of the town lies a green island of trees and gardens. Kamloops was built by defiance of the climate, by the insistent pouring of water on this cracked soil, by the cultivation of every available foot, by the determination of all the inhabitants to subdue the common enemy drought.

They have succeeded in peopling their patch of river bench with a forest of shade trees along every street, with masses of flowers in every garden. They have built what must be the perfect river community and the two rivers, with their farms, timber and railways, support it well. By the generosity of the rivers alone 10,000 people live the ideal small-town life in Kamloops.

The Thompson is the central economic fact of Kamloops and a very comfortable social fact as well. It provides the site of the waterside park that is the heart of the town. It affords safe swimming for the children in the calm water close to the southern bank. It nourishes fine groves of trees along its edge. It helps to cool the fierce summer heat and moderate the winter. It supplies the city's waterworks. Above all, its presence here relieves the sense of surrounding drought, while two lavish valleys give the inhabitant, at every turn, a new glimpse of distant beauty.

For all the modern look of the place, and all the efforts of the chamber of commerce to promote what is known in America as progress, there remains in Kamloops some feeling of its origin. Real cowboys in high-heeled boots, not the denizens of

bogus dude ranches, and Indians from the reservations are plenti-
ful on the streets any Saturday night. Stores display stock saddles in their windows as ordinary articles of commerce. The
horse has not become a curio.

These exhibits mark Kamloops as an old cattle town, but
the marks of an earlier time, the days of gold, are still faintly
visible. Lolling on the benches of the river park you will find the
inmates of the provincial old men's home, a few of them ancient
enough to remember the last of the Cariboo rush. Many of the
original Argonauts died in this refuge after spending the fortunes reaped around Barkerville. The present inmates, from all
parts of the interior, represent, in the unnoted record of their
obscure lives, the labor of ranch, of forest and mine, that has
made British Columbia.

At one time and another I have spent a good many days lis-
tening to these unsung patriarchs as they told their little stories of hardship and adventure, and I have often wished that their
recollections could be set down in the official archives at Victoria before it is too late.

Every month, I suppose, as some forgotten pioneer dies in
the old men's home, a fragment of our history, some local incident which would enrich or might alter the chronicle of Canada,
is lost beyond recovery. In the busy tide of progress few people
have time for the wrecks and derelicts, the old men who blink
in the sun, who find no listener for their tales, who cannot express the magic of a better time, and have learned, in a proud
silence, to take their secrets with them.

Kamloops, located by its rivers at a key point in the interior
economy, has always been as well a fulcrum in the political balance of British Columbia. What fierce, forgotten battles have
been fought on the Kamloops hustings! How often have the
great figures of the nation paused here, to win the interior vote,
on their campaign tours across the country! What Kamloopian
will ever forget that three provincial party leaders and two future premiers were chosen in convention here? And how can

British Columbia ever hope to see again any spectacle like the famous Conservative Party convention of 1926, with its days of ferocious deadlock, its sudden deliverance under Dr. Simon Fraser Tolmie, whose father was Douglas's physician and who bore the name of the great river's discoverer—bore it with honor and unequaled friendship in the politics of the province and nation?

Those departed glories are for old men like me. That they sound trivial and far off to the present generation in British Columbia shows how far the tide of progress has rolled.

The Dry Belt air is not only a refreshment to the stranger but a tangible asset to Kamloops. The earliest settlers realized that lung troubles yielded to this climate and doctors have confirmed this discovery. Western Canada's most important tuberculosis sanitarium was therefore placed just outside Kamloops, on the north bank of the Thompson, with a productive farm around it.

The success of the farm having established the worth of the soil for fruit and vegetable, truck gardening has spread along the bench east and west, making the city more and more a farming as well as a ranching center. When the Thompson can be pumped and all the good land used, Kamloops should become a city. (We oldsters like it as it is.)

You move up the Thompson eastward through a mixed farming country which suddenly leaves the Dry Belt behind. The river road now enters a forest of pine, larch, birch and poplar at the edge of the lake region.

The sharp boundaries of the Dry Belt, the quick transitions into moist and wooded country—all governed by the chaotic mountains and their freakish effects on the precipitation of clouds from the Pacific—are always surprising to the stranger. The Dry Belt, the accepted term in British Columbia, is seen, as you move toward the mountains, to be something of a misnomer. This is no belt but a relatively small tangle of valleys which the ocean clouds pass by before they hit the mountains. A few miles from every dry valley, on the higher land, there is ample rain to support the unbroken dark line of timber. The Thompson, from Kamloops upward, is navigable and thus comes within the authority of the national government. This fact was long forgotten after roads were built and the early stern-wheelers beached. When an enterprising Chinese merchant of Kamloops acquired one of these steamers a few years ago and launched it upon the river to carry farm products, the government of British Columbia discovered that it could not block the old channel with its highway bridges. At large expense, to permit the passage of this single craft, the government was compelled by federal law to install a lift span in its bridge above Kamloops.

This was a famous legal victory for the Chinese navigator and a reminder of the better times before the advent of progress, when men were free to voyage where they pleased. A reminder also of the Thompson's capacity as a carrier of goods. For that purpose, as farm production and population increase, the river may be used again.

Forty-three miles from Kamloops the sources of the Thompson appear. An area of deep, clear lakes is the reservoir that gathers the rain and melting snow from the western slopes of the Selkirks and consigns them to the river for transport to the ocean. Less than forty miles eastward, on the far side of the Monashee Mountains, the Columbia is moving to the same destination by a longer, southern route. A drop of moisture in the Monashee Range, you would think, must pause and wonder whether it should join the Thompson or the Columbia, whether it should remain Canadian or become American.

The first lake in the ascent of the Thompson is Little Shuswap, a catch basin for the waters pouring in from Shuswap Lake itself, to the east, and from the Adam River system, directly to the north. On the map the Thompson begins at Little

Shuswap. The channel that joins this lake to Shuswap is called Little River though it is, of course, the Thompson, and notable at this point mainly for its trout.

Shuswap, the true origin of the Thompson, is a lake extraordinary in its beauty and its shape. Its waters are clear and deep, its shores heavily wooded, its beaches shiny with clean sand. In fact it is two lakes, the western 45 and the eastern 37 miles long, lying almost parallel but joined in the middle, like a pair of Siamese twins, to form a crooked letter H, which lies on a slant from northeast to southwest. Roughly parallel to Shuswap, Adams Lake, on the west, completes a three-pronged waterway large enough to keep the Thompson filled.

Such a substantial body of water as Shuswap, set in valuable timber, affords easy transportation to the local lumber and pole industry. It offers also, on its southern shore, a water grade for the Canadian Pacific Railway's main line into the Selkirks. It supports, as its main center of commerce, the growing town of Salmon Arm.

At Salmon Arm, on the southern lake shore, one reaches the northern extremity of the Okanagan fruit valley which, being tributary to the Columbia, has no place in this book. The long chain of Okanagan Lakes, directly to the south of Salmon Arm, empties into the Columbia in Washington, but the foaming Okanagan orchards flow north as far as the banks of Shuswap. Salmon Arm and its surrounding fruit lands and mixed farms, though geographically part of the Thompson Valley, belong economically to the Okanagan community, whose almost unbroken line of orchard thus joins the Thompson and Columbia systems.

Salmon Arm has only some 3,000 people but it has produced a notable western figure. This is the town of Rolf Bruhn, a kind of Paul Bunyan among the loggers of British Columbia. As a Swedish boy he sailed before the mast, immigrated into Canada, walked across the country with frozen feet in the dead of winter, farmed in a remote valley from which he carried out his potato crop on his back, made a fortune in lumbering, was almost destroyed by the explosion of his boat on Shuswap Lake, was patched up by plastic surgeons, made a second fortune in mining, and died a minister of the crown. Today in the Shuswap valleys they are taking a second crop of timber from the forest that Bruhn logged thirty years ago.

The area of forest and lake is friendly to the camper and fisherman. We used to drive out from Kamloops to Little Shuswap in the first warmth of the year to loll on the miles of sandy beach, and where we drove in the morning through a forest of bare tamarack and birch, by evening, on our return, the first buds would be opening in a shower of green lace. Spring comes here overnight on its passage from the coast to the Rockies and settles down on the lake shores for a long pause before it assails the cold mountain rampart.

Before losing itself in the Thompson at Kamloops, the North Thompson maintains a dark and violent character of its own. That is not immediately apparent as you move up the tributary. The valley is broad and fertile, the river quiet, as the Overlanders found, to their relief, at the end of their awful journey. But, as everywhere, the Dry Belt ends suddenly at the fringe of the forest, the valley narrows in a few miles, and the North Thompson reveals that streak of wickedness which almost destroyed the Overlanders' rafts. The current is rapid now, its course is twisted and its canyons, hidden in heavy timber, are rocky and precipitous.

Until recent times the North Thompson country was among the loneliest in the traveled areas of British Columbia. The Canadian Northern Railway, now part of the Canadian National system, was built from the Yellowhead Pass by the water grade of the North Thompson at the beginning of World War I and its trains were almost the only travelers here. Even today only one village, Blue River, has managed to rise out of this somber wilderness. Settlement, pathetic little farms cleared out of the river flats, is only beginning. Some pockets of rich land and the great forests of cedar, fir and spruce almost as large as the coastal timber support a few small sawmills.

Where the road dwindles to a forest track some 170 miles north of Kamloops and then disappears altogether, the traveler begins to understand the feelings of the Overlanders who found themselves trapped in this jungle. Seen from the windows of the train, the only present mode of conveyance, the valley has a look of brooding monotony. The hills, hardly mountains yet, are black with evergreen growth, each exactly like its neighbor. There are no carved rock faces as in the Fraser canyon, no wide vistas as on the Thompson, nothing but the black forest, unbroken, unchanging, a blanket which rounds off and hides the shape of the earth. The disease of claustrophobia, I dare say, originated here.

Into the North Thompson flows water from the very edge of the Fraser to the west. The range of Clearwater Mountains, standing behind the forested hills of the North Thompson's western bank, separates it from the Cariboo plateau but cannot quite dam up the plateau's waters. By a sinuous chain of lakes and rivers, as the map shows but no stranger could guess, rain falling within sight of the Fraser is finally sucked eastward through the Clearwater Range into the North Thompson about halfway between Kamloops and the Yellowhead.

A family of half a dozen substantial Cariboo lakes thus drains eastward and some of their tributary creeks actually rise west of the Fraser's own tributaries in the Lac La Hache country. Among these lakes are Canim and Mahood, which belong to the Cariboo but have thrust their waters with a violent fall into the Clearwater River and thence into the North Thompson.

At Blue River the train enters the western defiles of the Rockies. Back of the timbered hills rises the bare escarpment of rock and snow. Within their clutch the river churns in furious rapids toward the right-angle turn of Hell's Gate. Seated in a comfortable observation car, you can hardly believe that thirty-two men, a pregnant woman and her small children rode this torrent on flimsy rafts and tried to drive oxen and horses through this tangled timber. The Overlanders' story can seem tame only to the reader who has not seen the river and the forest beside it.

Since it left Kamloops the train has been climbing steadily but imperceptibly. The C.P.R. line crosses the Rockies on laborious grades by spiral tunnels and often demands the power of two locomotives. The C.N.R. follows a grade so easy that a single locomotive can mount it without a gasp.

When the stranger peers out the window to behold a new valley on the left-hand side he can hardly realize that the little creek below him is the upper Fraser. The North Thompson has lost itself in the timber, the divide has been crossed, and the water is flowing north instead of south.

19   The First Inhabitants

FOR AEONS OF TIME BEFORE MAN SAW THE FRASER, PERHAPS before man lived anywhere upon the earth, the river channels, from the sea to the creeks of the farthest tributary, were navigated by salmon in unvarying autumnal migration. Essentially the story of the river, by length of occupancy, by the test of endurance, and by the ordeal of adventure belongs to the salmon, not to man.

Of all species living in and beside the river, including man, the salmon is in character the bravest; in body, pound for pound, the strongest; in shape and color the most beautiful; in its scheme of life the noblest; in its instincts the most mysterious.

Man studies the salmon's flesh under his microscope. He charts the salmon's wanderings on his graphs, maps and statistical tables. After he has almost destroyed the fishery by his folly, he sets up treaties, administering authorities and police regulations to protect the salmon for the uses of his commerce. Around the salmon he has constructed one of the most satisfactory projects of international co-operation in North American history. He packs the salmon in cans and ships them all over the world. But he never grasps the secret hidden somewhere in the salmon's tiny brain.

Always the central question remains: By what power, mechanism or sixth sense can the salmon, lost for years in the Pacific Ocean, return in exact time to the river, ascend it to the same stream, the same brook, the same nuptial sand bar where it hatched from its mother's egg and there, after reproducing its kind, give up its own life? Without charts in this labyrinth, without the faculty of reason, almost without sight in these opaque waters, how does the salmon pursue this blind, sure journey of hundreds of miles to its home?

Man finds no answer in his laboratories. Perhaps it is better so.

The scientists who have pried at the secret are humble in the presence of a wonder greater than their knowledge. The salmon's insatiable lust for life, its honorable appetite for death when the work of life is done, teaches these men the furious futility of human life, its overshadowing fear, its ignorance of the daily, unseen miracles around it.

The scientists I have known upon the river, men as great as they are obscure, came almost to worship the salmon and hid their worship under scientific jargon. Watching the inscrutable quest of the salmon, recognizing a principle beyond their power to explain, these men (though they would be the first to deny it) turn into religionists of a queer, incommunicable congregation.

The greatest of them, a man who had spent his life and genius on the study of these fish, once said to me, as we watched them surge up the river: "We really don't know anything about them. I don't think we ever will." Secretly, I suspect, he did not want this final knowledge lest he reduce a miracle to a formula. He preferred to glimpse here something larger than his science, a token of the common creaturehood in all living things.

There are few men like my friend who pause in wonder at the salmon horde. For most men the salmon has been only an easy source of food. Since their first coming to the Pacific coast men have lived on the salmon.

On the Fraser the original races of men, old beyond record, found swarms of fish more prolific than in any other river in the world. A minute fraction of the unfailing annual migration was enough to feed all the Indians living on the riverbanks and far beyond. A crude net of tree roots or bark could lift from the crowded current enough food to keep a man and his family for a year—food more nourishing, with more calories in it, than beef. Smoked over a fire, it would keep indefinitely.

When the white man reached the Fraser he discovered an entire Indian society and a primitive economic system living almost exclusively on smoked salmon and trading it to the remote tribes of the interior. There was no need to grow anything, or even to shoot game. After a few days' work in the autumn the Indian brave could devote himself without interruption to the pursuit of politics, war and women. Century after century the salmon provided a soft life for all human beings who cared to lift it from the water.

The white explorers ate the Indians' diet and could hardly have survived without it. The settlers who followed learned to turn the salmon, like the furs of animals, like the trees of the forest, into money.

No one knows when the first fish cargoes moved out of the teeming sea waters at the Fraser's mouth, but as early as 1835, even before Fort Victoria was founded, the thrifty Hudson's Bay Company was shipping salted salmon in barrels to Asia and the Hawaiian Islands. Thanks to the Frenchman, Nicholas Appert, who learned to can food in 1795, Americans were canning salmon on the Sacramento in 1860. Ten years later the first cannery was built on the Fraser at Annieville, just below New Westminster. By the turn of the century the Fraser was the world's largest salmon fishery.

The early fishermen called the Pacific fish salmon because they resembled in visible form, flesh and flavor the salmon of Atlantic rivers. The Atlantic fish derived its name from the Latin verb "salire," to leap. The Pacific fish possessed this same leaping power. It could propel its body over drops in the current six feet high or more. It could travel longer, fiercer waters than the salmon of the Atlantic ever encountered. Like the Atlantic salmon, it seemed to repair to fresh water at regular intervals of spawning.

In fact, the Atlantic and Pacific salmon were different creatures in structure and in life.

So long as they could sell their catch as "salmon," a universal delicacy which could never satisfy the demands of the trade, the fishermen asked no more. But the scientists soon discovered that the fish of the Pacific were a distinct race, far more numerous than the relatively minor race of the Atlantic.

The Pacific salmon, the scientists learned, has more rays in the anal fin than the Atlantic, more gill rakers, branchiostegal rays and pyloric caeca (the fingerlike pouches attached to the intestine). These were minute though decisive scraps of evidence which would escape the ordinary man. He could not fail to observe the basic difference between the life cycles of the two fish. The Atlantic salmon ascends the rivers from the sea, spawns and returns to the sea again. The Pacific salmon makes only one journey to the river, spawns and dies.

Both fish belong to the huge family of Salmonidae which, in its many branches, inhabits a large part of the world's oceans and bears many local names. The scientist calls the Atlantic salmon Salmo Salar. To the Pacific salmon he gave the appalling name of Salmo Oncorhynchus. No one but a scientist ever uses it.

As even the Indian knew, Oncorhynchus contains five distinct species. All are of about the same shape, beautiful of line, deepbellied, broad backed. All bear a shimmering metallic blue on the back, fading into the silver of the belly. But they vary sharply in size, slightly in color, and distinctly in methods of feeding and times of migration.

The largest among them and the most succulent is Oncorhynchus tschawytscha—the mighty "Spring" or "Tyee" in British Columbia, the "Quinnat" or "Chinook" in Washington and Oregon, the "Quinnat" or "Sacramento" in California, the "Quinnat" or "King" in Alaska.

The Spring, as we call it in Fraser waters, averages 25 pounds in weight and 38½ inches in length, but often reaches 50 pounds and has been known to weigh 80. The ridge of its back is almost black, its sides steely blue, its belly silver white.

This is the fish that attracts sportsmen from all parts of America to the Pacific coast in late summer. Around it has been built a thriving tourist industry, a rich legendry, an endless debate on rods, reels and trolling spoons, a strange dark ritual of angling.

Commercially the Spring is a relatively unimportant species, though in its fresh form it is highly prized, is shipped in ice across the continent, and makes better eating than any other species.

The fish on which the Fraser fishery was built is the prolific Oncorhynchus nerka—the "Sockeye" or "Alaska Red." It weighs on average only 7 pounds and is 28 inches in length. In coloring it is more blue than the Spring and in some areas is called "Blueback." It will not heed the angler's lures and must be taken in nets. Since it travels farther inland than any other species and is equipped with bountiful oils to nourish it on its journey, it is the ideal fish for canning. In the Fraser it far exceeds in number any other species. Until fairly modern times other species were seldom canned. The Fraser is the Sockeye's river.

Oncorhynchus kisutch, the "Cohoe" or "Silver," averages 9 pounds in weight, 28½ inches in length, and is the liveliest member of the family. It alone will take a fly in salt water, to the delight of the superior angler, who is above the mean uses of the troll. The Cohoe has an upper covering between blue and green but is easily distinguished from its cousins by the silvery sheen of its scales. On the Fraser (to add to the confusion of names) the Cohoe is a "Blueback" to all commercial fishermen. Like the Spring and Sockeye, it is fine food and its numbers make it valuable commercially.

Oncorhynchus gorbuscha, the "Humpback" or "Pink," is a

humbler breed. It weighs on average only 4 pounds and is about 2 feet long. The extraordinary hump growing upon the back of the male in spawning season explains its popular name. Canned, it makes valuable food but in quality it cannot be compared with the Spring, Sockeye or Cohoe.

Lowest in the estimation of fishermen is Oncorhynchus keta—the "Chum" or "Keta." Its average weight is 10 pounds, its length 32¼ inches. It was long despised, as food fit only for dogs and Indians, but nowadays it sells readily in the world's markets.

All five varieties live in the same general life cycle, but the length of the cycle varies a little.

From spring until the first days of winter the various local races of salmon within the five species begin their migration from the ocean to the Fraser, as to other Pacific rivers. Each race knows where it is going and moves in a body. The experts can predict, within a few days when the different waves of migration will appear off the coast. Most of the Fraser races move through the Strait of Juan de Fuca and, by circling southward through United States waters before they cross the boundary again into Canada, create a nice international problem in the regulation of the fishery. A minor movement rounds the northern tip of Vancouver Island and follows the Gulf of Georgia southward to the river mouth.

The general migration begins with the Springs, their name marking the season of their arrival. The Sockeye come in early summer and the various races of that species continue to appear until the end of October. The successive waves of Cohoe are off the river until late summer, with the Humpbacks. The Pinks sometimes remain in the sea until the eve of winter.

Since the Sockeye is pre-eminently the Fraser fish, its migratory movements are worth watching.

Except for a small procession around Vancouver Island, the Sockeye swarms up the Strait of Juan de Fuca in compact schools by well-defined routes. It travels always on floodtides and close to the surface. Leaping into the air for no apparent reason—perhaps some inner ecstasy before its approaching death —it reveals itself to the fisherman who follows the moving school. On the ebb of the tide the fish disappears. Its hiding place, between tides, is unknown. With the return of the flood it emerges where it sank and continues on its way toward the river.

Only in the sea are white men permitted by law to catch salmon. Indians, by ancient treaty, may take them from the river.

When the salmon appear off the coast, a numerous fleet of fishing craft, American and Canadian, sets off in pursuit. Hours of fishing are strictly regulated by Canada and the United States through a joint authority to permit a sufficient escapement of spawning fish.

The fisherman has three methods of capture.

He may troll in a small powerboat for Spring and Cohoe, which will take his spoon. For this laborious business he carries two or more stout rods attached to his mast and lowered into horizontal position when fishing commences. From each pole at least two trolling lines are rigged. They are hauled in by a mechanical winch which the fisherman calls a "gurdy."

As only Spring and Cohoe will take bait, the other species are caught by gill nets or purse seines.

The gill net is rigged by cork floats to hang in the water like a wire chicken fence, across some known fish channel. The salmon, never turning aside in its quest, pushes against the net, thrusts its head through one of the apertures and is helpless. If it tries to retreat, its gill covers are caught in the mesh.

The purse seine, operated from substantial boats some 60 to 75 feet in length, and with crews of seven to ten men, is just what its name suggests—a kind of purse, open at the bottom. It is drawn around a school of surfacing salmon, and, by a neat arrangement of rings and lines, its sides are quickly pulled together under the fish. A powerful winch is required to lift a well-filled seine aboard.

The fisherman takes his catch to the cannery, where he has made a contract in advance, or transfers it at sea to the tender of a fish company. Some boats are owned by canneries and operated on a share basis. Others are owned by individual fishermen. Every fisherman sells his fish at a price agreed upon between his union and the fish companies before the opening of the season. If the run is heavy, he may make enough in a few weeks to live comfortably for a year. In a season of light runs he may earn little. His life is hard in his cramped boat, is often perilous if he goes out to sea to meet the salmon, and is always a gamble.

If they escape the fishermen, the Sockeye enter the Fraser on the flood tide, the last tide they will ever know. It bears them up the lower reaches of the river and when it subsides they do not turn back or hide themselves, as in the sea. Close to the surface and hugging the side eddies by the bank, they start their final toil up the current.

They have been well equipped for the ultimate adventure. In their years at sea they have eaten and grown prodigiously. Their bodies are crammed with fat and oil. They never eat in fresh water, but their store of energy will carry them to the end of the road.

As it approaches its own spawning river a race of salmon turns suddenly off the main channel as if directed by a traffic light. Another race will pass all the lower tributaries, ascend farther to the mouth of its home waters, and there leave the Fraser. The great upriver races never pause for a moment at any side stream. Their destination is the Shuswap Lake country, within the western flanks of the Rockies, or the Chilcotin plateau, lying to the east of the Coast mountains, or Stuart Lake, not far south of the Alaskan Panhandle. Seven hundred miles of fast water are not too much for the Sockeye. They will not rest until they have reached their own sand bar. If they are blockaded by the freaky river current, if they cannot spawn at home, they will die unspawned, still struggling upward while a remnant of life is left.

The first hundred miles of broad river channel are easy. When it enters the canyon at Hope the salmon meets the first challenge of the current. At Yale it must swim through water which man cannot navigate with the power of steam. As the canyon narrows, the water deepens and the river, increasing its speed at every mile, is swirled into a chaos of conflicting currents. The salmon, knowing the path from the inherited knowledge of its ancestors, seeks every back eddy, unerringly finds the easiest water, and does not halt until it reaches the smooth pool just below Hell's Gate, 130 miles from the sea.

There a shoal of Sockeye, already turning crimson in the first stages of dissolution, will lie packed together, on the surface, in a single mass, spreading like a stain of wine across the brown water. A few yards above, the river writhes between the narrow, smoothly chiseled walls of the Gate in a convulsion which, you would think, must extinguish all organic life.

The salmon know, as their ancestors knew, that the ordeal of the passage is ahead. They pause to rest and gather strength. Then of a sudden they rush together at the mouth of the gorge, throw themselves high above the foam, dive down into some well-known whirlpool, leap again and perhaps reach the slower current above the gate. There they wriggle into the gravel at the water's edge, stunned and spent. In a little while they will move on again.

Or, if they have miscalculated the current by half a second, they are tossed out of the water like chips, high up against the bare canyon rocks, to drop back dead. Those which fail in the first attempt and still live are swept into the pool below. After resting, they will try again. They will fight the waters of the Gate until they get through or die. The eggs within these inland fish will never be laid except in the home waters, far above.

Once through the Gate (where the passage may be relatively easy at certain water levels), the migration moves steadily upstream at the rate of twenty to thirty miles a day. There are more barriers to cross—the powerful Scuzzy Rapids just above the Gate, the fiercer rapids at the mouth of Bridge River, and many narrow places on the tributary spawning streams. But in the end, with many casualties on the way, each band finds its particular river, enters some upland lake, and seeks out the brook where its ancestors have always spawned.

The final event is now at hand. A female fish, a male close beside her, pushes into shallow water at the stream edge. With a fluttering motion of her fins she hollows out a depression in the sand. The dislodged sand begins to form a little mound behind her. Having built her curious nest, she presses her belly against the hollowed sand and squeezes out her scarlet eggs. The male dashes in to pour his seminal milt upon the eggs, which fertilized and viable, sink into the sand and lodge in the little mound already prepared. Many eggs float away, are gobbled by trout and other fish, or find no hatching place, but some are safely covered by the sand that the mass of spawners has set flowing in the current.

Already the salmon, male and female, are near their end. The silver livery of the salt water has dulled. Their bodies are mottled brown and black, and streaked with hectic red. Their flesh is half rotten. The nose of the male has become hooked and grotesque. Lying numb, half out of water on the sand bars, the salmon wait for death. In a day or two the bars are covered by windrows of decay. The stench of autumn by some lonely brook proclaims the seeding of another crop.

Safe in the sand of a moving current, the eggs gradually come to life. How many months they will need to reach the moment of hatching will depend upon the temperature of the water. But in some 130 days, early in the new year, the infant fish, a speck of life attached to the tiny transparent balloon of the yolk sac that nourishes it, will be hiding in the sand. When the yolk sac has been absorbed, the fish, now an inch long, emerges from the sand and swims boldly into the current. A new cycle is under way.

The young of all five salmon species remain in fresh water for varying periods. The Pink and Chum migrate to sea early in their first year, almost immediately after hatching. The Spring remain in the stream for somewhat less than a year, the Cohoe for a year. The Sockeye, which has swum farthest in fresh water, does not leave it until a full year at least has passed. Some remain there for two and even three years. These, however, are general rules which the habits of certain races within the species may violate in some exceptional areas.

The young salmon, varying in length from 3 to 8 inches, slip unnoticed down the Fraser and, if they escape their natural enemies, reach salt water. There they disappear until they are ready to spawn again. Where they go in the sea man has not fully discovered but their range is wide. Springs caught off the west coast of Vancouver Island have been tagged and re-captured within a year off the coast of California. Growth at sea is rapid. The 50 pounds of a big Spring, say, usually must be constructed in three or four years. This requires voracious feeding on a diet of small fish, pelagic shrimps and other marine life.

Each species has its own time of return to the river. The Springs in their various races set out on their spawning journey in their third, fourth, fifth, sixth or even seventh year; the Sockeye in their fourth; the Cohoe in their third; the Pink in their second; the Chum in their third, fourth or fifth. These rules are not invariable. Some Fraser Sockeye spawn in their fifth year.

In all species a few specimens called "grilse" develop prematurely and appear in the spawning run a year ahead of their time.

Generally speaking, the largest fish in the run will be the oldest but not always. A gigantic Spring of 80 pounds, caught in a trap off Vancouver Island, was four years old.

These elementary facts of the salmon's life span were discovered slowly. The early fishermen knew that the fish came to the river every year and the run, they agreed, was indestructible. They knew how to can the salmon's flesh, which the whole world seemed eager to buy. This seemed to them an adequate knowledge. The important thing was that, by the turn of the century, they were canning over a million cases of Sockeye, 48 one-pound cans to the case, each case requiring 78 pounds of live fish.

In 1902 a stranger appeared on the river, one of the most remarkable men who ever lived beside it. He was destined to change the whole course of the fishery and thereby some of the joint affairs of Canada and the United States.

John Pease Babcock was an American who loved fish of all kinds as he loved human beings, and about equally. He had come to California as an official of the state fish commission when the government of British Columbia heard of him and asked him to move north. The provincial authority could not regulate the Fraser fisheries, which came under federal jurisdiction, but it considered them a part of the province's natural wealth and it had begun to receive disturbing reports about their future. Babcock was put in charge of the provincial fisheries department with orders to find out if the Sockeye run was in decline.

Babcock was young then. I knew him only in his later years, when he was a brisk, weather-beaten man, quiet of speech, philosophical of disposition, with the energy, the quick look and the bristling white hair of a terrier.

He knew it was impossible to gauge the future of the salmon by watching them, as the fishermen did, at sea. What was happening on the spawning grounds among the distant mountains? Babcock traveled the whole length of the river and its tributaries on foot and horseback, living like an Indian. Even when he was old and almost blind he continued his annual tour. From the beginning he paid settlers and Indians to make a rough count of the fish entering local streams. Presently he was hazarding a shrewd guess as to the total number of spawners in each season. His forecasts in general were remarkably accurate but this was crude work. There could be no method of conserving the fishery until the life habits of every species were fully known.

The fishing industry saw no need of Babcock's inquiries. There had been a brief decline in the run toward the end of the old century and the annual catch varied sharply, with a well-marked "big year" in every four. But the fisherman never expected any serious depletion and on the tributary streams of the interior the settlers, almost walking on the massed carcasses of the spawners, loaded them into wagons with pitchforks and used them to fertilize the land.

Babcock, who had no wife or family and had married the science of marine life, was becoming, in his quiet way, exceedingly alarmed. Why the varying run from year to year? If there could be a decline between 1897 and 1903, might it not occur again on a larger scale? And more disturbing, what would be the effect of settlement, railway construction and industry along the river on the fish that inhabited it?

He had no time to discover the answers for himself. He needed a scientist who could devote himself exclusively to the study of the salmon's life. Just such a man he found in Dr. Charles H. Gilbert, of Stanford University, who, by tagging salmon, already had learned about their homing instinct in a general way. Dr. Gilbert came to the Fraser and began the study that his successors still carry forward.

His work was based on an extension of the tagging experiments he had carried on in northern California. Tagging was a primitive business in those days, a mere clipping of fins as cowboys cut wattles in the loose flesh of cattle. A fish thus marked downstream, and recovered after spawning up the river, told the story of its movements.

By now Dr. Gilbert had learned to read the age of a salmon, the first essential in mapping its life span. By examining a scale just above the lateral line of the body and behind the pectoral fin, he could tell the fish's age just as easily as a woodsman can tell the age of a tree by counting the rings of growth.

The scale under a microscope looks very like a sawn tree stump; but whereas two rings, the winter and summer wood, mark a year's growth in a tree, the salmon's annual growth produces some seven rings. As the tree, by wider or narrower rings, records its varying expansion in wet and dry years, so the rings of the scale, narrow in winter and broader in summer, indicate the fast summer growth, the slower growth of winter.

Now that scales could be read like a book, Dr. Gilbert mapped out the different life spans of the five species and noted the exceptions among them. At the same time the homing habit was studied on sufficient individual spawning grounds to show that the salmon was not content merely to reach the parent stream, as had been thought before, but would return to its own particular tributary.

Dr. Gilbert died in the midst of his study. The work was carried on by Dr. W. A. Clemens, a Canadian, and his wife, Dr. Lucy Clemens. To this married partnership in science Canada and the United States owe much.

While the scientists worked in their laboratories and along the river, governments in Canada and the United States at last were beginning to catch Babcock's alarm. They had noted the striking fact that the Sockeye pack of the two countries had totaled 1,172,507 cases in 1897 and dropped without apparent reason to 372,020 in 1903. This seemed more than a passing accident. Even before that, as early as 1892, Canadian and American officials had conferred on the possibility of limiting the catch jointly, but nothing had come of it, for depletion had seemed impossible then.

The annual reports of Babcock, a river Cassandra who constantly pinpricked the federal authorities, and the confirmatory findings of federal officials, finally persuaded Canada to begin, in 1908, new negotiations with its neighbor. Nothing would serve, of course, but international action, for if Canada restricted fishing and saved the fish, the unregulated American fishermen at the mouth of Puget Sound would only catch more; if the United States imposed restrictions without Canadian co-operation, the Canadian fishermen would do the same.

The common sense of the thing was perfectly clear. Fishery

officials on both sides of the line understood from the beginning that they must establish a joint authority of regulation. Such an obvious arrangement was accepted by both national governments in the treaty of 1908, which proposed to establish a Canadian-American commission with power to restrict fishing north and south of the boundary. By allowing a sufficient escapement of fish to the river the commission would assure the restocking of the spawning basin—or so it was thought.

Here Babcock, the true author of this futile attempt to save a great international asset, encountered his first experience in pressure politics.

The Canadian Parliament approved the salmon treaty and the United States Senate appeared ready to approve it. But the fishing industry of Washington State, eager to exploit the fishery to the limit, persuaded the state legislature to oppose the treaty, on the doubtful constitutional argument that fishery regulation was under state and not federal jurisdiction. Enough pressure from Washington was exerted upon the Congress to prevent ratification. By 1914, having waited six years for American action, Canada repudiated the treaty.

In the meantime the Fraser fishery had almost perished overnight from a single man-made blow.

Through the passes of the Rockies, down the North Thompson, westward along the Thompson, and then south in the chasm of the Fraser, the Canadian Northern Railway had been crawling slowly toward Vancouver. In the summers of 1911 and 1912 the railway builders blasted a trench for a single track through the canyon and bored a series of tunnels. The debris of their quarrying slid into the river. Much of the rock was quickly removed. The river seemed to flow as usual by the spring of 1913.

That was the "big year" of the four-year Sockeye cycle, the year when the heaviest run could be expected. It swarmed in that summer, bigger than ever. The fishermen could laugh at Babcock's alarm when they packed 2,392,815 cases. But Babcock was not watching the congested canneries on the coast. He was sitting on a rock above Hell's Gate in tears.

Down below the Gate he could see the Sockeye milling in the big pool, rushing at the fury of the gorge and dropping back, helpess against a current they could not gauge or navigate. The railway debris had increased the speed of the river at the Gate, turned it into new courses deep below the surface, and created a caldron which few fish could survive.

Day after day Babcock watched a handful of stronger fish somehow break through the Gate and then, depleted by their struggle, perish in Scuzzy Rapids, three and a half miles upstream. For ten miles below the Gate the salmon were packed together in a writhing mass which already was beginning to die. Every sand bar down to the sea was foul with stinking flesh.

Babcock knew he was witnessing not some minor mishap in the history of the river but an international disaster, perhaps the end of the Sockeye. Only a driblet of the run would spawn in that "big" year. Four years later their progeny would return to the river but it would not be a "big" year then. The "big" year of the Fraser was finished.

During the spawning months of 1913 the Canadian and British Columbia governments desperately blasted at the debris in the river and managed to save a precious remnant of the run. They had hardly finished this work when, on February 23, 1914, a single slide from a railway tunnel on the east side of the Gate filled almost half the river channel. This seemed to complete the calamity.

To repair it would require years of work, an international agreement, and a large investment of money, as Babcock well knew. Until that project could get under way some of the 1914 run somehow must be moved past the Gate. More rock was blasted. A little wooden flume carried some fish around the new barrier. Others were lifted by hand in dip nets. It was a pathetic attempt to undo man's damage, but it kept the 1914 run alive.

In 1917 the offspring of the ruined 1913 run appeared off the Fraser mouth. The fishermen saw then that Babcock had underestimated, if anything, the damage of the railway slides. In what should have been a "big" year only 559,702 cases were packed by both countries, a quarter of the 1913 pack. An industry once worth $30,000,000 a year was now worth, on the average of the four-year cycle, only three millions and might soon be worth almost nothing. The loss in the 1913 run and in the subsequent years of that cycle up to 1945, not counting the smaller years, is now calculated at $297,000,000.

Man had scoured the mountains of British Columbia for minerals, he had started to clean off the forests, but this depletion took time. In the Fraser, with a few sticks of dynamite, he had destroyed one of the precious food resources of mankind in a matter of minutes.

This blow should have been enough to bring the Washington State fishermen to their senses, but even now they were not ready to see beyond the year's profits. Canada and the United States negotiated another treaty. It suffered the same fate as the treaty of 1908—ratification by Canada, rejection by the United States Senate at the behest of Washington State.

In those years I had come to know Babcock well and wrote up his annual reports for the newspapers. In his Victoria office, surrounded by his collections of Indian baskets, stuffed fish and bottled minnows, he suffered like a man who sees his family being murdered one by one. That his native country refused to end this crime was the final blow to the old man's hope. Yet, after a few weeks' brooding, he would go back to work again. Year after year, when nobody listened, he trudged the riverbanks, calculated the size of the run, and returned to write another report more alarming than the last, which few would read. Who cared about the Sockeye in the dreadful autumn of 1918, or in the debacle of the postwar years? Nevertheless, Babcock's lonely fight went on, he gathered increasing support on both sides of the line, and in the end the man with a single idea broke down all the obstacles of politics in both Washington and Ottawa.

In 1928 his worst predictions were fulfilled. The whole Fraser River pack sank to 90,343 cases. Such figures could be ignored no longer by fishermen or politicians. In 1930 a third treaty was negotiated and was ratified by Canada. Seven more anxious years Babcock waited while the United States Senate annually considered the treaty and pigeonholed it. In 1937, thirty-five years after he had begun his crusade, the Senate acted. The treaty at last could operate.

Babcock already was in charge of a Canadian-American commission which would soon restore the halibut fisheries of the North Pacific, but in the Sockeye treaty he felt that his life work was done. From now on the two countries that had jointly prospered on the Fraser fisheries and jointly ruined them would carry on the slow sure work of repair. "Babs," as we called him —truly Canada's Old Man River—coud take things easier.

The treaty of 1937 was another milestone on the long and difficult road that the two great nations of North America learned to travel together. By it each surrendered a minute fraction of its sovereignty to create a joint sovereignty adequate to protect the mutual interest. The International Pacific Salmon Fisheries Commission—three men from each nation —was given power to regulate fishing in Canadian and American waters after eight years of scientific study, and generally to do anything necessary to rebuild the fishery. Since other varieties were relatively unimportant, the commissions's powers covered Sockeye only.

Never in all the numerous international authorities created by Canada and the United States have men of both states worked more closely together or with better results than in the Sockeye commission. Had all the members and experts been of the same nationality they could not have lived in greater harmony. For them the international boundary had ceased to exist. Babcock's dream had fallen into safe hands.

The first job, by the terms of the treaty and by the logic of the problem, was to carry through the scientific studies long under way. For this undertaking—much greater and more complex than even Babcock had suspected—the commission appointed Dr. William F. Thompson, an American, who had distinguished himself in the fisheries of California. He, like Babcock, Gilbert and the two Clemenses, was a remarkable man—quiet, shy, patient and selfless.

His approach to the restoration of the Sockeye was called scientific and it was that, as results proved; but there was more of reverence in it than science. This was a man, as anyone could see after watching him work by the river, who felt profoundly but would never try to articulate the mysteries of nature, too deep for his explanation.

Dr. Thompson worked in an unobtrusive fashion and the

public soon forgot him. He had a suspicion from the beginning that the study of his predecessors had only touched the fringe of the Sockeye's life. It was true that the fish spawned in their native stream, that the "big" run had been destroyed by a blockade at the Gate. But why, when the blockade had been removed, did the runs of the other years remain small? Why had there been a period of depletion in the last years of the nineteenth century? Was it true, as Babcock supposed, that depletion, apart from the 1913 disaster, was caused by overfishing? Or was there some other cause, so far overlooked?

Thompson was soon convinced that a larger process was at work but, being a meticulous scientist, he would give no opinion until he had tested this process by years of research.

His method was that of Gilbert in all essentials. With ample funds to spend, he and his staff tagged thousands of Sockeye at selected points along the river. The fish was lifted from the stream in a dip net, such as the Indians had always used. A nickel pin was pushed through the upper edge of the body below the dorsal fin. To the pin was attached a white celluloid disk, bearing a number. For speed in identification later, the disks were devised in a kind of code, those used at one point on the river carrying a red spot, others a black spot, and others a combination of spots of different colors.

A few weeks after being tagged and released in the lower waters the fish appeared in the inland spawning streams. There Thompson's watchers, as well as settlers and Indians in search of a reward, would rescue the tags from the dying spawners. By checking the dates of these discoveries against the numbers of the tags, Thompson began to construct the first detailed anatomy of the fishery.

It was a laborious job. In 1941, for instance, 20,000 fish were tagged and about 30 per cent of the tags were recovered. The taggers soon developed a high degree of skill. In ten seconds or so they could dip a salmon out of the current, lay it on a table, fasten a tag to its body and throw it back, uninjured, into the water. During the migration this went on from dawn to dark in the recesses of the Gate, where men in rubber boots and slickers, to protect them against the enveloping foam, risked their lives on the slippery ledges. In a shack on the mountainside above them, Thompson's ichthyologists and statisticians compiled the results of the tests, as the tags came in from he upper tributaries, and began to draw graphs which would provide an entirely new concept of the salmon's life.

By now Thompson was working on the theory that Sockeye are more than a single species. Within that species, he had begun to realize, many distinct races existed, each with separate times of migration. If this were true, it was not enough to say that a species had been almost wiped out. It might be that certain races, encountering blockades in the canyon, suffered destruction while others, after the blockade had ceased, went unscathed. This would mean, in turn, that fishing regulations would have to be devised not to protect the incoming migration at large as if it were a single movement, but to protect each successive wave of migrants, lest intensive fishing in a single day deplete a whole race.

The race theory fitted into the other basic theory that Thompson was slowly evolving. He believed that blockades on the river were not all man made, that they had occurred frequently from earliest time. The railway blast perhaps had been the worst of these accidents but it was only man's imitation, on a larger scale, of nature's continual war on the fish.

In 1941 nature suddenly confirmed Thompson's theory in the kind of startling demonstration that a scientist might have awaited vainly for a lifetime.

There had been no fall of rock into the river in 1941. To the passer-by the water seemed to flow as usual through the Gate that autumn. And yet the fish began to pile up below the Gate just as they had done in 1913. For no visible reason a new blockade was under way.

No one who saw this spectacle is likely to forget it

From the cliffs above the Gate we could watch the swarm of fish in the lower pool, massed on the surface of the water in a solid, reddish island. Now and then a few fish would break away and swim toward the Gate, but the mass lay stationary, too tired to move.

When we had climbed down the cliffs and stood a few feet from the current we began to grasp the dimensions of the blockade. Through Hell's Gate the power of hell seemed to be pouring that day. The tide of water and foam, suddenly compressed in a channel of not much more than a hundred feet, welled upward, twisted in the fashion of a corkscrew, and rose and fell again in a steady pulse. The foam fell on us like a heavy rain. The wind almost lifted us off our feet. Against the sound of the water we could not hear a man shouting directly into our ears. After staring at the current for a few minutes we felt giddy and had to turn away, clutching the rocks for safety.

The unconscious life of the river surely must exclude all other life within it. But as we watched, a salmon would leap out of the middle of the caldron, high above the froth, its great body wriggling, fall back again and instantly disappear, to be sucked into the lower pool. Some of the fish did not escape so easily. Deflected in their leap by a sudden upsurge of the water, they were tossed twenty feet through the air against the walls and instantly killed. All around us, within our reach, these glistening creatures hurtled upon the rocks, squirmed for a moment, and fell limp into the froth.

Most pitiable of all was the sight of a fish somehow leaping over the worst point in the current into the somewhat smoother water above, only to be caught and overwhelmed there by the huge white wave that, at regular intervals of about a minute, rolled down through the Gate. Still, hour after hour, more salmon flung themselves at the current in quick darts of black above the foam.

All these fish could have spawned comfortably on a thousand sand bars below the Gate but the compulsion that drove them toward their own stream was stronger than the current and stronger than death.

Miraculously some got through. When we had slithered along the cliffs to a point a few yards upstream from the Gate we found a few fish which had gained the quiet water at the very edge of the river. They wriggled almost up on the gravel bank, hiding between the stones, half their bodies out of water. There they rested before entering the current again. Sometimes, just as they seemed safe, the pulse of the river would beat again, the great wave would roll down and sweep them from their refuge.

For weeks on end Dr. Thompson and his experts watched this massacre. At times no fish appeared able to pass the Gate. At others the observers could see little bands breaking through and moving upstream. These changes in the movement of the fish followed changes in the level of the water, just as Dr. Thompson had suspected. Evidently a blockade would occur whenever the river reached a certain level and, in this particular volume and speed, created currents too powerful for the fish.

From this two conclusions followed: First, that mere curtailment of fishing at sea would never restore the Fraser runs, for the fish that escaped the fishermen could perish in the river if the water reached the fatal depth. Second, that the whole problem of depletion was concentrated in a single spot, the Gate. There might be other danger points on the river but it was useless to cure them if this main barrier could not be broken.

The experts went back over their studies of the Gate itself. Their information, long known to government engineers, showed that the Gate was 120 feet wide at low water; that the drainage of 91,000 square miles was compressed upright, as it were, in this narrow gut, 85 feet deep at low water; that the river rose and fell as much as 90 feet and on average about 60 feet in a season; that its speed through the Gate, at the center of the current, reached 20 feet per second; and that within the Gate it dropped 7 feet. By studying the fish run, as revealed in their tagging operations, the scientists realized that blockade occurred when the river level rose 25 feet above low water, with a brief spell of passable current between 40 and 50 feet. The river could reach the point of danger at any time in late summer or autumn, depending on rainfall and on temperature, which governs the melting of snow in the interior mountains. Without physical control of the upper tributaries, which was far beyond its power, the salmon commission could not control the water level at the Gate. If a new channel were created by dredging or blasting, still worse currents might result. Therefore, a way must be found to carry the fish through the Gate regardless of the river level. Having reached that conclusion, the commission undertook to build its own channel and the most remarkable fishway yet devised.

At the University of Washington engineers constructed an exact model of the Gate in concrete, on a scale of 1 foot to 50 feet. All the contours of the sides and the river bottom, all the outthrust rocks and grooves, were carefully reproduced. When they had a miniature Gate the engineers poured a stream of water through it and, at various levels, observed all the freaks of the current. Finally they built a model fishway which, they hoped, would provide an easy passage for the salmon, regardless of conditions in the Gate.

At low water in the autumn of 1944 construction began. Essentially the Gate fishway was to consist of two gigantic concrete flumes, one on each side of the canyon, through which water would flow quietly enough to offer the fish sure passage.

It was easy to plan such flumes on paper and build them in laboratory models. When it came to the job of fastening them into the walls of the Gate and anchoring them to the river bottom against the current, not only ingenuity and the power of machinery were required but a high degree of courage. Every man working on those slippery rocks knew that he might fall into the river, and every man, looking at the current, knew that he would not come out alive.

To cut the footings for the concrete, men were lowered down the 90-foot cliffs on ropes. They pecked out steps in which other men could stand and drill holes for blasting. Yard by yard grooves were cut along both sides to hold the fishways and the debris was laboriously removed so that it would not fall and block the river.

Surprisingly enough, not one man lost his life in this work. A steam shovel slid down a patch of loose shale into the river one day but its driver caught a rope thrown from the shore just as he was sinking into the water—probably the only human being to survive a moment's immersion in the Gate.

After two years' work, interrupted by the high-water periods, the fishway was finished. It is a strange and ugly contrivance, which has greatly damaged the wild beauty of the Gate. On each side of the river a square concrete pipe is welded into the cliffs. The pipe on the left bank is curved to accommodate it to the bend in the river. The pipe on the right bank is straight and shorter than the other. Below it a tunnel has been bored through an outthrust promontory to guide the salmon from the lower pool to the entrance of the fishway.

The fishway is thus a device to suck a portion of the river through the pipes and then to slow this water down by a series of cross walls, or baffles, 18 feet apart. Each baffle creates a relatively quiet pool and the surface of each pool is a foot higher than the next pool downstream. The salmon swim from one pool to the other through slots two feet wide cut in the baffles. The amount of water entering the pipes can be regulated by entrance gates and the velocity of the flow within the pipes can be kept uniform by the manipulation of gates on the baffles.

From the hill above the canyon these concrete structures look small and they are so much a part of the walls that the distant traveler might overlook them. But in comparison with their passengers they are of enormous bulk. The fishway on the right bank is 20 feet wide and 222 feet long. The other is 20 feet wide for 160 feet and 12 feet wide for the remaining

300 feet. This is a lot of steel and concrete. In places it runs down 40 feet below the surface of the water. The tunnel, through the rock on the right bank, is 134 feet long, 12 feet wide and 42 feet high.

The whole scheme, fishways and tunnel, is designed to serve the fish at any water level which obstructs them. At highest water the structures are immersed 20 feet below the river surface but the fish can easily use the river current then. At low water, which also offers safe passage, the pipes are almost entirely exposed.

The whole project cost less than a million dollars. If it works it can save many times that amount every year in the increase of the salmon run. The commission is a cautious group of men. It makes no claims that it cannot justify by undoubted figures. Until it can see the result of the fishway's operation four years after the first fish were carried past the Gate in the concrete pipes it will not say that it has solved the ancient problem of the Fraser run. But the experts do know that, with the new passage at the Gate and a smaller, $200,000 fishway of a similar sort at the Bridge River Rapids, a much larger run of spawning fish than in former years has been moving into the upper tributaries since 1945, in which year, it is estimated, seven billion eggs were laid in the spawning basin.

The restocking of the Fraser has begun. Safe passage around the blockades and reasonable regulation of fishing at sea should complete the cure over a period of years.

The problem is more complicated than it appears from the condition of the run as a whole.

The vital new fact discovered by the scientists of the commission is the existence of the various salmon races within the species, a separate race with its own spawning time in each of the big tributaries; and the additional fact that some races, encountering the blockade, have been almost wiped out, while others, reaching the Gate at a favorable water level, have passed undamaged.

If the species had been uniformly depleted, the problem of restoration would be simple—the release of enough fish past the fishing fleet to assure ample spawning. But when the position of each race must be considered individually in relation to its strength or depletion, the regulation of fishing must be more complicated and difficult. When is the depleted race passing through the leagues of fishing water? How many of these fish can the two partner nations afford to catch? Up the river, what escapement actually has occurred by the end of the season?

These are the detailed problems that the salmon commission is still studying, now that its main problem has been solved. It has behind it two national governments, a state government in Washington, and a provincial government in British Columbia. It has the support of the fishing industry. It has the scientific knowledge and administrative experience of the excellent federal fisheries department of Canada and the British Columbia department under George J. Alexander, Babcock's able young successor, who inherits the old man's love of fish.

But the real force in the river, the force that antedates man's coming and perhaps man's life on the earth, is the instinct of a creature which lives its allotted span to the day, arranges its succession, and quietly dies. Here is no confusion of aim, no doubt, no complaint, regret or fear. The cycle of life and death, and life again, is unbroken, unchangeable, inscrutable, perfect. And the mystery within the salmon is beyond the grasp or guess of the superior animal called man.

20   For Anglers Only

UP TO THIS POINT ONE OF THE GREATER FACTS OF THE FRASER'S life has been suppressed. Now, though it goes against the grain to reveal it (for what angler wishes to attract competitors to his own preserves?), that fact must be revealed—the Fraser system is one of the largest reservoirs of game fish in the world.

This is not always apparent to the stranger. Trout, like women, are temperamental and neither, I suppose, would be interesting without this common quality. Thus it happens over and over again that foreign fishermen come to the fishing ground of the Fraser and, having only a day or so to spare, leave with empty creels, while others, fishing the same waters, return to the United States reporting that they have discovered the ultimate miracle.

In temperament the trout of the Fraser system, I fancy, are even more mercurial than those of other rivers, but perhaps ill fortune has soured me. At any rate, except in a few overpopulated lakes, you can never be sure of a catch. To say that the tributaries of the Fraser are teeming with trout, which is strictly true, is not to say that they always provide good fishing. It is only to say that there can hardly be any more trout in any equal volume of water, or larger or better trout. And yet, at certain seasons, the shallow upland lakes draining into the Fraser contain as worthless trout, for both catching and eating, as will be found anywhere.

The angler must know where he is going and he must go at the right season. A slight knowedge of angling also will be useful. I do not speak here as an authority. A humble and clumsy fly caster, I am not fit to be numbered among the giants like Bryan Williams, Harry Pooley, Panther Pitts, Torchy Anderson and that demigod of Fraser fishermen, the fabulous Bill Nation. Those who require exact and scientific information must study the methods of such men as Mr. Williams, in his definitive work *Game Trails in British Columbia.* I shall set down here mainly what I have seen with my own eyes and felt on my own rod—no very exciting tale—or what I have heard, under oath of secrecy, from the oracles.

The Fraser and its complex of rivers and lakes contain only two species of native trout, the Rainbow and the Cutthroat. The few Brown trout imported into British Columbia from time to time are so seldom seen and held in such low esteem that they are hardly worth considering.

The Rainbow (Salmo irideus), as all educated men know, is the noblest specimen of the trout family. His body is deep and fat, purplish on the back, silvery on the belly. His sides are striped by the radiant colors of his name. His muscles are strong, his heart dauntless. When hooked, he fights with such spirit, in the air almost as much as in the water, that the sensitive angler is impelled to reward him with release—a temptation which most of us have learned to overcome at the last moment.

While he belongs to fresh water, in lake and river, the Rainbow goes to sea from time to time if he can. In coastal waters, where he enters the rivers on the rising tide, he is sometimes known as a Sea trout. In Kamloops Lake, where the name originated, and in other lakes of this district, the Rainbow is called the Kamloops, and special virtues of strength and intelligence are attributed to him there. In other places he is called the Silver.

In some lakes the Rainbow reaches and even exceeds a weight of 15 pounds and even in such sizes has been taken on the fly. A 2-pounder will provide all the sport a reasonable man requires. It may take ten minutes to land one half that size in fast water.

The largest trout of all, the Steelhead, is now accepted by the experts as a member of the Rainbow family. To the angler he is chiefly interesting in coastal rivers on his migration from a spell at sea. The ordinary angler, catching him in some inland lake, will take him for a big Rainbow, which, in fact, he is. The Steelhead (Salmo gairdneri) runs from 8 to 20 pounds.

The second breed of Fraser trout is the Cutthroat (Salmo mykiss), so called for the streak of blood-red flesh on either side of his throat. He is inclined to be thinner than the Rainbow, shallower through the belly, and notably less agile as a fighter. Where the Rainbow fights on top of the water, the Cutthroat usually goes down deep. You can usually detect at once what kind of trout you have hooked.

But much depends, in the quality of your sport, on the condition of the individual fish. A small Rainbow may fight harder than a much larger Cutthroat, but the reverse will be true if the Rainbow is out of sorts. The variation between fish and fish, depending mostly on the condition of water and feed, is remarkable.

A third fish, the Dolly Varden (Salvelinus malma), is sometimes numbered erroneously among the trout and perhaps deserves that honor by its size and quality, but it is in fact a char, usually caught by lake trolling or, more or less by accident, in the pursuit of river trout with a fly. The Great Lakes trout (Cristivomer namaycush), caught on the troll in the larger Fraser lakes, is a char also.

The two breeds of true native trout inhabit all Fraser waters from the sea to the Rockies. They are seldom visible, however, close to the sea or, indeed, in any part of the main channel of the Fraser. Few anglers fish in the muddy river itself, preferring the clear side streams and lakes, but there is a tribe of queer old men, much like the ageless anglers of France, who sit for days on the banks of the Fraser, 50 miles from its mouth, dangle worms in the current and sometimes, it is said, catch trout and species unknown to the purists.

Serious trout fishing begins in the first tributaries of the Fraser: in the wicked Vedder, which enters the Fraser from the south; in the Pitt, Stave and Harrison, on the north bank; in Silver Creek, a southern tributary equal in color to its name; and in various smaller streams. Each has its little band of worshipers.

The Coquihalla, which joins the Fraser at Hope, where the canyon begins, also is fished successfully but I have no personal knowledge of its worth. If this book were not strictly confined to the Fraser, I should like to pause at the Coquihalla junction, ascend its pass through the mountains, and conduct the reader into the headwaters of the Skagit, which rises on the eastern slope (just missing the Fraser drainage basin) to flow into Puget Sound. Its icy waters, in my experience, provide the ultimate in trout fishing, as to both quantity and quality.

Though the Skagit itself is outside our bounds, the Hope Mountains around it are studded with little lakes of the Fraser family and alive with brooks from which the thoughtful angler, who is not overawed by size, may extract innumerable tiny trout on a stick, a string and a bent pin—the most tasty specimens of all.

There is much to be said for this humble branch of the great sport, though few fishermen will say it, since size has become the measurement of angling, as of everything else in America. In the mountain brook, with your pack horses grazing in some fragrant upland meadow, your creel well filled with sandwiches and an essential bottle of medicine, Izaak Walton can ask no more.

No important fishing rivers enter the Fraser (apart from the Thompson, whose fishing we shall examine later) until the Lillooet system is reached.

The little creek that drains Anderson and Seton Lakes to

the west was once a happy fishing place but few trout remain there now—only an immortal Indian who stands forever on the bridge, trailing a spoon in the fast water and, it is said, sometimes landing a substantial Rainbow or a powerful Dolly. Such waters, close to the roads, have usually been fished out long since, but back in the hills, above Seton Lake, in the drainage basin of Bridge River, are prolific trout lakes, where a Royal Coachman and I have often done well. In hot weather, though, these trout are muddy.

On the east bank of the Fraser, in this same general region, the three vivid blue and green Pavilion Lakes nourish gigantic trout but they are so crammed with fresh-water shrimp that they seldom bother your fly. These, I think, are the most intelligent of all the British Columbia trout and only the expert is likely to attract them. No spectacle can be more infuriating than the high-leaping Pavilion trout, too wise to accept your lure and then, if hooked in a moment of absent-mindedness, too powerful to be landed. More gut leaders, I would guess, have been broken in these little lakes than in any waters of similar size in British Columbia.

Harry Pooley, whose word must be trusted as the most venerable of British Columbia anglers and a former attorney general, asserts that there are bigger fish in the westernmost Pavilion Lake than in any other water he has ever fished. For all his skill (and even with the use of a spoon in a moment of final desperation) he has never caught a single fish there. Nevertheless, other fishermen of less experience have been successful. I have watched my fourteen-year-old son pull two trout, each over 3 pounds, out of the second Pavilion Lake in fifteen minutes while I failed to attract one.

Not far off, up Hat Creek Valley, I have found some of my happiest hours. Hammond Lake (which actually flows into the Thompson by an obscure creek but is, for fishing purposes, part of the Lillooet region) never raised a large-sized trout. It swarms with 12-inch Rainbow which, in summer, are fit food for cats.

Here one can afford to throw them back and, in this lovely basin, below the shoulder of a granite mountain, practice one's casting in a thoroughly educational fashion. I never left Hammond without a full creel and if I came here in spring or autumn the trout were prime on the table. When I fished in midsummer it was for religious reasons only, a lonely worship where no human eye could distract my devotions.

Since reverence is lacking in the more sporting angler, he will prefer Kelly Lake, that deep, dark eye blinking on the far slope of Pavilion Mountain and emptying westward to the Fraser. Kelly Lake water is so cold and clear that even in the hottest days of summer its trout are sweet and hard. How many thousand travelers, I wonder, have paused on the road beside the lake, cast their flies over the bank, and departed in disgust? The Kelly trout is elusive, even when you degrade yourself with a spoon. Yet Bryan Williams once caught a famous 16-pounder from the north shore, with a wet fly, in a driving November blizzard, and watched it break his leader and escape, after an hour's fight, only to die of exhaustion.

As a rule the fish rise in the last minutes of the dusk, when a Royal Coachman is your best bet. There used to be a wonderful old Irishman who rented boats on Kelly Lake for a living, but lived only to stand waist deep on the sand bar in the twilight, long after his customers had gone away empty handed. He seldom failed to land a 2-pounder, though he was a rough-and-ready caster. Better fishermen could stand beside him and never feel a strike.

If you manage to catch a Kelly Lake trout, he is worth a dozen others from most lakes, for his substance and flavor. Harry Pooley gives it as his opinion that these are the finest trout in British Columbia.

So far we have touched only the outer and inferior fringe of the angling country. We get near the heart of it farther north and roughly 50 miles east of the river in the plateau of the Cariboo. Some of the lakes here flow into the Fraser, some east-

317

ward into the North Thompson. For the fishermen they are all part of a single fishing ground. The scores of useful lakes are too numerous for individual mention. I speak with personal experience of only some half dozen.

Lac La Hache, a long, shallow splinter of water beside the Cariboo Road, shows the dimple of trout rises in the summer evenings but affords no first-rate fishing—not, at least, to me. However, it may well be the only lake in America where the local inhabitants on skates have been known to beguile the lonely winter by chasing the fish into the shallows and harvesting them when they are too exhausted to escape. This you could hardly call angling, though.

In the smaller neighboring lakes, the little reedy basins that are reached by almost impassable roads, the trout population actually deserves the adjective "teeming," which is too loosely used in tourist advertisements. If you can persuade Percy Ogden to take you to his secret places, far in the hills, you can hardly fail to prosper.

One night from Meadow Lake I extracted more than fifty pounds of fish in an hour, hardly one of them under three pounds, but the monotony of a strike on every cast, on any kind of fly, proved depressing. It was midsummer, the water was warm, and the fish, when I cooked them, tasted like dirt. In the end I buried most of my catch but this was no serious waste. Many of these small Cariboo lakes are overpopulated. The trout, lacking sufficient feed, finally dwindle to a uniformly small size. Heavy fishing is necessary to prevent this deterioration.

The embarrassment of riches at Meadow Lake is not a common experience. It never happened to me again. In general the stranger can disregard the advertisements and assume that he must work for every fish.

When you move on to Canim Lake, for example, you will almost certainly get fine sport, but not without honest labor. Canim and Mahood, below it, flow into the North Thompson but they are approached from the west through the Cariboo country. Their waters are deep and clear, their trout firm of flesh and fierce in battle.

I know nothing more delightful in the life of the fisherman than to camp at the eastern end of Canim and fish the creek mouths where, as I can testify, one of the largest Rainbow in British Columbia is still swimming about with one of my Grizzly Kings in his mouth. He owes his life to the mountain scenery, which distracted my attention, on a summer dawn, at a critical moment.

From Canim an angry little green river flows down to Mahood. You may descend it for a mile or two by boat, but no farther, or you will be sucked into a smaller edition of Niagara. The falls are reached by a trail which drops down into a canyon hardly a hundred yards across. The river, compressed in a bed only 20 feet wide, is too deep and swift for wading at its upper end and is difficult to fish, but at times I have seen more trout in it per foot of water than anywhere else.

In such swift water, where you balance on a slippery rock over a whirlpool, with no room for a back cast, it is more fun to catch a single fish than to take your legal limit in any lake. The Mahood trout are not large by British Columbia standards—a 3-pounder was my largest—but among these rocks and snags a 1-pounder will fight longer than a 5-pounder in quiet water. Since he can easily overbalance you into destruction, the sport is worthy of that name.

Mahood River offers an experience still more exciting, which I do not recommend.

The falls drop into a caldron perhaps 50 feet in diameter. In this perpetual boil it is difficult to believe that any fish or any insect can live. Harry Pooley had told me that this pool offered the best fishing in British Columbia. On seeing it, I began for the first time to doubt the oracle.

Though my faith was shaken, I weighted my leader with

lead (for it was impossible to cast otherwise against the whirl-wind) and crawled on hands and knees over the slimy rocks to the edge of the vortex.

It was desperate work. The wind almost dislodged me, the spray blinded me, the thunder of the falls and the churning of the pool turned me so dizzy that I did not dare to get to my feet. Crouched on the rocks, I threw my weighted fly, telling myself that Harry was a liar.

The fly had hardly touched the white foam before I felt the electric shock of the Rainbow. He was a 1-pounder only but he felt like a Spring salmon. I could not play him, nor could he maneuver. He was tossed about the pool like a chip and, I think, was literally drowned. In a few minutes, unable to handle a landing net, I dragged him up on the rocks. This performance I repeated three times, one fish for every cast. By then I was almost as helpless as the trout and glad enough to crawl down-stream to dry out in the sun.

However, my other experiences on Mahood should warn strangers who imagine that our fish are always easy to catch. My big days on the river occurred in June. In August an Ameri-can friend of mine, inflamed by my story, flew all the way from New York and between us we took only two fish from Mahood. Even the caldron pool was a washout. We failed along the whole seven miles of the river, which we followed with infinite labor. The fish had descended to the cool waters of Mahood Lake.

A few years later my experience was the same until, at dusk, only my boy and I out of a party of six remained on the river, hoping stubbornly for a night rise. It was almost dark when the rise came without notice. For half an hour we pulled in fish as fast as we could cast. When we had a total of thirteen between us we could no longer see the river and I had broken my rod on a back cast. If we could have remained half an hour more we would have doubled our catch, I suppose, but by then our chief concern was to find the trail through the woods. We crept along it somehow, found our boat, lost ourselves in the side channels of the upper river, and reached camp on Canim long after midnight, just as our friends were organizing a search party. But we had trout for breakfast.

To the west of the Fraser, and corresponding to the Canim country to the east, lies another system of lake and river draining the Chilcotin plateau. Harry Pooley tells me it offers without doubt the finest fishing in British Columbia. For the record of his slaughter on the Chilko River, just below the lake of that name, I have only his word, which has never been impeached, but even he was baffled until he tried a bumblebee, a fly seldom used in these parts. The results of this experiment were astounding.

Chilko and other lakes that feed the Chilcotin River are becoming famous among American fishermen, despite the difficulty of travel over Model T roads. It is folly to take a good car into many of the best fishing places and much cheaper to hire the local jalopies.

I am bound to say that my own experience of the Chilcotin country has been disastrous.

Years ago, when the road past Redstone was studded with round boulders like a streambed, Ernest Carson drove me past Kleena Kleene at five miles an hour until we looked out over a waste of sand, dwarf pine and marshy puddles to the eastern flank of the Coast mountains.

Here, since no one fished them, we expected the lakes to yield an unexampled harvest. On One Eye Lake we did indeed witness the most extraordinary rise of trout. On a space of water a mile long and half a mile wide the rises were never more than ten feet apart. They appeared like bubbles in a kettle. This eruption started at dawn, all the fish seeming to rise at the same instant, and it continued not more than five minutes, when a wind blew the insects from the water.

In that space of time we caught several fish but they were hardly large enough to keep. Had we come a year earlier we would have been properly rewarded. In the previous autumn, as a settler told us, all the big fish had died and lain in a deep layer on the shore. Nature, with some cyclical disease, had reduced an excessive population.

Apart from Carson's ruined automobile, we had little to show for that trip. It was our own fault. Instead of bearing west into the badlands of swampy lakes and stunted vegetation, we should have turned south to Chilko Lake.

It was on this ruinous expedition that I first met the Kokanee, a fish which will puzzle the stranger. All the lakes here seemed to swarm with a trout never larger than 12 inches, peculiarly slim, ravenous for any kind of fly. On catching one of them I perceived that it was neither Rainbow nor Cutthroat, but it tasted good enough. The natives called them fresh-water herring.

Actually the Kokanee (which is its most popular name) is a land-locked Sockeye salmon which probably ceased to go to sea centuries ago. Like the other Sockeye, it turns red at spawning time but never grows to the size of its seagoing ancestors. This dwarf of a noble breed is worth catching if you are hungry, not otherwise.

The shallow interior lakes also contain suckers and yellow-bellied squawfish, which will take any lure and sometimes can be a great nuisance to the angler. They are voracious destroyers of young trout.

North of the Chilcotin the next major tributary, flowing in from the east, joins the Fraser at Quesnel. The cold and furious Quesnel, I am told by Harry Pooley, is the best trout stream west of the Rockies. Many Americans share this opinion. I have never fished it, nor the great two-forked lake that is its source, but considering the testimony of Al Williamson and other reliable denizens of the region, I am ready to believe that the entire Quesnel system is heavy with fish.

The same may be said of the Blackwater system on the western side of the Fraser, just north of Quesnel. I have gone toward the Blackwater country only as far as the lakes near

Quesnel, which yielded me, in the scant hour at my disposal, a Rainbow of 4 pounds.

Perhaps the largest accessible reservoir of trout in America lies in the lake region west of Prince George, which Simon Fraser found so fascinating. A map of this area shows almost as much water as earth. The circle bounded by Stuart and Babine Lakes on the north, by Eutsuk on the south, cut through the center by Ootsa, François and Fraser, and splintered by scores of other lakes, converts the land into a series of islands.

Within the larger circle the British Columbia government has preserved the smaller circle of Tweedsmuir Park, named for a Canadian governor general (John Buchan) who knew how to cast a fly. The park is almost entirely surrounded by the water of lake and river.

The tales of trout in this virginal territory are staggering and, I believe, quite true. I have seen only the titanic specimens of Stuart and François Lakes, which are invaded annually by Americans. But this country is so large, its waterways so numerous, its reputation so fabulous that it deserves a whole book to itself. I add only the stated opinion of Harry Pooley (after he had lost every leader in his fly box) that the Endako River is beyond question, the supreme fishing water of the world.

This record, like all fishermen's tales, is stretching out too far. It must be concluded by a brief inspection of the Thompson fishing grounds which, being easily accessible, are congenial to an old hand.

The Thompson itself is a fishing river, though few people will risk wading in its fast waters. A small cult of fishermen like Pooley, Panther Pitts, Jack Cornwall and the ubiquitous Dr. Bobby Hunter (the wildest certifiable lunatic among all British Columbia fishermen) take 5-pounders almost anywhere between Ashcroft and Kamloops Lake. Even with such craftsmen the sport is spotty and unreliable. The visitor who cannot afford to await the trout's convenience will seek out one of the numerous mountain lakes surrounding Kamloops. Again, there are too many of them to mention but most are prolific in their season.

On the north side of the Thompson, such lakes as Paul, Pinintan and Knough and, on the south side, Peter Hope, the Surrey Lakes, Stump and Nicola, and many little-known ponds hidden in the dark spruce forest of the higher hills have sometimes bored me with excess and, at others (especially in the hot summer days when the fish sulk down deep) have grudged me a single rise. The troller, however, can seldom fail anywhere— that is, if the murder of fish by spoon and worm can be considered success.

The warning against seasonal fluctuation applies especially to the Kamloops region. June, before the Dry Belt heat has descended, and again in September, after the first frosts have chilled the water, are the only thoroughly reliable seasons. If one climbs high enough by arduous car tracks or, better still, by pack horse, the cool upland lakes are usually good even at midsummer.

A few years ago I drove into the hills from Cornwall's to a lake which must remain secret, under promise to its owners, and at dusk was just pulling in my first 5-pounder in preparation for the record catch of all time, when my wife called from the shore that the gas tank of our car had sprung a leak. There was nothing for it, since we were 20 miles from any habitation and must get the car out of here before it ran dry, but to pack up and abandon the supreme chance of a fisherman's lifetime. Driving back in the darkness over a track unfit for a deer—gas tank plugged with chewing gum, chassis permanently distorted—I resolved to return by horse someday to what, despite Harry Pooley, must be the finest fishing in the whole Fraser system. May it long be preserved from a good road, a secret known only to the elect.

The Kamloops country was long the undisputed kingdom of Bill Nation. That extraordinary man, who knew trout better than any other British Columbian and had spent his life studying the insect life on which trout feed, chose to call himself a guide. Careless of fame or money, he would row you around Paul Lake, his favorite, or any other lake you fancied for a few dollars a day. After an hour's fishing with him the richest American tycoon was subdued and humble in this shy man's presence. Beside his life of innocence and content, the perfect companionship of man and nature, your own life suddenly appeared for the failure it was. And what could you say for your skill when he could cast a fly and pierce the tail of any fish you pointed out among the autumn salmon horde?

The machinery of civilization, as perhaps was inevitable in such a creature, finally killed poor Bill. He died from the poison of a spray gun while painting his boat.

His memorial is the Nation Special, the fly he constructed out of his unequaled knowledge of insect life and the appetite of the Kamloops trout. No fisherman can afford to be without Bill's masterpiece. With it, throughout the Fraser system, one should carry the Grizzly King, the Royal Coachman, Queen of the Waters, Teal and Red, Claret and Mallard and Bucktails of various designs.

Considering its length, the Thompson system affords surprisingly little good river fishing. Its great trout reserves are its lakes. To this rule Little River (actually the upper waters of the Thompson itself) is a notable exception. Though it is notoriously moody, superb one day and sterile the next, it commands the loyalty of a distinguished company which, by a secret code, is informed of the morrow's prospects and rushes up from Vancouver overnight.

Harry Pooley, who can read the smoke signals all the way to Vancouver Island and thus arrive at Little River on the witching hour, has taken his oath as the patriarch of all anglers that there can be no other fishing like this in the world. But Harry has never heard of my secret lake and, from my lips, he never will.

There is another secret unknown to him and to most Canadian fishermen, though a few Americans have discovered it.

I insert it here, at the end of this chapter, with the book already half printed, because I have just stumbled upon it myself. The North Thompson valley, which seems so dark and forbidding from the train, broadens out before the motorist, the horseman, and the foot traveler into a labyrinth of side valleys, full of gleaming lakes and rushing torrents, over which broods the curious presence of Bill McGarrigle, a reformed professional baseball pitcher, who discovered the Rainbows long ago and dedicated his life to them.

Without a cent to his name, with a bag of porridge and a can of condensed milk for his only food, he walked up from his cabin at Little Fort to Tuloon Lake year after year and built there with his own hands a fishing camp commanding a string of other lakes where, in an October snowstorm, I recently took my limit of fat Rainbows, up to five pounds, in an hour, and watched Mac smoke them, with an eleven-pounder, over his alder fire.

This, Harry Pooley notwithstanding, must be the ultimate in fishing as Mac is the ultimate in guides, hosts, fish lovers, and natural philosophers. Under the protection of men like him the lakes will never be fished out and under the care of his wife, Arline, no fisherman will ever be hungry or cold.

Or, if you prefer fast water, drive north from Little Fort to Dutch Lake and put yoursef into the competent hands of Dorothy Bell and Grace McGraw, reformed newspaperwomen, who turned a decayed ranch into the most delightful resort in British Columbia. With them explore the foaming canyons of the Clearwater, whose fish descend, hard and cold, out of the great lakes above.

These facts I reveal grudgingly, for when the North Thompson is rediscovered, with its towering scenery, coastal forests and heavy freight of Rainbows, every perceptive fisherman in America will invade it. But, praise the gods of angling, old Mac will still be there, never allowing more than a dozen rods on his lakes and guarding the Rainbows like a father.

21 The River's Railways

WHEN SIR JOHN A. MACDONALD PERSUADED THE PACIFIC COAST colony to join Canada his chief bargaining counter was a transcontinental railway. Without the Fraser passage through the Coast Range such a railway could have been built, but it would not have been in the right place to anchor the national boundary or serve the national community which Sir John envisaged.

If there had been no Fraser, the railway would have reached the coast far to the north of its present location. It could have followed the present route of the Pacific Great Eastern Railway, from Squamish, north of Vancouver, and hence northeast into the interior, far from the forty-ninth parallel. There was also Mackenzie's route to the sea, a long way up the coast and useless in maintaining the Canadian-American border. No route but that of the Fraser would support the boundary and serve the existing coastal settlements.

"Old Tomorrow," as the greatest statesman in Canadian history was called, had his troubles with the Canadian Pacific Railway. A matter of campaign funds from railway builders, known as the Pacific Scandal, actually smashed the Macdonald government, the first after the Confederation of the Canadian provinces. It would have smashed a lesser man than Sir John for good. But he came back after five years, pressed ahead with his railway, and remained as the nation's leader until his death in his old house on the Ottawa River.

The railway took longer and cost more than he had expected. It cost so much and took so long that Sir John's enemies expected it to bankrupt the new nation. In Britain, where investors were invited to put their money into the project, and did, the public was warned in the press that the railway would never pay for its axle grease, that it would perish in the defiles of the British Columbia mountains. The C.P.R. became, of course, one of the largest and most successful transportation systems in the world.

The days of its prosperity were far ahead when the railway builders pushed into the Rockies and finally hit the Fraser system on the upper Thompson. It was relatively easy to carry the line down the Thompson but in the Fraser canyon the engineers faced the same difficulties as Fraser in his canoe, as the miners on foot, as Douglas and his contractors on the Cariboo Road.

The C.P.R. engineers used the best route available. They followed the left bank of the Thompson to Lytton and just below it, at Cisco Creek, swung their line to the right bank of the Fraser, cutting it out of the solid rock along the high bluffs around Yale. In the wide flats below the canyon they found an easy grade through the coast jungle. With bridges over the lower tributaries of the Fraser they had no further difficulty in pushing the line to Port Moody, on Burrard Inlet, and then, as an afterthought, on to Gas Town, the beginnings of Vancouver. Once out of the Rockies, the C.P.R. was a Fraser River railway.

Walter Moberly, of Toronto, apparently was the first engineer who seriously studied the Fraser as a possible railway route. Already he had urged Governor Douglas to build his gold road along the Fraser and, long before British Columbia thought of any transportation but freight wagons, wrote to Douglas that the Fraser might become "at some period in the future the line of a railway from Canada." Moberly's views were rejected by the engineers who undertook the first C.P.R. surveys. One of them, indeed, reported to the Canadian government that a railway could never be built through the British Columbia mountains.

In 1865, six years before British Columbia decided to join Canada, Moberly decided to prove his theory. He had seen the Cariboo Road built up the Fraser canyon and knew a railway could be built beside it, but east of Kamloops, by the headwaters of the Thompson, there was no known pass through the Selkirk Range. Moberly, almost by accident, found the missing link in a route from the prairies to the coast.

> I arrived [he writes] at the Eagle River and on the top of a tree near its mouth I saw a nest full of eaglets and the two old birds on a limb of the same tree. I had nothing but a small revolver in the shape of firearms; this I discharged eight or ten times at the nest but could not knock it down. The two old birds, after circling round the nest, flew up the valley of the river; it struck me then, if I followed them, I might find the wished-for pass.
>
> I explored the valley for two or three weeks afterward, and having been successful in finding a good pass, I thought the most appropriate name I could give it was the Eagle Pass.

Moberly's discovery proved that a railway, ascending the Fraser and the Thompson, could cross the Rockies. At that time no one was interested in building such a railway, but when Sir John undertook his final work of nationhood he sent for Moberly, then in Utah. Moberly rode up to British Columbia, pausing only to change horses, and hurried on to Ottawa to tell the prime minister where to locate his railway—by the Pass of Eagles and down the Fraser. After extensive surveys by Sanford Fleming, famous engineer in chief of the Canadian Pacific Railway, Moberly's opinion was confirmed.

In these decisions the strategic importance of the Fraser route, as a barrier against American expansion, emerges clearly on the face of official documents. A memorandum by Major General R. C. Moody, military commander of the British Columbia colony, says bluntly that a railway along the Fraser would offer British Columbia the chance to defend itself—a decisive argument with Sir John, who was convinced that Manifest Destiny, now armed by its own Civil War, was pushing northward again.

While the C.P.R. was crawling westward across the prairies and through the Rockies, construction began in the Fraser canyon. The firing of the first shot of dynamite, between Yale and the Alexandria bridge, is described in the Montreal *Gazette* by an eyewitness:

> The memorable day was showery, which did not interfere with the gathering of interested spectators. After some congratulatory remarks for the Conservative Government and the Pacific Province by persons present, Mr. Onderdonk (the contractor) . . . ordered the foremen to light the fuse—a grand success; the loud noise resounded in the Fraser Valley, besides causing a downpour of rain. . . . After the blast Captain John Irving, of Fraser and Thompson River fame, used the whistle of his sternwheel boat, the Enterprise, to add to the ceremony.

The C.P.R. was conceived in national ecstasy but born of long labor. H. J. Cambie, the engineer in charge of the Fraser section, has left this record:

> We were confronted with new problems almost every day. One of our great troubles was the old waggon road, which ran for miles alongside the railway and which had to be kept open, as it was the only means of access to the upper country and continued so until the railway took its place. . . . Outside the Chinese there were very few foreigners in the country and most of the men on the construction work were English-speaking, many of them Eng-

lishmen. I was often surprised by the great number of them who were well informed men who had drifted through most parts of the world, many of them highly educated. They were good workmen, too. Onderdonk supplied excellent camps and good sleeping quarters, and the food in his camps was of really good quality and well served. I often dropped in and had a meal in the camps. The wages were $2.00 and upward per day.

By 1880 Onderdonk had 7,000 men at work between the sea and Lytton. "The loud roar of enormous discharges of powder has almost constantly reverberated among the mountains," says a contemporary newspaper account. "Fifteen tunnels have been bored, one 1600 feet in length, and millions of tons of rock blasted and rolled with the noise of an avalanche into the rushing, boiling Fraser; workmen have been suspended by ropes hundreds of feet down the perpindicular sides of the mountains to blast a foothold; supplies have been packed in upon the backs of mules and horses, over trails where the Indians were accustomed to use ladders, and building materials landed upon the opposite bank of the river at an ernormous expense and crossed in Indian canoes. It is estimated that portions of this work have cost $300,000 to the mile."

Onderdonk was a daring builder. To save the expense of hauling supplies by wagon and pack horse, he built the steamer *Skuzzy* and finally the Smith brothers, river pilots from the Columbia, pushed this tiny craft past Yale and through Hell's Gate to Boston Bar—surely the most remarkable voyage in the record of Canadian steamboating. A steam winch and 160 Chinese tugging on a rope were required to drag the *Skuzzy* past the worst of the canyon water. For this feat the Captains Smith received $2,250.

The gold rush, it would seem, had been a mild and orderly affair compared to these riotous construction days on the river. After the well-behaved Englishmen noted by Cambie, a crew of

a different sort now swarmed along the railway from Port
Moody to the Rockies.

The labor, according to Dr. George W. Campbell, chief
timekeeper, consisted of "any kind of a human being who could
handle a pick and shovel; and as the best of wages were paid, the
line was flooded with some of the toughest characters on the
coast, not a few of them being men who had done time at
St. Quentin. Police protection was an unknown quantity. . . .
Of course there were gamblers and other loose characters hanging
on the tail of the work, and as everything ran wide open at Yale
the town was the scene of many a riotous night, and not a few
men found death or injury as a consequence. The hospital for the
whole grade was at Yale, and the transportation of the wounded
men to that point, especially from the upper divisions, was often
attended with harrowing incidents."

The contractors could not find enough white labor and,
against the protest of the new provincial government in Victoria,
imported Chinese, the founders of the present thriving Chinese
community in British Columbia. Tom MacInnes, in his *Chinook
Days*, says the

> Chinese had built a bit of old China along our waterfront,
> [at New Westminster] bizarre and necromantic; and I re-
> call how, with dried lichee and Pekin dates and kumquats
> and preserved ginger and firecrackers, they made glad the
> hearts of small boys who went to visit them during the
> nine-day festival of the Chinese New Year. . . . New West-
> minster was unique then in having the authentic atmosphere
> of the early American west, mingled with the atmosphere of
> the early Victorian England.

On July 29, 1885, Onderdonk finished the section from Port
Moody to Savona's Ferry, west of Kamloops. When the link between Savona's Ferry and Eagle Pass was completed on September
30 the Fraser and its tributary, the Thompson, were lined with
steel. The last spike of the transcontinental railway was driven

in the Rockies on November 7. The locomotives were now chuffing into Port Moody and meeting, on Burrard Inlet, the ships of the Pacific Ocean.

Onderdonk paid off his army at Yale on October 8, as recorded by the Port Moody *Gazette:*

> The scene at Yale on Saturday last beggars description. A thousand white men lately employed on the railroad rushed out of the cars and into the saloons. In two hours the streets were full of lunatics; they roared and raved and attempted to force their way into private houses. Twelve hundred Chinese arrived by the same train and went into the woods and cooked their rice. It is amusing to see the difference between Pagans and Christians.

Pagan, Christian and lunatic, they had extended Canada to the Pacific, drawn the line against Manifest Destiny, and completed the work of Simon Fraser on his river.

The engineers of two more transcontinental railways could find no better route than the Fraser.

In the halcyon days before World War I, having long since digested the cost of the C.P.R., Canada embarked on a second spree of railway construction. It seemed a good idea at the time and, a little later, was judged a disaster. By World War II, Canada found that it had not overbuilt, that without its web of transportation it could never have attempted its gigantic war program.

The two transcontinental lines projected in the first decade of this century were called the Canadian Northern and the Grand Trunk Pacific. Both were built at enormous cost by private capital, with large state underwriting.

The Canadian Northern cut through the northern sections of the prairie provinces, crossed the Rockies by the Yellowhead Pass, and turned south by an easy divide to the North Thompson. It ran downhill by the Overlanders' route to Kamloops and turned west on the right bank of the Thompson to Lytton. The C.P.R. having taken the right bank of the Fraser canyon, the Canadian Northern was forced to the left bank, which it followed to New West-minster. Crossing the river there, it reached what was then the southern edge and is now the center of Vancouver.

The Grand Trunk Pacific paralleled the Canadian North-ern through the Yellowhead Pass, followed the big bend of the Fraser into the central interior of British Columbia, ascended the Fraser's western tributary, the Nechako, and dropped down to the coast at Prince Rupert by the water grade of the Skeena.

This northern railway used not only the grade of the Fraser but its current. Supplies and laborers for its construc-tion camps were rafted down the big bend on the route of the Overlanders' main party. The current was just as dangerous as in the gold-rush days. How many scowloads of freight and immi-grant laborers sank in the Grand Canyon and along the other rapids of the bend no one will ever know. No one cared much either. In those days anything went. The brawling railway town of Prince George, which had replaced the old fort, was a set out of Hollywood so long as construction was under way. It col-lapsed immediately afterwards in the first years of the 1914–1918 war.

The Canadian Northern and Grand Trunk Pacific were too big and expensive for the frail economy of Canada. The national government had to take them over from their bank-rupt private owners and merge them into the vast system of tracks, rolling stock, ships and hotels called the Canadian Na-tional Railways, one of the world's most successful experiments in public ownership. By World War II every yard of track and every piece of equipment in the National system was required.

The fourth of the Fraser's railways was a white elephant from the start.

Just before the first war a private contracting firm offered to build the Pacific Great Eastern Railway from the north side of Vancouver harbor, westward along the harbor bluffs, up Howe Sound, along the Squamish Valley into the interior, and then by the Fraser trench across the Cariboo plateau to Prince George. The scheme did not appear as crazy then as it does now, for the P.G.E. was to serve as the freight outlet of the Grand Trunk Pacific into Vancouver. But when the G.T.P. was merged with the C.N.R., and the new National system thus acquired a convenient route to Vancouver by the North Thompson and the Fraser on the C.N.R. tracks, the only good reason for the P.G.E. disappeared overnight.

The P.G.E. promoters went broke and dumped their half-finished railway upon the doorstep of the British Columbia government, which boldly undertook to complete the original project. Year after year the cost of carving a railway out of the Howe Sound cliffs and extending the unfinished line to Prince George increased, until the treasury could no longer bear the load. The section from Vancouver to Squamish was abandoned. No further attempt was made to build north of Quesnel.

For nearly thirty years the government operated a railway without real beginning or end, from Squamish to Quesnel, always promising at election times to finish it to Vancouver and Prince George, and even to push it still farther north to the Peace River farm country. The white elephant emerged now and then with some gaudy new scandal or, in election campaigns, with promises of general opulence if a few more millions could be found for the Peace River extension.

These promises were for election purposes only. The truncated railway, at last under efficient management, barely earned operating costs, contributed nothing to the support of its swollen debt, but served the mines of Bridge River and the cattle ranches of the Cariboo. It was a cozy and well-run little railway, on which you knew every engineer, conductor and brakeman, and traveled as in a family party. The white elephant was a comfortable beast of burden.

As this book is written the provincial government at last has taken its courage in its hands and is starting the Quesnel-Prince George link. It is also building an automobile road from

Vancouver to the Squamish terminus. By truck to Squamish, and then by rail to Prince George, Vancouver freight will move into the interior and, it is hoped, newly developed products of forest industries, mines and ranches will move down to the coast.

Once through the Coast mountains by the Squamish canyons, the P.G.E. follows the Fraser northward, swinging away from the river in places and then back again beside the great trench. Essentially it is the product of the Fraser, the successor of the old steamboats, the competitor of the Cariboo Road, the freight carrier of the whole river region north of the Thompson.

As a three-forked artery of travel the Fraser has come a long way since the days of its first white explorer. Four railways use the passes it has carved through the mountains. The main highways linking British Columbia with the rest of Canada follow the same river grades. The map of the Fraser thus is largely the transportation map of Canada west of the Rockies. Without the Fraser this transportation system could never have been built. Without such transportation there would be no Canada as we know it now.

22   The Future of the River

A RIVER WHICH DESCENDS FROM THE ROCKIES TO THE COAST and spills some 3,000,000,000,000 cubic feet of fresh water into the ocean every year must waste in mere motion an almost unimaginable power. It is is not unimaginable to the engineers. They say the Fraser, when harnessed with dams and turbines, can give man 6,000,000 horsepower of electricity. It is probably the largest source of unused power left in the whole of North America. Not long will it remain unused.

The power potential of the Fraser was long suspected in a rough way. In recent years it has been measured in detail.

Almost from its beginning Vancouver was lighted and its industries propelled by electricity manufactured on three of the Fraser's tributaries, close to the mouth—the Stave, the Coquitlan and the Alouette, which produced together some quarter of a million horsepower.

These lower tributaries, however, are among the least important as a source of power. It is when he ascends the main river, sees its total flow and the steady drop in its level, and then the chance to divert it into new courses that the engineer dreams big. Someday, he knows, the Fraser, with rich manufacturing materials around it, can create one of the great industrial centers of the world.

This process may be said to have started in a serious fashion in the latter part of 1948 when the Bridge River, above Lillooet, was dammed and diverted through a 13,000-foot tunnel down to

337

Seton Lake, a drop of 1,200 feet, to produce 62,000 horsepower, which is carried by 130 miles of transmission line to the hungry industries of Vancouver. Nine more units of the same size will be added to the Bridge River scheme and finally produce 620,000 horsepower, which Vancouver ultimately will need.

Still this taps only the fringe of the Fraser's power. Its main body is to be found within the parent stream and its great western tributaries. Engineers know precisely how it can be tapped.

Between Prince George and Quesnel the Fraser drops 200 feet and between Quesnel and Lytton 1,080 feet, a total of 1,280 feet or four times the height of Niagara Falls. If that head, with the volume of water composing it—a flow of over 20,000 cubic feet per second—could be put under control Canada would have 1,690,000 extra horsepower to add to its present total electrical supply of 11,000,000.

As the engineers have planned it, the head would be captured in three or four traps.

The first dam would be built at Lillooet, backing the current up to the ramparts of Pavilion Mountain. The second and highest dam would be built at the base of the mountain, on a site called Moran. It would be over 700 feet high and comparable to Boulder Dam, which is 730 feet high and 1,000 feet along the crest of its brim. The Moran dam would pond the river back 150 miles to Quesnel, creating a lake perhaps 5 miles wide in places and thus swamping some ranches but irrigating a large dry area. Above Quesnel a third and a fourth dam could be built close to Cottonwood canyon and at Fort George canyon, ponding the river back to Prince George. Instead of a river a narrow lake would bisect the Cariboo plateau.

By this means the whole current of the main river, except its last stretches in the coastal canyon, would be put to work. The canyon, too, could be dammed below Lillooet, but this would be impractical since there is plenty of power farther upstream

338

and any rise in the canyon level would submerge the only passage for railways and road.

All the damsites have been studied by government engineers and geologists. No part of the Fraser's vast anatomy is a mystery to them. Men like R. C. Farrow, British Columbia comptroller of water rights, who has trudged the riverbanks on foot, paddled its current by canoe, and followed its remote tributaries into the mountains, regard the Fraser as quite the most wonderful thing in the world—not a river merely, not just a source of wealth, but something much greater, a kind of living, organic force, a mysterious manifestation of nature, almost a god. This god, like that of the salmon experts, has its faithful band of worshipers, the unknown engineers who risk their lives in its exploration, who compute its behavior on charts and graphs, and for meager pay, are ready to deliver it to men's uses.

An expert like Farrow, I suppose, finds the main stream of the Fraser a fairly simple problem in engineering. The western tributaries offer possibilities larger and more exciting.

As we observed in traveling over the Cariboo plateau, the western tributaries rise on the eastern flank of the Coast Range. Only a few miles off, other rivers rise on the western flank and rush wildly to the sea. To an engineer the important thing is that the interior rivers lie some 3,000 feet above the upper reaches of the coastal rivers. If the interior rivers could be diverted from the Fraser and guided through the mountains directly to the sea, they would fall over half a mile, creating a gigantic head of water. This diversion, which appears fantastic to the layman, will be undertaken before long.

Engineers have been working on this project for a long time. As early as the first days of the rush a shortcut into the gold fields from the coast was attempted through the narrow canyon of the Homathko River, some 130 miles up the coast from Vancouver. A remarkable engineer named Waddington built a trail up the Homathko in 1864 and thought he would beat Douglas's road builders into Cariboo. Just as he was nearing the last pass into the plateau his Chilcotin Indian packers murdered most of his crew in Tragedy Canyon. The survivors fled down to the sea and did not return.

The Homathko saw no more white men until engineers of the Canadian Pacific Railway started looking for a route to the Pacific in the eighties. The railway explorers realized at once that this was not a practical passage to the coast and wisely decided to build down the Fraser.

While modern engineers had surveyed the upper tributaries of the Chilcotin and were confident that these waters could be turned coastward, no white men since the C.P.R. engineers walked from the plateau down to the sea by the Homathko route until Farrow and a small party undertook this almost impossible journey in the summer of 1928.

They started from the Cariboo on horses. When the horses could go no farther over the mountains they were sent back and a party of five struggled ahead on foot, across snowfields and glaciers, through tortuous canyons and down perpendicular mountainsides. In places the engineers had to stop for days to build a log bridge over some unmapped stream. Often they turned far off their course to avoid some impossible chasm. Sometimes they covered only a hundred yards in a day of labor. But in the end they got down to the headwaters of the Homathko.

Their surveys had proved the essential fact that less than ten miles of rocks separated the headwaters of the Chicotin system from the headwaters of the Homathko. A tunnel could carry the water of the Chilcotin directly to the sea with a head of some 3,000 feet and create over a million horsepower of electricity.

For years after that the engineers pursued their studies and mapped out a power plan in detail. It has many possible variants, depending on the needs of any industry established on the coast to use the power. The most satisfactory scheme seems to be the diversion of the Taseko Lakes into Chilko Lake, the damming of the latter's flow and its diversion by tunnel to the Southgate River, which, like the Homathko, enters the head of Bute Inlet. Such a diversion would provide a head of 3,005 feet and 1,100,000 horsepower.

One serious difficulty arises in this project. The Chilcotin system is probably the largest spawning area of Fraser River salmon. A third of the total run is believed to originate there. If the salmon spawned in Chilko Lake or its creeks, they could be lifted easily over the low dam required to impound the lake waters. Unfortunately they spawn in the river below the lake and their young swim up to the lake to spend the first years of life there. How to lift millions of tiny salmon fry over a dam is more than engineers or ichthyologists know yet. It might prove impossible.

Even so, a government must consider the relative values of various resources. If it has to decide between a million horsepower of electricity, operating a gigantic tidewater industry, and a portion of the salmon run, its choice is obvious. In developing the Fraser it will be necessary to use every known device to lift salmon over dams and get their young down again, to invent new devices and, when these are unworkable, to divert the spawning of the fish, by regulation and artificial reproduction, to rivers where no obstructions are required. These prospects alarm the Sockeye commission. A clash between fish conservation and power development is certainly ahead.

Having established the practicality of the Chilcotin diversion, the engineers moved north. There they found that the headwaters of the Nechako system also could be turned westward to the coast. They have mapped out two northern schemes. One would take the waters of Eutsuk Lake through the mountains, drop them 2,400 feet into Kimsquit River, and develop 1,500,000 horsepower. The other, farther north, would repeat the same process between Tahtsa Lake and Kemano

River, with a head of 2,550 feet, to produce 850,000 horsepower.

These figures would vary upward or downward depending upon the precise plans followed among the many alternatives available. Altogether the engineers believe that the coastal diversions should give Canada some 3,700,000 horsepower, more than half the potential of the Fraser system.

With all the possible diversions under way, most of the water of the Fraser system would move as before. The diverted lakes and rivers would still deliver the largest part of their flow into the parent stream, whose volume would be reduced on average by only 9½ per cent.

Three relatively simple tunnels through the mountains and some inexpensive dams, creating 3,700,000 horsepower, offer an opportunity unequaled on this continent, in the view of the British Columbia authorities. The dimensions of these schemes will be better understood when it is remembered that Boulder Dam produces 1,835,000 horsepower.

Apart from the coastal diversions and the development of the main Fraser channel, the remainder of the potential 6,000,000 horsepower of the whole river system would come from dams on various tributaries like the Quesnel and the Adams and from various small local projects. The damming of the Thompson, the largest tributary, is hardly practicable in foreseeable time, though it offers no engineering difficulty, because such an undertaking would flood two transcontinental railway lines and the main highway.

It is not easy to calculate the value of the Fraser's power in dollar terms. At wholesale, the provincial government engineers reckon, 6,000,000 horsepower is worth $180,000,000 a year. But the amount of real wealth that the use of this power would produce in manufactures of various kinds cannot be estimated. When 750,000 horsepower now used in British Columbia industries produces goods worth more than $600,000,000 a year, it may be reckoned that the Fraser can produce $5,000,000,-

ooo a year, if markets are available. As Canada's national income, at this writing, is about $15,000,000,000, the size of the Fraser as a national asset is evident.

Such figures show that the Fraser, as probably the largest undeveloped source of power among all the rivers of America, is no longer a British Columbia asset. Since it could increase Canada's total electrical supply by more than 50 per cent, it is a national asset of the first magnitude, comparable in its industrial possibilities to the St. Lawrence in the East (though not, of course, for navigation).

The national government has no power over the Fraser, except in the regulation of navigation and fishing, but clearly only the national government is rich enough to put the river under control for power purposes. In the past few years the two governments, national and provincial, have grasped the importance of the Fraser in the future economy of Canada. They have begun the construction of what should someday be a comprehensive river authority.

The Dominion-Provincial Board, Fraser River Basin, a committee of four representatives of the dominion and four of the province—engineers, irrigationists and fishery experts—is now completing the immense task of mapping the Fraser not only for the production of power but for the irrigation of land, for the protection of fish, and for the control of floods. This committee of advisory officials is the nucleus of an executive body such as Canada has never established in the past. The Fraser is accepted at last as a national responsibility and a national opportunity, one of the largest facts in the nation.

It may be asked why British Columbia is even thinking about the development of huge new power sources when, at the moment, its million people are using only a million horsepower. A province of this population, it may be thought, is suffering delusions of grandeur. In fact, extra power on a scale never thought of in western Canada before is being sought by industry already. At this writing various plants to produce 300,000

343

horsepower are under construction. Two of the largest corporations on the continent, one Canadian, one American, are studying the westward diversion schemes, at heavy cost, with a view to establishing tidewater industries convenient to ocean shipping. Even one of these industries would require about a million horsepower. If aluminium is manufactured on the British Columbia coast, as one company plans, the subsidiary fabricating industries could use still more.

The development of the Fraser's potential power will occur in steps, probably over a long period, as electricity is needed in different places, but the experience of America in the last generation shows that almost nowhere has power production kept up with the demand for it. British Columbia is proceeding on the general assumption that where power is created industry and the market for power will follow.

If this assumption is sound in the future, as it has proved in the past, the industries ultimately powered by the Fraser will be at least the second factor in the Canadian industrial economy, the other being the industries of the Laurentian Valley. The effect of this shift in economic balance from east to west, on the economics, the politics and the living standards of the nation, is beyond calculation.

This is some time off, though perhaps not so distant as might have been supposed before Canada became a leading industrial nation. In the meantime the Fraser is a liability as well as an asset. Every so often it floods its lower banks, deluges its delta, and swamps its railways and roads.

From their first days on the river white men watched its annual freshet with anxiety, as the Indians had watched it for centuries. A crude system of measuring the water's level was devised and gradually improved, until now daily, or even hourly, measurements are taken from gauges at fixed points like Mission and Hope. Water officials at Victoria know, day and night, how the river is behaving, and by studying the snow in the mountains and the weather that dissolves or holds it frozen can foresee the approach of floods.

This is a tricky and fairly unreliable business, since a rise of a few degrees on the thermometer can instantly unloose the runoff of the mountains, while a drop in temperature, even in the middle of a flood, can reduce the river's level in the course of a day or two. Since it lives by snow on steep slopes, the Fraser operates by a delicate thermostat.

Probably worse occurred in unrecorded times, but the greatest flood known to the early white men was that of 1894. Since then the river level during the usual freshet of late May and early June has been generally considered in relation to the '94 peak. It is the danger mark watched by all engineers and farmers in the Fraser Valley.

At the time of the '94 flood there were few farms along the lower reaches of the Fraser. Damage, reckoned in dollars (though not in human misery), was relatively small. When, in the spring of 1948, the engineers saw the water rising fast on the Hope gauge, when they looked at the gigantic load of snow in the mountains, and learned of sudden hot weather throughout the interior, they knew they were in for trouble. Though a drop of a few degrees in temperature could arrest it, the engineers predicted a flood.

The temperature did not drop. The snow sluiced down the Rockies and the Coast Range. The river rose on the gauges to the '94 mark and passed it by just over 12 inches. Bruce Dixon, the veteran commissioner of dikes, a dark and quiet man whose warnings had long gone unheeded, knew that the disaster he had feared was upon the valley at last.

Modern Canada had never seen a flood like this. Quietly, slowly, inexorably the brown water rose beside the farm land below the canyon and the delta at the river's mouth. Before it earth dikes crumbled and dissolved like sugar, or suddenly, under pressure from below, exploded, tossing trees, stumps and barns

345

into the air. A cargo of uprooted trees and flotsam from the interior poured out to sea, and with it poured the carcasses of milk cows, horses, pigs and sheep to be washed up on the rocks of the gulf islands and even on the beaches around Victoria. The two transcontinental railway grades were submerged. Except by air Vancouver was isolated from the rest of Canada.

Farms were abandoned. Barns rode out to sea. Farmers worked day and night to shore up the dikes with sandbags. Bulldozers pushed more earth and rock into the weak places. The army took to shovels. The navy sailed its mine sweepers and landing craft up the river and across the deluged farms to rescue the people of stranded villages. Thousands of refugees were housed in New Westminster and Vancouver, having lost everything they owned. All animal life fled before the water and a cat was actually seen swimming down the river with a mouse riding on its back.

The flood covered more than 50,000 acres of the best farm land in Canada. Its damage to houses, farms, barns, orchards, crops and livestock has never been estimated accurately but probably amounted to $20,000,000. It could easily have been much worse. A cooler spell in the mountains slowed the runoff and eased the flood at its peak. But for that relief the key dikes above Rosedale probably would have broken and exposed the main farming area around Chilliwack and Sumas on the south bank. The dikes held there and on the delta, where the wide, deep channel of the river could carry its extra load.

Looking at this spectacle of ruin, the national government finally recognized the Fraser as a national responsibility. It combined with the provincial government, paying three-quarters of the cost, to rehabilitate the flood victims and to prevent another flood. The two governments agreed to spend $5,000,000 for rehabilitation and $11,000,000 for dike construction. Some 200 miles of new dikes between the canyon and the sea are being built at this writing, to a level 2 feet above the 1948 flood peak and much stronger than the old dikes.

Such a flood may seem minor and such expenditures modest to those who live along the Mississippi. They seem large enough to the small population of Canadian farmers and to the hard-pressed provincial treasury at Victoria. The engineers knew that this was not the last flood and that dikes alone could not guarantee them full protection against another.

If the Fraser is to be brought safely under control along its lower reaches, its freshet must be controlled at the source. That project is on the agenda of the federal-provincial commission of experts. They will produce a plan by which the main lakes of the Fraser can be dammed and their spring runoff released slowly. This scheme will take time and money, but not so much as the layman might suppose. A few low and inexpensive dams at strategic points on the great natural reservoirs of the upper river could feed the snow water into the main stream in tolerable quantities. In places flood control could be combined with power development. By a system of dams the Fraser's annual rise, it is hoped, can be held to its average of about 16 feet, well below the dike level.

Thus man undertakes to plan the future of the Fraser.

His occupation of its banks has been a brief time, a moment only, a fraction of a moment, in the river's life. Men of white skin have seen the river for hardly more than a century. Already they have taken its gold, cut its timber, gutted its salmon run, ridden on its current, lined it with railways and roads, drained a patch or two of its swamps, diked its lowlands, poured its water on their fields, and turned a particle of its motion into electricity. They have used it to contain Manifest Destiny, to build the nation of Canada and divide the continent by an imaginary line of sovereignty.

All this—and the forgotten adventures of Spanish navigators, British explorers, fur traders, gold miners, dance hall girls, freighters, lumberjacks, settlers, road builders, railway builders and builders of cities—has been accomplished almost without design or conscious purpose—a prodigy of labor without recognition by the world or even by the nation it so largely made, a process of history without a record, an epic without a song, a poem or a folklore.

But everything that man has done along its channel, everything he will do with steel, concrete and mechanical power will soon be forgotten in the memory of the river.

So long as the planet turns, mountains stand, snow falls and water runs downhill, the Fraser will move, dark, brown and furious, to the sea. There is ample time to complete its work. A force of water which could sweep off the mountain snow at the beginning of the world, cut the interior trench, and bore through the coastal mountains will scour away the bridge piers, breach the dams, and block up the tunnels of men at leisure. The river has millions of years before it to remove every frail mark of man's presence, to rebuild its banks and shift its channel to its own designs, when there is no eye to see them.

Short as the story of man must be here, by the river's measurement of time, he will alter temporarily its current, modify its fury, and soon destroy every trace of the several curious little civilizations that have flourished on it in times of Indian and white. By man's measurement, indeed, the old days already are finished and the new days have begun.

How fast the time has gone! How little left of the river life we knew in our boyhood, yesterday! All crushed beneath the marching foot of progress, improved beyond recognition, civilized in shape and spirit alien to us. Do not grudge the memories of old men, helpless to stay the birth of the new time and entitled, surely, to the past, which no one else will covet.

For us it is enough that we knew the days before the engineers came, traveled the lonely road, saw the light of the mile house in the storm, watched the shadows engulf the canyon, beheld the sunrise on the peaks, smelled the spring growth and autumn drought, rode the empty rangeland under the stars, and listened to the river telling us of remote time past and unlimited time to come.

348

Enough that we lived upon these banks, looked down at the moving water, felt the motion of blind force, sensed the substance of a continent, and caught a glimpse of the reality of the earth, which it is the chief business of men's society to disguise. Enough that we knew for a moment the power of mindless, inorganic life, beside which all organic, man's among it, is the fragment of a passing dream.

We have had the best of it. We have seen the river, naked and virginal, when we were young.

Bibliography

ANGUS, H. F., ed., *British Columbia and the United States; the North Pacific Slope from Fur Trade to Aviation*, by F. W. Howay, W. N. Sage, and H. F. Angus. Toronto: Ryerson, 1942.

BEGG, ALEXANDER, *History of British Columbia from Its Earliest Discovery to the Present Time*. Toronto: Briggs, 1894.

BOUTILIER, HELEN R., "Vancouver's earliest days," *British Columbia Historical Quarterly*, April, 1946.

British Columbia Department of Lands—Geographic division, *Geographical Gazeteer of British Columbia*. Victoria, B. C.: Banfield, 1930.

BURT, ALFRED LEROY, *A Short History of Canada*. Minneapolis: University of Minnesota Press, 1942.

CHITTENDEN, NEWTON H., *Health Seekers', Tourists' and Sportsmen's Guide to the Seaside, Lake-side, Foothill, Mountain and Mineral Spring, Health and Pleasure Resorts of the Pacific Coast*. San Francisco: C. A. Murdock & Co., 1884.

CREECH, E. P., "Similkameen Trails, 1846–61," *British Columbia Historical Quarterly*, October, 1941.

CREIGHTON, DONALD GRANT, *Dominion of the North, A History of Canada*. Boston: Houghton, 1944.

351

FLEMING, SIR SANDFORD, *Report of Progress on the Explorations and Surveys of the Canadian Pacific Railway up to January, 1874.* Ottawa: MacLean, Rogers & Co., 1874.

——, *Report on Surveys and Preliminary Operations on the Canadian Pacific Railway up to January,* 1877. Ottawa: MacLean, Rogers & Co., 1877.

FRASER, SIMON, "Journal of a Voyage from the Rocky Mountains to the Pacific Coast, 1808," in L. F. R. Masson, *Les bourgeouis de la compagnie due Nord-ouest,* 1889.

FUTCHER, WINIFRED M., *The Great North Road to Cariboo.* Vancouver, B. C.: Wrigley, 1938.

GIBBON, JOHN MURRAY, *Steel of Empire: the Romantic History of the Canadian Pacific, the Northwest Passage of Today.* Toronto: McClelland, 1935.

HANNA, D. B., *Trains of Recollection.* Toronto: Macmillan, 1924.

HARVEY, NETTA, *History and Finances of the Pacific Great Eastern Railway.* A graduating essay submitted March 27, 1935. University of British Columbia.

HACKING, NORMAN R., "British Columbia steamboat days, 1870–1883," *British Columbia Historical Quarterly,* April, 1947.

——, "Steamboat 'round the bend," American steamers on the Fraser River in 1858, *British Columbia Historical Quarterly,* October, 1944.

HOWAY, F. W., *British Columbia, the Making of a Province.* Toronto: Ryerson, 1928.

——, "Coal-mining on Burrard Inlet, 1865–66," *British Columbia Historical Quarterly,* January, 1940.

——, "The Discovery of the Fraser River, Second Phase," *British Columbia Historical Quarterly,* October, 1940.

BIBLIOGRAPHY

———, *Early History of the Fraser River Mines*. Victoria, B. C.: Banfield, 1926.

———, *Work of the Royal Engineers in B.C., 1858–1863*. Victoria, B. C.: R. Wolfenden, 1910.

LAUT, AGNES C., *The Cariboo Trail*. Glasgow: Brook, 1916.

———, *Pioneers of the Pacific Coast*. Glasgow: Brook, 1916.

LEACOCK, STEPHEN, *Adventurers of the Far North*. Glasgow: Brook, 1914.

LE BOURDAIS, LOUIS, "Billy Barker of Barkerville," *British Columbia Historical Quarterly*, July, 1937.

LOWER, ARTHUR R. M., *Colony to Nation; a History of Canada*. Toronto: Longmans, 1946.

MacINNES, TOM, *Chinook Days*. Vancouver, B. C.: Sun Publishing Co., 1926.

McINNIS, EDGAR, *The Unguarded Frontier; a History of American Canadian Relations*. New York: Doubleday, 1942.

MacKAY, DOUGLAS, *The Honourable Company; a History of the Hudson's Bay Company*. Indianapolis: Bobbs-Merrill, 1936.

McKELVIE, B. A., *Fort Langley, Outpost of Empire*. Vancouver, B. C.: Vancouver Daily Province, 1947.

MacKENZIE, SIR ALEXANDER, *Voyages from Montreal through the Continent of North America to the Frozen and Pacific Oceans in 1789 and 1793 . . .* Toronto: Courier Press, 1911.

McNAUGHTON, MARGARET, *Overland to Cariboo*. Toronto: Briggs, 1896.

MEANY, EDMOND S., *Vancouver's Discovery of Puget Sound*. New York: Macmillan, 1907.

MILTON, W. W. F., VISCOUNT & CHEADLE, W. B., *The Northwest Passage by Land*. London: Cassell, 1865.

353

NEWCOMBE, C. C., ed., *Menzie's Journal of Vancouver's Voyages.* Victoria, B. C.: Cullin, 1923.

PETTIT, SYDNEY, "Sir Matthew Baillie Begbie," *British Columbia Historical Quarterly*, January, April, July, October, 1947.

POPE, SIR JOSEPH, *The Day of Sir John Macdonald.* Glasgow: Brook, 1915.

REID, R. L., *The Assay Office and the Proposed Mint at New Westminster; a Chapter in the History of the Fraser River Mines.* Victoria, B. C.: Banfield, 1926.

RICHARD, T. A., *Historical Backgrounds of British Columbia.* Vancouver: Wrigley, 1948.

ROBERTS, MORLEY, *The Western Avernus.* London: Smith, Elder, 1887.

ROBINSON, NOEL, *Blazing the Trail through the Rockies.* Vancouver: News Advertiser Press, 1915.

ROSS, MARGARET, *Amor DeCosmos, a British Columbia Reformer.* A thesis submitted 1931. University of British Columbia.

SAGE, WALTER N., *Sir James Douglas and British Columbia.* Toronto: University of Toronto Press, 1930.

SCHOLEFIELD, E. O. S., *British Columbia from the Earliest Times to the Present.* Vol. 1. Vancouver, B. C.: S. J. Clarke publishing company.

SHORTT, ADAM, AND DOUGHTY, A. G., eds., "The Pacific Provinces," in *Canada and Its Provinces*, Vols. 21–22, 1913–1917.

SKELTON, OSCAR D., *The Railway Builders.* Glasgow: Brook, 1916.

TALBOT, FREDERICK A. A., *Making of a Great Canadian Railway, the Story of the Search for and Discovery of the Route, and.*

the Construction of the Nearly Completed Grand Trunk Pacific Railway . . . Toronto: Musson, 1912.

WADDINGTON, A. P., *The Fraser Mines Vindicated, or, the History of Four Months.* Victoria, B. C.: De Garro, 1858.

WADE, M. S., *Mackenzie of Canada.* Edinburgh: William Blackwood, 1927.

WADE, M. S., *Overlanders of '62.* Victoria, B. C.: Banfield, 1931.

WALKER, DR. JOHN F., *Memorandum on the Geological History of the Fraser River.*

WALLACE, W. STEWART, *Dictionary of Canadian Biography.* Toronto: Macmillan, 1926.

WHEELER, A. O., *The Selkirk Range.* Ottawa: Government Printing Bureau, 1905.

WOOD, LOUIS AUBREY, *Red River Colony.* Glasgow: Brook, 1915.

Index

dairying, 179, 181, 206
dams. *See* power, water
Dean River, 29
Deighton, Captain John, 155, 182
Deitz, William, 71-72, 163, 171
delta of the river, 12, 49, 178, 179,
    181, 346
    drainage by Oliver, 180
depth of the river, 11
Destiny, Manifest. *See* Manifest Des-
    tiny
Devil's Gap, 73, 83, 86
Devries, Captain Henry, 155
dikes, 12
direction of the river. *See* course of
    the river
divide between Fraser, Mackenzie,
    and Athabaska Rivers, 264
Discovery, 19
discovery of the river, 13-20
Dixon, Bruce, 345
Doane, Captain W. G., 154
Dominion of Canada. *See* Canada
Dominion-Provincial Board, Fraser
    River Basin, 343
Douglas, Governor James, 53-56, 66,
    71, 73, 74, 76-83, 87, 115-17,
    128, 129, 133, 134, 140, 142, 144,
    150, 152-55, 163, 177, 182, 187,
    212, 246, 268, 278, 328
    on the Cariboo Road, 76-77
Douglas Lake, 267
Douglas Road, 195
drainage area of the river, 8, 12, 239,
    261, 264
Drake, Sir Francis, 13-14, 17
Drake, W. T., 123
drought, 276
Dry Belt, 11, 220, 222, 225, 239, 252,
    260, 267, 269, 275, 278-79, 281,
    324
duel, Molly Devers and Nellie Bell,
    173
Dufferin, Lord, 126
Dutch Lake, 326

Eagle Pass, 329, 332

Eagle River, 329
Edmonton, 93
electric power. *See* power, water
Eliza Anderson, 156
Emily Harris, 150
Endako, 260
Endako River, 323
Enterprise, 152, 154, 156
entrance to the river. *See* mouth of
    the river
epidemic, smallpox, 112
Eutsuk Lake, 341
expansionism, United States. *See*
    Manifest Destiny
explosions, steamboat, 158
expressmen and routes, 84-87

falls of the Mahood, 254
Family Compact, 140, 144
farm, experimental, 201
farming, 12, 78, 179, 181, 197, 205-10,
    268, 278
    crops, 206
    fruit. *See* fruit growing
Farrow, R. F., 339, 340
ferries, 80, 82, 159, 201, 267, 332
"Fifty-four Forty or Fight," 116
Finlay River, 25
Finlayson, Roderick, 55
fishing (angling), 311-26
    anglers, famous, 312
    "best in the world." *See* Pooley,
        Harry
    lakes and rivers, 314-26
    salmon, 288
    trout, 238-39, 267, 280, 311; vari-
        eties, 312-14
Fleming, Sanford, 329
floods and flood control, 206, 344-47
flora, 11, 77, 237
Flying Dutchman, 156
force, continental, 7
force of the river. *See* power of the
    river
forests. *See* timber
Fort Alexander, 153
Fort Alexandria, 152

Overland Transit Company. *See* British Columbia Overland Transit Company
Overlanders, 89-106, 281-83, 334

Pacific Great Eastern Railway, 223, 224, 245, 252, 254, 327, 334-36
Pacific Ocean, race for control, 14, 16, 18-20
Pacific Scandal, 327
Pack Rat, the (J. Stevens), 169
packing of freight, 74-76, 84-87
paper (pulp) industry, 254
Parsnip River, 25, 36
passes, Rocky Mountain. *See* Rocky Mountains, Canadian
Pattullo, Thomas Dufferin, 196
Pattullo Bridge, 196
Paul Lake, 325
Pavilion, 226, 230, 232, 234, 236, 239
Pavilion Indians, 227, 234
Pavilion lakes, 239
 fishing in, 316
Pavilion Mountain, 73, 80, 226-28, 233, 240, 241, 246, 317, 338
Pavilion trail, 230, 270
Pavilion Valley, 274
Peace River, 22, 24, 25, 33, 36, 38, 261, 335
Pear Lake, 230, 241
penitentiary, British Columbia, 197
"Pentrelew," 144
Perry, Harry, 257
Peter the Great, 14-15
Pettit, Sydney, 129, 131, 142
pilots, river, 146-59
Pioneer, and mine, 172, 224
pioneers. *See* Overlanders
Pitt Lake and River, 200
 fishing in, 314
Pitts, Panther, 312, 323
place names, 271
planes. *See* airplanes; airport
plants. *See* flora
poems by James Anderson, 169-70
police, early, 137
politics, 277-78

Pooley, Harry, and "the best fishing in the world," 312, 316, 317, 319-26
Port Alexander, 153
Port Douglas, 151, 155
Port Moody, 183, 328, 332, 333
Port Moody *Gazette*, 333
portages, 36, 66
potato and tomato crops, 268
power of the river, 5, 10, 11, 41, 43, 47, 196, 212
power, water, 12, 224, 239, 244, 270, 337-45
 or salmon preservation?, 341
 value, actual and potential, 7, 342-43
precipitation. *See* rainfall
prices in gold-rush days, 171
Prince George, 69, 147, 159, 217, 255-57, 261, 323, 335, 338
Prince Rupert, 260, 261, 334
Puget Sound, 19, 20
pulp industry, 254

Queenborough. *See* New Westminster
Queenston, 98, 100
Quesnel, Jules, 38-39, 69
Quesnel, 75, 80-82, 84, 85, 105, 131, 137, 139, 147, 149, 152-54, 159, 169, 252-55, 335, 338
Quesnel Lake, 69-70, 253-54
Quesnel River, 8, 27, 29, 39, 69, 73, 253-54, 322, 342

railways, 10, 123-26, 159, 179, 183, 184, 193, 195, 197, 211, 222-23, 260, 261, 271, 275-76, 327-36
 See also names of railways
rainfall, 206, 278
ranch life, 242-43
ranches. *see* cattle
Rankin, Philip, 122
rapids, 8, 26, 28, 40-47, 97-98, 100, 101, 109-10, 148, 151, 244, 254, 261, 272, 293, 299, 309
Rebellion of 1837, 115, 140, 142

CPSIA information can be obtained at www.ICGtesting.com
Printed in the USA
LVOW10s0004210315

431427LV00002B/72/P